HISTORIOGRAPHY AND CAUSATION IN PSYCHOANALYSIS

An Essay on Psychoanalytic and Historical Epistemology

HISTORIOGRAPHY AND CAUSATION
IN PSYCHOANALYSIS

*An Essay on Psychoanalytic
and Historical Epistemology*

Edwin R. Wallace, IV, M.D.
Medical College of Georgia

 THE ANALYTIC PRESS
1985

Distributed by
LAWRENCE ERLBAUM ASSOCIATES, PUBLISHERS
Hillsdale, New Jersey   London

Distributed solely by

Lawrence Erlbaum Associates, Inc., Publishers
365 Broadway
Hillsdale, New Jersey 07642

Library of Congress Cataloging in Publication Data

Wallace, Edwin R.
   Historiography and causation in psychoanalysis.

   Bibliography: p.
   Includes index.
   1. Psychoanalysis—Methodology.   2. Historiography.
I. Title.
BF175.W27   150.19'5   84-13543
   ISBN 0-88163-015-2

Printed in the United States of America
10 9 8 7 6 5 4 3 2 1

To My Teachers
George E. Gross   Philip Rieff

My worthy friend, gray is all theory,
And green alone life's golden tree.

Goethe, *Faust*, Part I, Scene 4.

Contents

Preface and
Acknowledgments

It might help the reader to know something about how this book came to be. It grows out of a lifelong passion for history and an attempt to integrate it with my psychiatric identity. History was my first love and governed my intellectual development until well into college, at which time I changed my course toward medicine. Aware of no particular interest in psychiatry, I entered its clerkship somewhat begrudgingly. There I was astonished to find physicians practicing what I understood as essentially the historical method. I was at home.

Through psychiatric residency and personal analysis, graduate work in history, study of the philosophy of history, and subsequent work as a psychodynamic clinician and historian, I have become increasingly convinced that the genetic method is the bedrock of psychoanalytic technique, that Freud's primary contribution is his historical approach to the study and therapeutic transformation of human behavior, and that history and psychoanalysis share methodological-epistemological issues which it is mutually advantageous for them to examine.

I have experienced the cross-fertilization between my clinical and historical identities to be of immeasurable advantage to both aspects of my work. In this monograph I attempt to convey what I mean by this, to demonstrate the relevance of each discipline for the other, and, most especially, to clarify and analyze certain psychoanalytic issues from the perspective of history and the philosophy of history.

In the painful and exhilarating attempt to meld my psychodynamic and historical identities several individuals have proved especially important. First and foremost are George Gross, of the New York Psychoanalytic Institute, and Philip Rieff, of the University of Pennsylvania, to whom this volume is gratefully dedicated. I am thankful to Lloyd Stevenson, formerly Director of the Johns Hopkins University Institute of the History of Medicine, for helping me to the therapeutic awareness that as historian and psychiatrist I am pretty much one and the same. To my late father, Edwin R. Wallace, III, M.D., I am indebted for providing me with a model of the physician-historian.

Conversations extending over a number of years with John Gach, of Columbia, Maryland, have assisted me in clarifying my position on many points. To George Gross and John Gach, again, go my appreciation for their careful and incisive reading of this monograph in manuscript. The former's comments and criticisms were particularly useful for the causation part of the monograph, and the latter's for the historiography section.

I wish to thank my department chairman, Mansell Pattison, for providing an atmosphere conducive to scholarly work and for his interest in methodology and epistemology. I want to thank Susan Kasmin Shrader for her role in the preparation of this monograph. My typists — Ms. Susan Brega, Ms. Becky Blount, and my mother — have been skilled and patient. My wife, Laura, and children, Laura and Win, have been, as ever, understanding with the trials and tribulations of my scholarship.

In the interest of readability I consistently use the masculine pronouns—he, his, him, himself—to refer to the generic clinician, historian, and patient. Please read this as what would more accurately, but clumsily, be expressed as he/she, his/hers, him/her, and himself/herself.

Introduction

Although the craft of history writing is an old one, it is only recently that historians have paused to reflect upon their methodology and theory of knowledge. With a few exceptions, such work did not begin in earnest until the 1920's. Subsequent decades have witnessed an extraordinary proliferation of critical and analytical treatments of historiography. Most have come from the pens of philosophers, not historians. Indeed, it can be argued that, alongside mind, language, and science, history heads the list of twentieth century philosophical preoccupations.

Though nearly a century old, until recently psychoanalysis, like history, enjoyed relatively little systematic reflection upon its methodology and epistemology. Monographs by Rieff (1959), Novey (1968), Sherwood (1969), Ricoeur (1970), Matte Blanco (1975), Schafer (1976, 1978), and Edelson (1975), critical reviews by Kline (1972) and Farrell (1981), anthologies by Hook (1959) and Wollheim (1977), and articles scattered throughout a number of periodicals and annuals exemplify a growing current interest in the philosophy of psychoanalysis. It remains to be seen whether here, as in the philosophy of history, philosophers rather than practitioners will do the bulk of this work. One thing is certain: those writing philosophy of history and those writing philosophy of psychoanalysis can ill afford to ignore one another. The methodological-epistemological issues involved in attempting to reconstruct the past from its traces in the present are basic to both history and psychoanalysis, as will become abundantly clear.

This monograph is an amplification and development of a previous paper on methodology in history and psychoanalysis (Wallace, 1983a)—topics with which, as a clinician and historian, I have been concerned for some time. In many respects, it is a reflection upon issues encountered in the preparation of two previous works—a textbook of psychoanalytic psychiatry (Wallace, 1983b) and an historical monograph (Wallace 1983c). As in the earlier items, I attempt to demonstrate that the procedure, problems, and possibilities of psychoanalysts and historians are similar and mutually illuminating. Indeed, I maintain, along with a growing body of writers, that psychoanalysis is a fundamentally historical enterprise and that acknowledging this carries no threat whatsoever to its scientific dignity.

Although this work is written from the standpoint of an historian, as well as a dynamic psychiatrist, and although it aims to alert the historian to the affinities between psychoanalysis and his discipline, its primary intent is to use history and the philosophy of history to cast light on epistemological and methodological issues in psychoanalysis. In short, historical epistemology is treated largely as a mine from which valuable ore can be extracted for psychoanalysis. If, from this process, the historian finds something useful to him, I shall be more than happy; however, my main objective is to heighten psychodynamic clinicians' awareness of the relevance of history and philosophy to the issues they face. In particular, I argue that psychoanalysts can acknowledge the role of theory, perspective, and interpretation without abandoning all claims to empiricism and embracing a radically subjectivist, relativist, and idealist point of view.

The book is divided into two parts, each consisting of two chapters. The first portion examines the parallels between history and psychoanalysis and points out the relevance of each for the other. A number of methodological and epistemological questions are treated, including: what is the nature of historical and psychoanalytic subject matter?; how do the data of historians and psychoanalysts compare and contrast with each other and with those of the natural scientists?; what is the relationship between data gathering and theorizing in history and psychoanalysis and, again, how does it compare with that in the natural sciences?; what do we mean by "interpretation" in history and in psychoanalysis and how does it relate to observation?; are history and psychoanalysis scientific?; do their explanations utilize covering laws?; can their propositions claim to be veridical—that is, are historians and psychoanalysts constructing or reconstructing the past?; can history and psychoanalysis be objective?; what are the positions of the analyst and historian vis-à-vis their subject matter?; what is the place of the analyst's or historian's personality in his work?; are historical and psychoanalytic theories of knowledge correspondence or coherence ones?; can the psychoanalytic method be used in the historian's work?

Because the literature often presents these and other issues as antitheses, I examine many of them as dichotomies: positivism versus historicism, idiographic versus nomothetic methodologies, theorizing or interpreting versus observing or data gathering, participation versus detachment, presentism versus antiquarianism, idealism and relativism versus realism, and subjectivism versus objectivism. I argue that these antitheses are only apparent ones, and that analytic and historical technique involves an ongoing interaction between the poles within each of these dichotomies rather than a one-sided cleaving to one or the other.

One item of historical and psychoanalytic epistemology—causation—is sufficiently important to warrant a section all to itself. It permeates virtually every major issue in the philosophy of history and psychoanalysis. Although for most of their history psychoanalysts and historians thought very little about their concept of causation, there is now a burgeoning interest in what historians and analysts mean by "cause" and even in whether they are entitled to speak of it at all.

The second part of the study examines this topic. I hope to illustrate that the concept and problems of causation in history and psychoanalysis are similar and mutually elucidating.

This part contains two chapters. The first (Chapter 3) traces the historical background of the issue in science, philosophy, history, and psychoanalysis; it examines Freud's five concepts of causation. The second (Chapter 4) continues the logical analysis of determinism begun in the first chapter and evaluates the criticisms of causal language in psychoanalysis. Because Schafer (1976, 1978) has addressed many of the issues, key here is a critique of his work, and that of his sources. I aim to demonstrate the inadequacy of the criticisms of psychoanalytic causation and to reassert the superiority of causal language in the study of human behavior. Among the questions addressed are: is causal language impersonal and mechanistic?; is psychic causality transeunt (i.e., a concept of causes acting upon the individual from without)?; do causal explanations involve one in an infinite regress?; what is the nature of psychic causes and how does one identify them?; what do we mean by "historical determinism" and how do historical and situational determinants relate to each other?; do causal explanations entail inevitability and invariability propositions? In line with this, I explicate a concept of meaningful, purposive, and intersectional multi-causality. The chapter ends with a look at the ramifications of the historical and logical analysis for the therapeutic relationship and for the age old dilemma of free will versus determinism.

Throughout the monograph I have presented numerous clinical examples of the points under consideration. While this may prove boring or distracting to many psychoanalytic readers, I have felt it necessary to include them for two reasons: (1) for the benefit of the nonclinical—historical and philosophical—reader; and (2) because in dealing with abstract and ambiguous matters it is incumbent upon an author to exemplify his concepts and link them to their referents as clearly as possible.

Let me emphasize that this monograph is not put forward as a history of the philosophies of history and psychoanalysis or of the concept of causation; nor is it a primer on historical or clinical technique. Rather, it develops certain ideas and criticisms regarding selected aspects of these topics. Although there is some attempt at synthesizing, the primary purpose of this study is analytical. It strives to raise psychoanalytic consciousness of the issues treated herein. The goal is to clarify problems, not resolve them.

HISTORIOGRAPHY AND CAUSATION IN PSYCHOANALYSIS

*An Essay on Psychoanalytic
and Historical Epistemology*

HISTORIOGRAPHY

In his 1935 introduction to Zilboorg's *Medical Man and the Witch in the Renaissance,* Henry Sigerist, the dean of American medical historians, remarked on the striking similarities in the procedure of academic historians and dynamic psychiatrists. The historian Hughes (1964, p. 47) concurs, asserting that "Psychoanalysis *is* history." Similarly, the former president of the American Historical Association, William Langer (1958), the philosophers of history Meyerhoff (1962) and Walsh (1969), the philosopher of psychoanalysis Ricoeur (1970), and the psychoanalysts Schmidl (1962), Wolman (1971), Novey (1968), Schafer (1976, 1978), and Leavy (1980) have written about affinities between the two disciplines. I believe that psychoanalytic clinicians have long sensed that they are practicing what Loewald (1977) has termed the "history of the individual."

Nevertheless, none of these authors has developed his ideas and observations into the systematic and comprehensive treatment that the subject deserves. In the next two chapters I articulate and attempt to support the thesis that there are point by point parallels between the two disciplines and that the implications of these are fruitful for both. The first chapter is divided into four sections: *Subject Matter, Theory and Data, Positivism versus Historicism, and Covering Laws*. The second chapter is likewise divided into four sections: *History and Psychoanalysis as Relationship, Idealism versus Realism, Art versus Science,* and *Mutual Contributions*.

1
Historiography

SUBJECT MATTER

How, at first blush, can there be any kinship between the psychodynamic healer, sitting empathically with a suffering fellow being, and the academic historian, probing diligently, if dispassionately, through moldering archives? After all, the first is dealing with a living individual, in the present, to whom he relates in a collaborative mode, to the end of alleviating his discomfort and perhaps restructuring his mode of being-in-the-world. The second, in contrast, works, by and large, with the documents and monuments of those long dead; is more concerned, unless he be a biographer, with cultures and periods than personalities; and, as opposed to the therapist's pragmatic and "presentistic" passion for history, has a purely academic interest in the past for its own sake.

In actuality, both historians and analysts are concerned with the same thing—human affairs. More precisely, they take as their subject the symbolically mediated behaviors of Homo sapiens, that which must be understood in terms of ideas, affects, purposes, desires, memories, interpretations, and more or less successful attempts at adaptation, as opposed to those aspects of humanity which are sufficiently explained as biophysical happenings. These latter, as well as the manifold events of the physical environment, interest both practitioners only insofar as they enter into the individual's and society's construction of,and action upon, reality. Furthermore, because of our peculiarly human propensity to representationally take our histories into us, where they consciously and unconsciously influence our present perspectives and actions, psychoanalysts and historians grasp that our symbolically mediated behaviors must be understood diachronically. They must be appreciated as they unfold over time, and not merely from within their contemporary context.

Inasmuch as their concern is with symbolically mediated behavior, both professionals are preoccupied with occurrences that are actually or potentially, explicitly or implicitly, intentionally or unintentionally, verbally or nonverbally communicative. Chronicles, documents, monuments, artifacts, and economic indices on the one hand, and fantasies, feelings, parapraxes, defensive maneuvers, and psychoneurotic symptoms on the other, are equally meaningful human activities and events. But they are intelligible, as we shall see in the next section, only to one who is prepared to understand, to ask the right questions and listen for the answers.

Such considerations move me to agree with Collingwood's (1946, p. 213) contention that a prime difference between the data of the historian and those of the physical scientist is that the former have an "inside," as it were—that is, meanings and motives that precede and accompany the observed and reported events themselves. Only the most plodding chronicler is satisfied with merely recording dates and occurrences. To know, for example, that one Julius Caesar crossed the Rubicon in 49 B.C. is to possess a mere piece of external data. To understand Caesar's history and intentions, and how these fitted into the political and sociocultural ambience of ancient Rome, is to begin to appreciate its proper significance, to get "inside" it. Similarly, in dynamic psychiatry, to know that a patient's mother was hospitalized for alcoholism when he was eight, that a year later she deserted the family for her lover, and that when the child was fourteen she returned home with a terminal illness and soon died is less than half the story. To get "inside" these events one must discern the patient's interpretations of, and reactions to, them.

A second peculiarity of the field of inquiry in history and psychoanalysis, as opposed to that in the experimental sciences, is its mediate, as opposed to immediate, relationship to the "observer." In other words, the historian works with the real event no more—or even less—than does the psychoanalyst. The past event in history, as much as in dynamic psychiatry, is irrecoverable, but its meaning in the present is not. Langlois and Seignebos (1898, pp. 63–67) correctly point out that the historian's observational data are, not the "facts of the past" themselves, but their "traces" in the present. Much of their treatise on methodology is an account of the process of reasoning by which the historian infers the facts from the traces. In the case of written documents these historians were aware that the "traces" are of "psychological operations," which must themselves be constructed before one can proceed to inferences about the events they report. Collingwood (1965, p. 101), as well, asserts that "it is the past as residually preserved in the present that is alone knowable."

As the historian Becker (1958, p. 48) has aptly stated, "the historical fact is in someone's mind or it is nowhere . . . the *actual occurrence* and the *historical fact* are two different things [my italics]." Even the records with which the historian works, he points out, are not the events themselves but only a pattern of ink on paper, left by someone with an image or idea of the events. Florovsky (1969, p. 351) concurs that "The knowledge of the past is necessarily indirect and inferential. It is always an interpretation. The past can only be reconstructed."[1]

---

[1]Nevertheless, if the historian or analyst is at a disadvantage to the natural scientist in lacking observational access to the events themselves, he is at an advantage in possessing "knowledge by direct acquaintance" of at least one member (i.e., himself) of that class of phenomena (humanity) he studies. This becomes a powerful tool in the historian's and the analyst's attempts to arrive at inferences about the structure of their subject matter. The problem of "other minds"—that we cannot know them directly, but only by inference or description (which Freud, of course, taught us is also true of

It is, in other words, the "historical fact," rather than the "actual occurrence," that engages the historian. All dynamic psychiatrists grasp this important distinction when they differentiate between the patient's "actual biography" and his "analytic" one. But here the analyst, in contrast to the historian, deals with both historical facts (memories) and with approximations to the actual events ("transference"—acting out, rather than recollecting, important themes from one's history). It is the intimate connection between the two that gives the psychoanalyst a route into the past (or rather, into the *reconstruction* of the past) that the historian does not have. This link and the opportunity to question the matrix of his historical facts (the patient), to test his hypotheses against the subsequent responses of the patient, give the dynamic psychiatrist certain advantages. On the other hand, since the therapist limits his transactions to the patient himself and does not usually encounter his friends and family members, he lacks access to a means of cross verification—the reports of contemporary witnesses—that the historian possesses, a handicap which Freud (1909, p. 207) himself acknowledged.

A third peculiarity, implied in the second, of both specialists' data is that they are themselves *interpretations*. In other words, historians and clinicians work, not with historical occurrences, but with the chronicler's or patient's retrospective interpretations of them. This is of course implicit in the differentiation of psychical from actual reality, the analytic from the actual biography. The patient's or chronicler's interpretation will depend on his history and the contemporary vantage point from which he speaks. In short, historians and dynamic psychiatrists are interpreters, not of actual events or flawless

---

important aspects of our own minds)—does not expose the psychoanalyst to epistemological difficulties that the natural scientist escapes. The natural scientist, too, knows his subject matter only by inference from his sense (or instrumental) data. In this respect, what the physicist or biologist studies is no more "real," no less "abstract," than the subject matter of the psychoanalyst or historian.

reports, but of interpretations—or rather, since the original historical occurrence itself was to some degree interpreted (and not merely passively perceived or undergone) by the analysand or by the chronicler's eye witness, *re*interpretations. (In this respect—and particularly as regards the analysand—it is correct to say that the original interpretation is an integral part of the historical event.) Analysts and historians select, order, and interpret interpretations that have themselves been selected, ordered, and interpreted. They are, strictly speaking, historiographers, not historians.[2] Freud (1909a, p. 206) himself demonstrated an appreciation of this, in a passage explicitly comparing the analysand to the historian:

> If we do not wish to go astray in our judgement of their historical reality, we must above all bear in mind that people's childhood memories are only consolidated at a later period, usually at the age of puberty; and that this involves a complicated process of remodelling, analogous in every way to the process by which a nation constructs legends about its early history . . . [and] just as a real historian will view the past in the light of the present.

In other words, we are dealing with four chronological levels of interpretation—(1) the original interpretation of the event, at the time of the event, by the participant (i.e., the patient or the chronicler's eyewitness), (2) the patient's or eyewitness's subsequent conscious and unconscious elaborations upon the original interpretation, and (3) such interpretive elaboration that occurs at the time the event is retold to the chronicler or analyst. (4) The historian or analyst then engages in his own interpretive elaboration of this retelling.

---

[2]Here I am using the term "historiography" to mean the "history of histories, the history of the historical enterprise." At all other points throughout this monograph I shall be using "historiography" in its other sense—to mean the methodology and theory of historical practice.

A fourth distinguishing characteristic of historical and psychoanalytic data is that, unlike those in physical science, they often intentionally conceal as much as they reveal. Both chroniclers and patients consciously and unconsciously delete, disguise, and distort, to ends both known and unbeknownst to them. In the transmission and successive recopying of documents, as in the conscious and unconscious reworking of childhood memories, considerable transmutation of the autograph or original impression - interpretation may occur. This confronts psychoanalysts, as well as historians, with the need for what scholars term "diplomatics" (i.e. the study of the nature and authenticity of documents), for weighing and sifting the evidence in their attempt to reconstruct an approximately accurate version of the events and (in the case of the analyst) the fantasies of the past.

Nevertheless, the dynamic psychiatrist is generally less concerned than the historian to distinguish sharply between psychical and actual reality. The clinician appreciates the inextricable and circular relationship between one's fears and fantasies and external reality itself. Psychotherapeutically, what is important is that the patient's (like everyone's) behavior is framed in accord with his psychic reality, his view of self and world. While the patient's conception of his history will bear considerable relationship to what has actually transpired, it will also be determined by his mental set (both at the time of the event's occurrence and at the time of retelling). But historians too are aware that myths and illusions can powerfully influence the past that they study. On the other hand, there are points in every treatment where it is manifestly important, as will be demonstrated, to unravel actuality from fantasy in the patient's recollections.

THEORY AND DATA

Methodological and epistemological considerations emerge logically from our treatment of the subject matter. We now examine a number of overlapping issues which, for convenience, are presented as antitheses: historicism versus positivism, idealism versus realism, theorization versus observation, idiographic explanations versus covering laws, subjectivity versus objectivity, participation versus detachment, *verstehen* versus observation, "presentism" versus antiquarianism, relativism versus psychic unity, and art versus science. When facing such dichotomies both historians and analysts are all too likely to take an either-or stand, rather than the middle way which, I shall repeatedly emphasize, does more justice to reality. Many of these dialectics are exemplified by reference to Freud himself.

In history and psychoanalysis, as in science in general, the *relationship between theory and data* is the issue that overarches all others. What are psychoanalytic and historical facts? Are they discovered or invented, organized or organizable? Should our approach be Kantian or Lockian?

There are those who view historians and psychoanalysts as first gathering the data, unburdened by theoretical preconceptions, and only later theorizing about them; while others act as if they imaginatively spin out what they study. Ranke (1973) in history, and Meyer (1906) in dynamic psychiatry, are the most famous exemplars of the view that data are rock-like entities which, if one only collects them, will animate and assemble themselves into coherent and accurate theories.[3] For Ranke (Ibid, pp. 30–31) the two cardinal characteristics of the historian are "a feeling for and a joy in the particular in and by itself" and the absence of preconceptions; his task is to portray the past "as it actually was [*wie es eigentlich gewesen*]."[4] More recently, phenomenological and existential

---

[3]Beard (1936, p. 31) quotes the sociologist Pareto as representing an extreme version of the inductivist position: "We are following the inductive method. We have no preconceptions, no a priori notions [itself an a priori notion!]. We find certain facts before us. We describe them, classify them, ever on the watch for some uniformity (law) in the relationship between them".

[4]In fairness to Ranke it must be acknowledged that he was not unaware of the fragmentary nature of historical evidence and of the

psychiatrists often write as if theories will spontaneously generate themselves if the patient unfolds his phenomenology in sufficient detail. Langlois and Seignobos (1898), whose handbook educated several generations of historians, were not so naive as to ignore the role of interpretation, but they drew an oversharp line between gathering and criticizing one's data on the one hand, and theorizing about it on the other. At the opposite pole, those like Beard (1934, 1935) and Collingwood (1946) in history, and Schafer (1976, 1978) and Spence (1982) in psychoanalysis, often write as if history and psychoanalysis are exercises in faith and speculative ingenuity, *con*structions rather than *re*constructions.

An erroneous and one-sided conception of the scientific method, based on a caricatured picture of the physical scientist, has kept many historians and dynamic psychiatrists from appreciating the interactive and mutually conditioning role of theorizing and data gathering in history, psychoanalysis, and science in general. Anxiety over whether they are "scientific," in a sense that would satisfy their most hostile critics, has led historians and analysts to cleave to a simplistic "observation before theorization" model long after natural scientists have abandoned it as illusory. Fortunately, many historians and psychoanalysts are coming to an honest appreciation of the fluid line between data collecting and theorizing; it is solely by refraction through the selecting and ordering lens of theory that data are reconstituted as facts.

As the philosopher Melden (1969, p. 193) says:

> Progress in empirical inquiry does not occur when minds that are freed of all prepossessions are exposed to the stimulus of fact in order that they may be led by some homing instinct to

---

need for imagination, intuition, and reconstruction—what he termed the "poetic" aspects of the historian's work. Furthermore, one must remember the historical context in which Ranke wrote (the early and middle nineteenth century). He was attempting to emancipate historical studies from thralldom to grand scale philosophical schemes such as Hegel's.

the truth. Facts do not announce their own existence and, even if they did, they do not come labelled with their varying degrees of importance. For history, as written, is no mere catalogue, arranged in chronological order, of past events. Even if such a catalogue existed, it would explain nothing because it included everything. The historian is concerned to explain; he must, if he consults the facts, be led to the facts by the hypotheses in mind, the information at hand; selecting these on the basis of his antecedent knowledge for their presumed importance and exploring in the limited manner possible for him the adequacy of his hypotheses. . .

In line with this, I believe that the distinction between "narrative" or "descriptive" histories on the one hand and "explanatory" or "interpretive" histories on the other, proposed by White (1963) and others, is an artificial one. The narrative in academic history, quite as much as that in psychoanalytic clinical history, is formed from data that have been selected and organized, not merely from an apprehension of their inherent structure or inner logic, but in accord with the theoretical presuppositions of the investigator. There may be a valid distinction between histories that explain more and those that explain less, but a history without interpretation or explanation would not be history, as Meyerhoff (1959, pp. 19–20) explains:

> Fact, theory, and interpretation form a closely knit complex in a historical narrative. The simple facts of history are not simple at all; or insofar as they are simple and elicit universal agreement among historians . . . they seem to be trivial and only reinforce the demand for an interpretation. . . . The facts of history invariably appear in a context of interpretation. There is no narration without interpretation, and there is no interpretation without theory.[5]

---

[5]In practice, it is often difficult to determine whether a particular work is more accurately denominated a piece of "history," "theory," or "criticism"—particularly since any history combines features of

The reader who does not believe Meyerhoff's comments apply equally to psychoanalysis is advised to pick up any of Freud's case histories, where he will see, as Ricoeur (1970) points out, that presentation of data and theoretical elaboration often go hand in hand. This even occurs in some instances where Freud explicitly attempts to separate data from theory—in the Schreber case report, for example, where the portion termed "Case History" is conditioned by theoretical principles very nearly as much as the section entitled "Attempts at Interpretation." In psychoanalysis, Schafer (1978, p. 10) expresses sentiments akin to those of Melden and Meyerhoff: "one cannot establish either the historical sense or the current significance of a fact outside of some context of questions and methods for defining and organizing the material in question."

One's theory of the nature of the historical process leads one to ask some questions but not others, attend more to certain kinds of data than others, view some connections as more important than others, and so forth. For example, it is insuffi-

---

all three. Often the more creative and synthetic histories run the risk of being thrust out of the category of history and into that of social theory, philosophy, or criticism. Consider, for example, two classic studies of Freud—Jones' (1953, 1955, 1957) trilogy and Rieff's (1959) *Freud: The Mind of the Moralist*. The former is presented in the traditional historical narrative format with interpretation weaving itself in and out of the chronologically arranged data. Rieff's book, by contrast, is organized around his thesis. It is not a biography or historical narrative and yet it is grounded in as thorough a knowledge of the history of Freud and his intellectual and cultural ambience as is *The Life and Work of Sigmund Freud*. Rieff's intent is not to write a biography of Freud—though no reader can come away from his book without learning a good deal of history—but to develop a novel perspective on Freud and Western society. Paradoxically, most would consider Jones' work more unequivocally a species of history than Rieff's, and yet Rieff's is the more penetrating and comprehensive analysis of that history.

ciently appreciated that but for theory no psychiatrist would take a longitudinal history or inquire into sexuality and the fantasy life. Before Freud provided a theoretical rationale (i.e., childhood determinism and the role of sexuality and psychical reality in neurosis) for such inquiries, this data was rarely obtained. In history, one could cite the role of Marxist theory in bringing scholars to ask the economic questions they had hitherto neglected. Every historian, like it or not, has an explicit or implicit philosophy of history which ineluctably comes to bear on the data.

Let me illustrate this further with the relationship between the psychoanalytic thesis of historical determinism and the apprehension of transferential behaviors. Behaviors which the analyst denominates "transferential" were observed by psychiatrists long before Freud, but were dismissed as puzzling, meaningless, irritating or, in the case of Breuer, frightening. Their proper significance was not appreciated until Freud elaborated a new theoretical framework—unconscious childhood determinism—in which they assumed crucial significance. In other words, transference is not simply observed, it is observed *and* interpreted.

Much the same point could be made with the Oedipus complex which, except in exotic cases like Oedipus or in psychotics is not observed directly, but rather is inferred from data that are themselves interpreted in accord with the theorem of the "Oedipus complex." What the French historian-political scientist Aron (1969, p. 275) says of the historian applies here to the psychoanalyst: "The historian of a particular sphere subscribes more or less consciously to a theory of his sphere— a theory more often borrowed from the philosopher than the historian. *It is not that the theory can be proved independently of historical data, but that these data never impose a theory, or at any rate, impose it only on condition of their being deciphered in a certain manner.* [my italics]." This applies equally to many natural science hypotheses—the theory of evolution, for example.

Nevertheless, it is not a matter of unwarrantable assumptions or of imposing a theorem such as the Oedipus complex on one's data. The following vignette illustrates that it is a matter of the construct's *interaction* with the data. (And it must be remembered that the Oedipus theorem itself did not spring Athena-like from Freud's head, but that it arose from the interaction between Freud's mind and his data.) It is an excerpt from a session early in the second year of the treatment of Mr. B., a 25-year-old graduate student with a string of disappointing relationships with women he termed "prick teasers" and a penchant for amorous triangles and strip-tease shows.

> He began by talking about stealthily creeping up to the counter of a pharmacy to purchase a pornographic magazine, following which he hurriedly stuffed it into his brief case and left. After conducting some business in the county courthouse he walked into the restroom where he masturbated to pictures in the magazine. When I asked how he felt, he responded, "excited, but afraid I would get caught by the vice squad or somebody." Some minutes later he passed a deserted building, "dirty and delapidated, sort of like a stable," compulsively entered and masturbated, getting his expensive clothes filthy in the process. Here again he expressed excitement, and yet apprehension about being caught. There was silence, following which he remarked that this feeling was similar to that when he masturbated in his bedroom as a teenager. Oftentimes he would not lock the door. When asked whom he feared would walk in on him he replied "well, it was usually right after school, so I guess my mother was usually the only one home." A silence followed and I asked him about the fantasies which accompanied his adolescent masturbation. He replied they were of three older women, friends of his mother. He became uncomfortable, and then laughingly recollected that one of them even had his mother's first name. A long silence followed, at the end of which he nervously recalled an occasion on which he had walked in on his attractive and hysterical mother while she was sun-bathing in the nude.

The themes of sensuality, guilt feelings and inhibitions related thereto, teasing, and the wish-fear of being caught—and catching others—are obvious, but they are not appreciated in their full genetic and dynamic context without application of the Oedipus construct. Furthermore, the material of this session emerged only because of countless prior interventions designed to diminish Mr. B's resistance to acknowledging it— *interventions which would not have occurred had I not appreciated the Oedipus theorem and the sorts of data which point toward the presence of unconscious incestuous strivings.* In short, the theory is neither demanded by the data nor does it create them; rather, it enables one to grasp the significance of the data more fully.

The concepts of the symptom as a "compromise formation" and of "anger turned against the self" as a mechanism of depression are further cases in point. Using such constructs one makes an initial, tentative organization of the data, which then serves as a guide in the subsequent search for information. Such theorems gain credibility from their explanatory power and from the convergence of multiple lines of evidence.[6]

The construct of anger turned inward, for example, receives its warrant, where it applies, from interacting with manifold data such as the following:

> the patient becomes consciously depressed and recounts no signs of anger in situations which would elicit anger in virtually anyone, or he is aware of only momentary anger and subsequent depression; he exhibits marked anxiety whenever anger is discussed; he experiences violent dreams; he engages in passive aggressive behavior or makes destructive paraprax-

---

[6]There is of course a conscious experiential base that helps us grasp the concepts of the unconscious defense mechanism and the compromise formation. Who has not experienced himself suppressing an unwanted memory or fantasy or displacing anger from a person onto an animal or inanimate object? Who has not placed himself in situations designed both to defend against and surreptitiously gratify strivings about which one is ambivalent? We assume that there is a continuum and commonality between activities such as these and their unconscious counterparts.

es; he relates a lifelong history of discomfort with anger; he was reared in a family where his expressions of anger were stifled and where one parent responded to the imprecations of the other with depression; his suicidal fantasies include thoughts about how remorseful and grief stricken certain friends and relatives would be at his funeral; the therapist begins to experience the patient's endless recounting of depressive symptoms and self deprecatory ideas as veiled complaints about the therapist and those whom he represents; the patient feels less depressed on occasions when he can acknowledge his anger; and interpretations consistent with the internalized aggression hypothesis elicit confirmatory responses, associations, and affects.

The following data were organized in the light of the psychoanalytic concept of "actively attempting to master the passively experienced trauma."

Ms. G. presented after a suicide attempt precipitated by learning of a former husband's terminal cancer and her current boyfriend's threat to leave her if she visited the dying man. Past history revealed: the father, to whom the patient had been very close, left the family when she was 9 and died soon after of cancer; in early adolescence she engaged in an ongoing sexual relationship with a doctor who was killed in an accident shortly after they had agreed to marry; in late adolescence she married a doctor who gave most of his attention to his mother and eventually divorced Ms. G.; she then married a merchant who died a few years later from a metabolic disease; she left her third husband, a prominent business executive, shortly after she learned he was still seeing his former wife; for the ten years thereafter she engaged in numerous short term relationships—nearly all of which terminated at her own initiative—and in prostitution from which she earned a considerable income. In regard to this she spoke somewhat proudly of the "sense of mastery and control I get from being paid for sex."

The clinician posited that prostitution and leaving men represented, in part, an attempt to actively master the traumata (of childhood seduction by the doctor and being left by the father and other important men). This construct was then tested against the patient's behavior, associations, and remembrances in the subsequent sessions.

With his construct of "displacement" Freud (1918, p.73) organized the Wolf Man's account of his reaction to his sister's death as follows:

> When the news of his sister's death arrived, so the patient told me, he felt hardly a trace of grief. He had to force himself to show signs of sorrow, and was quite coolly to rejoice at having now become the sole heir to the property . . . . It was to be assumed, no doubt, that his grief over the loss of the most dearly loved member of his family would meet with an inhibition in its expression, as a result of the continued operation of his jealousy of her and of the added presence of his incestuous love for her which had now become unconscious [the data for all this comes from other portions of the narrative]. But I could not do without some substitute for the missing outbursts of grief. And this was at last found in another expression of feeling which had remained inexplicable to the patient. A few months after his sister's death he himself made a journey in the neighbourhood in which she had died. There he sought out the burial place of a great poet, who was at that time his ideal, and shed bitter tears upon his grave. This reaction seemed strange to him himself, for he knew that more than two generations had passed by since the death of the poet he admired. He only understood it when he remembered that his father had been in the habit of comparing his dead sister's works with the great poet's. He gave me another indication of the correct way of interpreting the homage which he ostensibly paid to the poet by a mistake in his story which I was able to detect at this point. He had repeatedly specified before that his sister had shot herself; but he was now obliged to make a correction and say that she had taken poison. The poet, however, had been shot in a duel (ibid, p. 23).

This is an excellent example of the explanatory power of psychoanalytic propositions, of the manner in which they interact with the data, and of the sort of evidence that converges to support them.

In the sphere of "applied psychoanalysis" one might allude to constructs such as the following: the similarities in form and content between dreams, jokes, myths, and psychotic thinking reflect an underlying commonality—i.e., regression to the primary process modes of childhood; religious and obsessive-compulsive rituals share similar unconscious determinants; and mental mechanisms such as "projection" can become institutionalized by whole societies to form animistic and mythico-religious systems (what Spiro [1965] calls "culturally constituted defense mechanisms"; see also Wallace, 1983c, pp. 217–232). Although it is difficult to conceive of quasi-experimental or quantitative research paradigms that could support or refute such hypotheses, they are powerful explanatory tools that tie many disparate facts together. One could subject such theorems to a species of empirical test by exploring the history and function of myths and rituals in a particular society and investigating , with the clinical psychoanalytic method, the meaning and functional relationship of the myth or ritual to the histories and mental economies of particular individuals. With such procedures one could determine the extent to which myths, rituals, dreams, symptoms, and certain childhood behaviors serve similar ongoing functions and share common mechanisms. However, one could not answer with any degree of certitude—despite Freud's intense desire to—questions concerning the origin of cultural institutions with this technique.

Turning to a slightly different aspect of the relationship between theory and data, it is important to point out that a certain amount of the analyst's evidence consists of what might be termed "second order evidence"—that is, data that are themselves interpreted as manifestations of other sorts of data. This was the case, for instance, when Freud (1909a) cited aspects of the Rat Man's transference as proof of Freud's hypothesis about the patient's childhood relationship with his father. In short, data available from the patient's adulthood (i.e., his relationship with Freud) were interpreted as standing for then unavailable data from his childhood. Testing clinical hypotheses against universal symbols would be another example of second-order evidence; inferring a castration complex from exhibitionism, or a primal scene from a fear of loud noises, still others. In practice, psychoanalysts rarely, if ever, build formulations around such evidence alone. Rather, they use it to alert them to issues they might otherwise ignore, and view it in the context of other lines of evidence.[7]

In history and psychiatry it is a question of theory on two levels. Each historian or clinician possesses both a theory of the historical process in general and of the culture, period, or individual he is investigating in particular. Competing schools of psychology and psychotherapy (such as the Freudian, Jungian, Adlerian, and so forth) may be differentiated according to the various philosophies of the history of the individual which they espouse.

Freud, raised in the mechanistic and positivistic climate of Helmholtz and Brücke, tended to view the line between data and interpretation as hard and fast. Data were substantial things and theory depicted their nature and arrangement. This was manifested in his numerous archaeological metaphors of psychotherapy, in which unconscious memories and impulses were portrayed as possessing artifact-like permanence; the analyst had only to unearth and describe them

---

[7]In instances, such as in some of the formulations of Kohut (1971) and other theorists about the earliest stages of infantile psychical life and object relations, the use of "second-order evidence" can favor a certain amount of circular reasoning. For example, in line with Kohut's principle of "the telescoping of analogous experiences" and his theorem about the nature of early mother-child relations in pathological narcissism, Mr. A's recollections of oedipal and latency age disillusionments with his father are taken as pointing toward much earlier disillusionments at the hands of the mother (any memories of which would be largely preverbal and essentially unrecapturable). These putative maternal disillusionments are then treated as the predisposing causes of Mr. A's pathological reaction to his father's disappointing behavior.

(see, for example, Freud, 1909a, pp. 176–177). In the Dora
case he (1901a, pp. 112–113) strenuously asserted the absence
of speculation: "the material for my hypotheses was collected
by the most extensive and laborious series of observation . . .
any one who sets out to investigate the same region of phenomena and employs the same method will find himself impelled to take up the same position." Freud seems not to appreciate that one's organization and interpretation of the data
invariably presuppose some theoretical perspective.

Nevertheless, Freud was quite capable of respecting the
knotty epistemological problems here entailed. He came to
comprehend that the analyst's task, like the archaeologist's,
is not merely uncovering but *reconstructing*. He (1909a, p.
207) appreciated, as we have seen, that patients, like nations,
refashion their histories from the vantage point of current
concerns. He possessed a fine tolerance for the ambiguity and
incompleteness inherent in the interpretation of dreams and
the analysis of personalities. Elsewhere Freud (1915, p. 117)
acknowledged, "Even at the stage of description it is not possible to avoid applying certain abstract ideas to the material in
hand, *ideas derived from somewhere or other, but certainly not
from the new observations alone* (my italics)." In arriving at
"generalizations, rules and laws which bring order into chaos
we cannot avoid falsifying [reality]," Freud (1937a, p. 225)
admitted; with tongue only partly in cheek Freud (ibid., p.
225) "almost said 'phantasying'" when referring to metapsychological theorizing. "But does not every science come in
the end to a kind of mythology?" he (1932) asked Einstein.
More often, however, Freud fancied himself searching after
the truth in a purely empirical mode; he was antipathetic
toward contemporary physicists who stressed the mystery of
nature and who threatened the Newtonian universe.

In practice, historians and dynamic psychiatrists approach
their subjects in a manner that allows free play between observation and interpretation, between a relatively passive re-
ceptivity (Freud's "evenly suspended attention") to the data
and an active restructuring of it. Historians and psychoanalysts go over and back over their patient or texts in ex-

quisite detail, saturating themselves in their sources. They encounter the same datum repeatedly—but often in slightly different contexts or connections with data already uncovered. Patterns and themes begin to appear, analogies are drawn, hitherto meaningless mounds of data are ordered; some of this is the fruit of the practitioner's preconscious and unconscious connections between, and elaborations upon, the material. From these arrangements, causal hypotheses will be constructed and tested. The whole process, absorbing and reconstituting, observing and interpreting, is such an inextricably interactive, mutually determining one that a unilinear cause and effect model does it no justice. The interpreter imposes himself on the data no more than the data impose themselves on the interpreter. The choice is not between Kant and Locke, but a recognition that each requires the other. Consider the following back-to-back sessions (with Ms. C, whom we encounter again in Chapter 4) as yet other instances of how the clinician's conceptualizing interacts with the patient's productions:

Patient: Joe [a long time friend of the family] told me that he thinks, from what he knows of Mama, that one reason she won't talk with me about Daddy is that she had no relationship with him. [silent shaking of her head]. I don't know. This struck a chord although I don't remember enough to know if he's right. [silence].

Therapist: What do you remember about your parents' time together?

Patient: Oh, I hardly remember them doing much together. Their interaction was usually with the whole family. They looked pleasant enough [silence]. Maybe one of the reasons they never argued is that they were indifferent to each other.

Therapist: How do you feel about the idea that your parents might not have had much of a relationship [her father was long deceased]?

Patient: [sighs] Sad, disappointed for Daddy—and Mama too, I guess. [silence]. But relieved too, I guess, in a way. If they didn't have much of a relationship then it means that there's not something wrong with me that I can't have a relationship with Mama either [silence]. [Her complete "ownership" of responsibility for deficits in the mother-daughter relationship had been repeatedly discussed in prior sessions.]

Therapist: I wonder if there might not be other reasons for your relief. I'm thinking about what you told me last week about the pleasure you took in your "special" relationship with your father and about your adolescent fantasy that you were not your mother's child, but rather your father's by a previous marriage.

Patient: Yes, you're right. There is some of that. In a way I do like to think I had something with Daddy that Mama didn't. You know, Daddy and I used to ride in the front seat and Mama and my brother and sister in the back [silence]. Yes, I hate to admit it, but I like to think I gave Daddy something that Mama couldn't [silence]. But it makes me feel bad that I might have kept Daddy from Mama.

Therapist: It makes you feel *guilty* [here clarifying her feeling]?

Patient: Yes [silence]. But then I think, "what about Mama?" She's controlling. She could have kept me from him. Maybe she said, in effect. "Here, he's yours." Maybe her being in the hospital so much was a way of getting away from him. I remember so well my becoming the woman of the house while Mama was sick. I resented her for it.

Therapist: But you may have enjoyed it too.

Patient: Yes, in a way I'm sure I did.

The hour continued in the same vein. The following session she began by talking about her depression over the weekend. She had no idea what was causing it. When asked to associate to it the following train of thought emerged.

Patient: What comes to mind is an angry remark I made to Mama on Friday. I feel guilty about it now [silence]. I'm thinking about an older friend—no, an acquaintance—of mine who died last week. She was a woman who often mistreated her children. She ended up putting those kids in an orphanage. At the funeral I was thinking mostly about those kids, not Alice [the deceased] [silence]. I felt guilty about not going to the show with Mama Thursday night. So I asked her over to dinner Saturday [silence]. I hadn't gone to temple. She picked up my next door neighbor and saw my car at home. Later she gave me hell about it, guilt tripped me.

Therapist: Did you know she was going to pick up your neighbor? [Ms. C and her mother attended different synagogues.]

Patient: I'm sure I must have. She often does [silence]. I see what you're getting at. That I engineered it so she could tell me how bad I am. Probably so.

Therapist: That you wanted punishment.

Patient: Hell, I probably did because Saturday I did think, "I wonder what Mama would say about this." I guess I did feel a little guilty about it.

Therapist: You felt guilty last session about something else—keeping your father from your mother.

Patient: [long silence]. Yes. [silence]. You know, I've wondered a lot why I moved back to K [her home town]. Mama used to bug me all the time when I lived in B [four hundred miles away]. I should have figured it would have been ten times worse back in K. But at least I didn't end up in the same area of town with her. I guess I came back to take care of her [silence]. I guess I was afraid that if I was away . . . [silence].

Therapist: That she might die? [In earlier hours she had talked about her intense sense of responsibility for her mother's well being].

Patient: Yes. And I need to keep her alive. I guess I felt like my independence might kill her, but [silence].

Therapist: But?

Patient: But I think in some ways it would be easier if she died.

Therapist: That's one of the things you've been feeling guilty about.

Patient: Probably [preoccupied silence].

Therapist: I wonder if, when your father died, you might have wished it had been your mother?

Patient: I don't remember thinking it then, but since then I've wondered if I might not have preferred my mother to die. It would have been easier. I do remember, when my grandfather died, wishing it had been my grandmother instead. After he died my grandmother actually accused me of keeping Granddaddy away from her. Sounds familiar, doesn't it?

Therapist: nods

Patient: [silence] I feel so bad, so guilty about all this. [There followed a good deal of self reproach about her feelings about her grandmother and mother and her "greedy" relationship with their husbands. She also related her recent guilt-laden apology to her mother (who was then temporarily bedridden with influenza) for a trivial incident *years* before—"accidentally" jostling the mother as the two were leaving a crowded theater.]

Therapist: It seems that your friend's death stirred up your anger at your mother and that you then turned this on yourself. I believe that this, and your guilt feelings, were causing your depression over the weekend.

Patient: slowly nods.

In the subsequent session much additional hostility and guilt feelings vis-à-vis the mother emerged. It was still several months before the patient became aware of the incestuous aspects of her "special" relationship with father—and the complex of guilt feelings associated with this.

Ordinarily there is a balance between interpretation and observation. Problems arise only where one's theory allows one to ignore vast quantities of relevant data—as Freud's (1939) psychological and biogenetic theories of monotheism permitted him to ignore the historical and cultural contexts of Judaism; as Sulloway's (1979) insistence on the a priori biogenetic and biological strains in Freud led him to overlook Freud's psychological and empirical side; as Kohut's (1979) version of metapsychology permitted him to miss potent oedipal themes in Mr. Z.; as Little Hans' father's preoccupation with his son's positive Oedipus complex allowed him to neglect clear manifestations of a negative Oedipus; as some historians' commitment to economic explanations allows them to ignore social, political, psychological, and ideological factors; and as Zilboorg's (1935, 1941) presupposition that all witches were psychotic or hysterical allowed him to ignore much evidence to the contrary. No point of view and one drowns in one's data; too strenuous a point of view and one never tastes them.

In his clinical work Freud generally anchored his fomulations to detailed histories; he (1909b), p. 64) criticized Little Hans' analyst father for allowing, at several points, the father's own presuppositions to interfere with the son's line of thought. The technique of "evenly suspended attention" was advocated, in part, to prevent the analyst's preconceptions from distorting his view of the patient's history and phenomenology. Freud (1909b, pp. 22–23) advised: "It is not in the least our business to 'understand' a case at once: this is only possible at a later stage, when we have received enough impressons of it. For the present we will suspend our judgement and give our impartial attention to everything that there is to observe." "The most successful cases are those in which one proceeds, as it were, without any purpose in view, allows oneself to be taken by surprise by any new turn in them, and always meets them with an open mind, free from presuppositions" (Freud, 1912, p. 114).

Nevertheless, there were occasions, as we shall see, when he suspended the gathering of phenomenological and historical data in order to speculate prematurely. This was particularly true in Freud's sociocultural work. In his studies of religious rituals and beliefs, for example, he did not trouble himself to learn their cultural history or to familiarize himself with the phenomenology of their practitioners. That telling rosary beads appears similar to the obsessional's counting and recounting the buttons on his shirt becomes sufficient to confirm the hypothesis that both behaviors are manifestations of isolation of affect and doing and undoing; the need to appreciate the historical and cultural context of the nun's behavior and whether her phenomenology is identical to the obsessional's is obviated (Rieff, 1953, p. 109). Such dangers are inherent in Freud's (1915–1917, p. 67) dictum that "phenomena as perceived must yield in importance to trends which are only hypothetical."

Even so, Freud is correct that we cannot dispense with "hypothetical trends." Phenomenological psychiatrists are naive to think that their patients' "shining forth," to use Boss's (1963) term, will be understood without the intervening selecting and organizing principles of the clinician. One need do no more than consult any of the phenomenological/existential case histories—Boss's account of "Dr. Cobling," for example, which he explicitly puts foward as an atheoretical narrative designed to illustrate the inadequacy of psychodynamics—to see that they are shot through with implicit theoretical presuppositions (many of them Freudian!). If psychodynamics without phenomenology is sterile and reductive, phenomenology without psychodynamics is presentistic and chaotic.

The key, as Hartmann (1927, p. 376) grasped, is maintaining balance:

> I heartily subscribe to Kronfeld's view: "Phenomenology is a preliminary approach necessary for any psychological theory which seeks to explain phenomena genetically. . . . It is on the one hand the precondition for the formation of the theories, and on the other hand it demands such theories; otherwise it remains essentially incomplete."

The following interchange with an obsessive-compulsive patient, Professor T, illustrates how phenomenology and psychodynamics can illumine one another.

> He spent the first few minutes of the hour talking about wanting to be "fed" by his parents and explaining that this involved

everything from being cooked for to being acknowledged (especially by his father) as one who is worthwhile and lovable; he spoke of his sadness, frustration, and anger at the "conditional" nature of such "feeding" as he received.

Thence he spoke of his wife's new evening job and his assuming the responsibility for preparing supper and getting his small children bathed and to bed. He merely touched on this, however, and was prepared to move on when I asked him to spell out what it was like with his wife away and his tending the children at night. Initially he gave me a mechanical report of his wife's new job and the evening schedule with the children. It was necessary for me to stop him and request that he flesh out those evenings. There followed a concrete description of his coming home from work and wanting to have a drink and unburden himself to his wife, only to encounter her as she rushed out the door to her job. The more concrete he became about the interaction, the harder it was for him to ignore his hurt, frustration, and anger at not being "fed" by her.

Thence he turned to his interaction with his children. He began dinner at 5:00 P.M. and spent a few frustrating minutes consulting recipes and hunting up ingredients and utensils. He became tense and irritated when speaking of the necessity to stop every few minutes to settle arguments between the children, then followed the struggle to get them to the table, refill their glasses, and so forth. He spoke of how hard it is to converse with them; he had to continually suppress a nervous urge to move away from the table. Then he spoke of the frustration of cleaning the kitchen and simultaneously answering their battery of childish questions. He described an incident the previous night in which he lost his temper over his son's relentless queries and spoke of his concern over the boy's response: "Daddy, you make me feel dumb alot." The patient then paused and tearily expressed his fear that he does not give his children sufficient affection—"but I feel like I have to overcome a tremendous block in myself to give to them." I responded, "It's hard to give what you yourself were denied [referring to his frequent descriptions of his father's hypercritical and unloving interactions with him]." He nodded and spoke of his anger and disappointment vis-à-vis his father and his desire to do better by his children. He closed by bemoaning the rigid and mechanical manner in which he puts his children to bed and of how he must suppress the strong urge to belt them when they take more than a few minutes to fall asleep.

Without the phenomenology I could not have delivered my genetic interpretation; without the interpretation the full significance of the phenomenology would have gone begging.

Analytic listening is a complex and sophisticated perception occurring simultaneously in several modes. On the one hand, the analyst's aim to elucidate the historically determined, unconscious dynamics of his patient's conscious experience does not lead him to ignore the latter or dismiss it as "mere resistance" or epiphenomenal froth. The contents of consciousness are quite as real as those of unconsciousness and must be grasped in their own right, as well as apprehended as indicators of an unconscious and genetic dimension. In many dreams, for example, it is as important to appreciate the dreamer's current, conscious and preconscious attitudes and concerns as it is to penetrate the latent dream thoughts and the genetic foundation. Ego psychology, it can be argued, has enhanced the psychoanalyst's appreciation of such points.

On the other hand, no analyst aims at the phenomenologist's goal of "hearing only what is said"—as if any human being could achieve such a feat anyway. One certainly strives to hear what the patient says, but in the context of all that he has said, and much that he has left unsaid, before. One attempts to appreciate each communication in and of itself and as part of a broader context comprising the themes in the patient's life history and the patterns of behavior throughout the treatment. One listens to what the patient says and consciously experiences, but in part as a pointer to what is left unsaid and unconscious. And he listens with an evenly hovering attention that facilitates access to the preconscious and unconscious aspects of his perception. Finally, as Reik (1949) made abundantly clear, the analyst listens to what the analyst is telling himself—as this often helps illumine what the patient is telling him (to be exemplified in the subjectivity–objectivity section). In sum, if one listens only for what is said, he will end up hearing far less than he is actually told.

POSITIVISM VERSUS HISTORICISM

Our discussion of the relationship between theory and data fans out in two directions: further consideration of the analyst's and the historian's encounter with their "material" and an examination of the controversy between nomothetic and idiographic explanations. Let us begin with the latter, and reserve the former for the next chapter.

The positivistic versus historicist debate has raged for decades in history and psychoanalysis (as in the other social sciences). Broadly speaking, the positivist is looking for regularities and universalities, and the historicist for concrete events and reputedly idiosyncratic lines of development. In history, positivism takes the form of large scale, linear or cyclical, speculative schemes such as Comte's, Spencer's, Marx's, Spengler's, and the cultural evolutionists', and of less grandiose attempts, such as Hempel's, to shunt particularist explanations through covering laws. Freud, as we shall see, had a strongly positivistic side, though he was historicist as well. In history, extreme historicism is represented by those like Ranke and in psychiatry by those like Meyer. In a sense, we can interpret the neo-Freudian defection of Kardiner and others as an historicist critique of the positivistic aspects of classical psychoanalysis.[8]

---

[8]It must be acknowledged that there has been considerable ambiguity and confusion in the use of the terms "positivism" and "historicism." Today the former is often used synonymously with "empirical" and "realist." At other times "positivism" refers primarily to preoccupation with the discovery-formulation of lawful regularities and generalities. Although empiricism and preoccupation with laws and general regularities can go hand in hand, nineteenth century

In history itself, outside Marxist circles, there is little attention to lawful schemes of universal development though there is an active controversy over covering laws. In psychoanalysis both issues are alive. Let us begin with a discussion of epigenetic, universalist schemes in Freudian psychology.

I (1983c) have recently attempted to document that Freud's theory of personality was partly determined by his infatuation with the ideas of those like Comte, Buckle, and Spencer. In this work I discussed Freud's running battle between historicist and ahistoricist (positivist) explanations of human behavior. The cultural evolutionists' tenets of psychic unity and the comparative method, their belief in fixed and unilinear schemes of development, and their tendency to espouse the biogenetic law and Lamarckism contributed to the ahistorical aspects of Freud's cultural and psychological work.

The idea of psychic unity assumes, as the American anthropologist Morgan (1907, p. 275) said, that "The human mind, specifically the same in all individuals in all the tribes and nations of mankind and limited in the range of its powers works and must work, in the same uniform channels, and within narrow limits of variation." The comparative method was founded on the idea of "survivals" ("processes, customs, opinions . . . carried on by force of habit into a new state of society different from that in which they had their original

---

positivists' concern to leap immediately to the latter often lent their work a markedly unempirical character. Twentieth century positivists, by contrast, continue to emphasize laws and regularities, but are much more empiricist and epistemologically sophisticated than their nineteenth century counterparts. It was the nineteenth century variety by which Freud was mostly influenced. Nineteenth century historicism, by contrast, was an empiricist counterbalance to the positivistic subsumption of particulars to universals. Nevertheless, some writers (such as Popper) have complicated the picture by using the term "historicism" to refer to preoccupation with universalist and lawful schemes of history, rather than with concrete data and idiosyncratic lines of development.

home" [Tylor, 1874, p. 16]), the notion that certain contemporary primitive cultures are a faithful reflection of those of prehistoric times, and the conviction that one can rank cultures on a scale of development. This device consisted in extrapolating from known stages of development in one culture to unknown stages in another (e.g., looking to nineteenth century Melanesians for information about what the prehistoric Greeks were like). Many of the cultural evolutionists also espoused the idea that psychological processes and memory traces could be transmitted through Lamarckian inheritance and that the psychological development of each individual biogenetically recapitulates that of his ancestors.

Freud was more ahistorical in his cultural and applied psychoanalytic than in his clinical-psychological work. In *Totem and Taboo,* for example, he applied phylogenetic (i.e., the primal parricide) and psychological theorems to institutionalized behaviors whose histories and cultural contexts he had not studied and whose practitioners he had not analyzed. Important aspects of the Judaic and Christian religions were explained as recapitulations of the putative murder of the prehistoric "primal father;" the Lamarckian transmission of the memory of and remorse over this deed was said to determine much of religious philosophy and ritual. Freud picked and chose his data from authors, such as Frazer, who had in turn picked and chosen their data from a welter of sources without regard to synchronic and diachronic context.

Freud's adherence to an exaggerated concept of psychic unity allowed him to ignore history, diffusion, and the role of cultural conditioning in psychology, and hence to feel quite confident in generalizing his discoveries with Viennese neurotics to the members of exotic cultures he had never visited. His allegiance to the comparative method permitted him to write a good deal of conjectural history about primitive institutions. He accepted without question the cultural evolutionists' positivistic schemes: that all civilizations must follow a regular developmental course from animism through magic to religion to science; that totemism everywhere precedes religion; that matrilineal kinship systems precede patrilineal ones; that monogamy grows out of group marriage; and so forth.

As Rieff (1959, pp. 234–235) says, "Freud the social theorist, so far as he was identical with Freud the natural scientist, showed the traditional positivist eagerness to eliminate the challenge of history by finding lawfulness in nature. . . . For Freud, psychological knowledge was the only necessary data; history was not evidence but exemplification, as in theological argument." It was Freud's penchant for analogizing, Rieff (1953, p. 108) tells us, that facilitated this cavalier treatment of culture history: "The analogy was sufficient to draw the inference. Concrete historical documentation was superfluous. Psychoanalytic analogies were to comprehend all the traditional disciplines of the social sciences."

For Freud, Weinstein and Platt (1973, p. 3) contend, "the oedipal drama is inevitably and immutably the decisive reality, and what is important in and for man occurs independently of specific social structures and without reference to historical time." Similarly, Ricoeur (1970, p. 243) opines that to Freud "there is no history of religion." Freud saw it not as a social institution with its own line of development, but primarily as an area of "emotive repetition" (e.g., the Oedipus complex, the primal parricide). Consequently, says Ricoeur, any gaps in this history were considered inessential.

The same criticisms could be brought to bear against Freud's psychohistorical work. For example, although Freud (in E. Freud et al., 1978, p. 224) himself advised Lytton Strachey of the impossibility of ferreting out the dynamics of historical figures, he analyzed Leonardo and Dostoevsky with a vengeance. His formulations of these individuals were constructed around embarrassingly little historical data and tell us, I have argued (1978, 1979), more about Freud than about his subjects.

From the historicism-ahistoricism polarity in Freud's cultural work, which I do not consider to be a valid example of the psychoanalytic method, we shall turn to this dialectic as it presents in his clinical and psychological theorizing.

For example, Freud cautioned against interpreting dreams on the basis of symbols alone, without regard to the dreamer's life story and associations; yet in later years he (1915–17, pp. 150–151) suggested that, as our knowledge of universal dream sybolism increases, we can dispense with the history and associations altogether. In regard to the incest taboo and the latency stage of psychosexual development, he (1905a, pp. 177–78, 241) alternated between viewing them as socially acquired and as transmitted through Lamarckian inheritance. He (1905a, p. 234) asserted that "the external influences of seduction are capable of provoking interruptions of the latency period or even its cessation" and yet opined elsewhere (in Jones, 1957, p. 354) that the duration of this stage was phylogenetically determined. Freud (1905a, p. 18) advised that "we are obliged to pay as much attention in our case histories to the purely human and social circumstances of our patients as to the somatic data and symptoms of the disorder," and yet in the Wolf Man report he delighted in demonstrating "the [phylogenetic] schema truimphing over the experience of the individual" (1918, p. 119). On the one hand he (1923a, 1938, p. 206) conceptualized the superego as the precipitate of one's childhood identifications and of the incorporation of aspects of the wider social ambience; on the other hand he viewed it as a biogenetic-Lamarckian memory trace of the tyrannical primal father (1930, pp. 130–131). He acknowledged the influence of environment and individual history on the nature and manifestation of the Oedipus complex, but at other times collapsed ontogeny into phylogeny and saw the complex as an irreducible biogenetic-Lamarckian given (Freud, 1918, pp. 86, 119). The same dichotomy is present in Freud's consideration of the other phases of psychosexual development (Freud, 1905a, p. 241). In short, if one views the phenomena of psychosexual development as manifestations of phylogenetically determined universal cycles, then one is free to ignore the vicissitudes of interpersonal experience. Fortunately, in clinical practice Freud did not allow his phylogenetic-Lamarckian bent to interfere with his appreciation of the concrete history of the individual.

A primary contribution of *Studies on Hysteria* was its insistence that neurotic symptoms be understood diachronically. Although in the early 1890's Freud's recognition of the role of history in psychopathology was limited to the immediate context of origin of the presenting symptoms themselves, he soon realized that the relevant history extended back to the first years of life.

In the Dora case, for instance, he (1901a, p. 27) noted that the adult trauma was "insufficient to explain or to determine the *particular character* of the symptoms . . . we must go back to her childhood and look about there for any influences or impressions which might have had an effect analogous to that of a trauma." Such findings led Freud (ibid, p. 16) to "begin the treatment, indeed, by asking the patient to give me the *whole story of his life* and *illness*" (1901a, p. 163, my italics). In the third chapter I examine the influence of Darwin and the cultural evolutionists on Freud's genetic method (see also Wallace, 1983c).

Let us focus on Freud's historiography as it manifests itself in one of his most famous case histories, the Rat Man. This case is also significant in that we possess Freud's day by day account of the treatment, which we can compare with the published report.

Here we find Freud at his most historicist and ahistoricist. As to the former, he began the treatment by gleaning a detailed anamnesis of the chief complaint—the Rat Man's obsessional ideas. There are many other instances in the treatment where we see Freud taking pains to set behaviors in broad current and historical interpersonal contexts. Few historicists would quibble with the following manifesto:

> The solution is effected by bringing the obsessional ideas into temporal relationship with the patient's experiences, that is to say, by enquiring when a particular obsessional idea made its first appearance and in what external circumstances it is apt to occur. . . . We can easily convince ourselves that, when once the interconnections between an obsessional idea and the patient's experiences have been discussed, there will be no diffi-

culty in obtaining access to whatever else may be puzzling or worth knowing in the pathological structure we are dealing with—its meaning, the mechanism of its origin, and its derivation from the preponderant motive forces of the mind (Freud, 1909a, pp. 186–87).

This theoretical statement is exemplified in a splendidly historicist piece of work that immediately follows. The patient had just informed Freud that he had great difficulty studying owing to his girlfriend's recent absence (because her grandmother was ill). In the midst of his studies, the Rat Man had the following thought: " 'If you received a command to take your examination this term at the first possible opportunity, you might manage to obey it. But if you were commanded to cut your throat with a razor, what then?' " (ibid, p. 187). There immediately transpired an impulse to harm himself, which was replaced by the uncomfortable thought: " 'No, it's not so simple as that. You must [first] go and kill the old woman [the grandmother]'."

Freud (pp. 187–88) reconstructed the history of this behavior as follows:

In this instance the connection between the compulsive idea and the patient's life is contained in the opening words of his story. His lady was absent, while he was working very hard for an examination so as to bring the possibility of an alliance with her nearer. While he was working he was overcome by a longing for his absent lady, and he thought of the cause of her absence. And now there came over him something which, if he had been a normal man, would probably have been some kind of feeling of annoyance with her grandmother: "Why must the old woman get ill just at the very moment when I'm longing for *her* so frightfully?" We must suppose that something similar but far more intense passed through our patient's mind—an unconscious fit of rage which could combine with his longing and find expression in the exclamation: "Oh, I should like to go and kill that old woman for robbing me of my love." Thereupon followed the command: "Kill yourself, as a punishment for these savage and murderous passions." The whole process then passed into the obsessional patient's consciousness accompanied by the most violent affect and *in a reverse order*—the punitive command coming first, and the mention of the guilty outburst afterwards [my italics].[9]

This case report also exemplifies the time honored historical technique of looking for themes, patterns, and parallels, and drawing causal inferences therefrom—the inductive aspect of the historian's work. This occurs, for example, with the themes of receiving commands, doing and undoing, and so forth. Of course *there is a sense in which this search for themes, as previously implied, is itself dependent upon adherence to a theory that tells one that there will be themes to be found and upon an experience and training that confirms this.* There is thus a circular relationship between the concept of historical determinism and the apprehension of themes: without the former one would often overlook the form and content common to otherwise discrete and idiosyncratic events; without the latter one would not be alerted to the necessity for a concept of historical determinism.

Freud's daily process notes contain much more historical data than the published case history, as well as a clearer demarcation between Freud's data and his interpretations. Nevertheless, even here it is at times difficult to separate the data from Freud's theoretical elaboration upon it; and we often encounter what would be considered, by today's standards, very premature formulations and interpretations indeed.

For example, in the third (!) hour, from data gathered about the Rat Man's relationship with his girlfriend and several paramours, and the context of some of his hostile obsessional thoughts (including their relationship to an elderly professor

---

[9]Another good example would be Freud's elucidation of the causes of Dora's *tussis nervosa* and aphonia by placing these symptoms within the context of Herr K's presence or absence. See also the Wolf Man case report (Freud, 1918, p. 23),

who had inadvertently frustrated one of the Rat Man's trysts), Freud (p. 263) presented the patient—at this point in complete absence of childhood history—the following reconstruction: "how before the age of six he had been in the habit of masturbating and how his father had forbidden it, using as a threat the phrase 'it would be the death of you' and perhaps also threatening to cut off his penis."

The Rat Man's subsequent associations and recollections, and history gleaned in later sessions, eminently support this hypothesis. At issue is not whether it proved correct, but Freud's procedure in arriving at it. This is a good example of deductive reasoning and the use of a device we shall consider in a moment—the covering law. In short, from generalizations derived from the psychoanalytic theory of psychosexual development and obsessional neurosis, coupled with specific (though fragmentary) current data about his patient, Freud retrodicted a particular set of circumstances in the Rat Man's childhood. Here, as elsewhere, Freud relied on the requirements of psychoanalytic theory as much as on the clinical data themselves. The Dora case contains many examples of this as well. Indeed, as Rieff (1959) remarks, the interchange between Freud and Dora at times resembled an intellectual combat.

Premature interpretations and reconstructions such as these, which Freud himself (1938, p. 178) later warned against, laid him open to the charge of suggestion. And unfriendly critics' suspicions were unlikely to be allayed by protests, however correct, that "the mechanism of our assistance [consists in] giving the patient the conscious anticipatory idea of what he may expect to find, and he then finds the repressed unconscious idea in himself on the basis of its similarity with the anticipatory one" (Freud, 1910a, p. 142).

Now retrodiction is something every psychoanalyst engages in and often, like Freud, with uncanny accuracy. Nevertheless, analysts do not ordinarily dispense with an inductive testing (i.e., history gathering, as well as the observation of transferential themes, patterns of associating, and so forth) of such reconstructions before feeling confident enough to communicate them to the patient who, in any event, would be resistant to hearing them early in therapy. Freud's penetrating intuition and conviction in the psychic unity of humankind allowed him to dispense, at times, with the empirical aspects of psychoanalysis. As Jones (1953, pp. 96–97) put it, "His great strength, though sometimes also his weakness, was the quite extraordinary respect he had for the *singular* fact . . . when he got hold of a simple but significant fact he would feel, and know, that it was an example of something general or universal, and the idea of collecting statistics on the matter was quite alien to him."

The Little Hans Case, while Freud was the analyst only at second hand, provides in some respects a more equitable balance between theorizing and data gathering than the Rat Man report. It is true that the observer—Hans' father—was a proponent of the psychoanalytic mode of organizing and interpreting experience. But it is equally plain that the son's preoccupations with sexuality, hostility, castration, and the origin of babies preceded any interpretations received from his father.

For example, Little Hans was engaging in masturbation from his third year, had received a castration threat from his mother at 3½, was very concerned with the size of his organ and whether all individuals have penises, and had been sexually stimulated by his mother's behavior (caressing and exhibitionism). Apropos evidence for his castration complex, independent of the father's interpretations, consider Hans' persistent denial of what he had actually observed on several occasions (with his sister and mother)—that women do not have penises—and his two fantasies: *"I was in the bath, and then the plumber came and unscrewed it. Then he took a big borer and stuck it into my stomach. . . . The plumber came; and first he took away my behind with a pair of pincers, and then gave me another, and then the same with my widdler"* (Freud, 1909b, pp. 65, 98; Freud's italics).

In regard to Little Hans' speculations about where babies come from consider the following:

Hannah [his baby sister, whose birth precipitated his neurosis] travelled with us to Gmunden in a box like that [his mother would have been pregnant with her then]. Whenever we travelled to Gmunden she travelled with us in the box. You don't believe me again? Really, Daddy. Do believe me. We got a big box and it was full of babies (ibid, p. 69).

Hanna just came. Frau Kraus [the midwife] put her in the bed. She couldn't walk, of course. But the stork carried her in his beak. . . . The stork came up the stairs to a landing . . . and he had the right key and unlocked the door and put Hanna in *your* [his father's] bed, and Mummy was asleep—no, the stork put her in *her* bed' (ibid, p. 71, Freud's italics).

Do you know how the stork opens the box? He takes his beak—the box has got a key too—he takes his beak, lifts up one (i.e., one-half of the beak) and unlocks it like this (ibid, p. 78).

The lock-key-box symbolism virtually explains itself from the context, with little need to invoke psychic unity or universal symbolism. Nevertheless, this case report also makes evident the role of theory. Without a prior appreciation of psychoanalytic developmental psychology and psychodynamics, Hans' father would not have grasped the full significance of the defensive aspects of Hans' behavior and the nature of the dangers he feared.

Since in the Little Hans case Freud had access, through the father, to events which would ordinarily (in the analysis of adult neurotics) have to be *reconstructed,* this treatment reflects a somewhat different species of history-writing—closer to contemporary chronicle than to historiography—than that in the Rat Man. Whereas the Rat Man and Little Hans case reports exhibit modes of clinical historiography that differ somewhat from one another, the Schreber case manifests traces of yet a third. Here the data have been collected by one—Schreber himself—ignorant of psychoanalytic modes of selecting and organizing them. The resultant disadvantage is that much psychoanalytically pertinent information is lacking (also because of the publisher's censorship) and that Freud cannot question his "patient" or test his clinical hypotheses against the patient's responses. The advantage is that Freud cannot be accused of having suggested Schreber's material to him. In this case the interpretations are laid on a data base fixed once and for all by the patient's absence.

Freud's hypothesis emerged from the interaction of his previously existing concepts of paranoia and psychosexual development with the themes in Schreber's memoirs. The information and themes that Freud adjudged as most significant were determined by the interaction between Freud's theoretical presuppositions and the configuration of the data themselves. The evidence upon which Freud founded his formulation is abundant. The autobiography makes it plain that: (1) Schreber's second illness (the topic of the memoirs) began after a series of dreams that his insanity (absent for 8 years) had returned, after repeated nocturnal emissions, following the half waking thought that it must be pleasurable to be a copulating woman, and during his wife's absence; (2) the initial delusion regarded the idea that Schreber's persecutor (from the context and other remarks, apparently his psychiatrist Flechsig) aimed to transform him into a woman and then abuse him sexually; and (3) the final transformation of this ego dystonic thought into the ego syntonic idea that God himself favored this turn of events so that Schreber might become divinely impregnated and produce a superior race of humanity; this delusion also manifested itself in cross dressing.

From such data and from Freud's theoretical presupposition that the projection of latent homosexuality is central in paranoia Freud concluded that (and I paraphrase and summarize):

Schreber harbored strong unconscious homosexual desires for his father and brother which were displaced, initially, onto his physician Flechsig. Stimulated by his wife's recent absence (with the concomitant frustration of his sexual needs and the removal of the individual whose presence protected him against his homosexual desires) and his ongoing frustration at their childless marriage, Schreber's repressed homosexual strivings and desires to be impregnated began surfacing—in dreams that his insanity had returned and that he was hence back with the beloved Flechsig, in repetitive nocturnal emissions, and in the transient thought that it would be nice to be a woman submitting to intercourse. In order to defend against these ego dystonic strivings (since they would entail the loss of his genital) Schreber projected them onto the person of Flechsig, who became the persecutor intent on abusing Schreber. Through the eventual substitution of God for Fleshsig, and the introduction of the idea that his sexual transformation was to be the preamble to an heroic act of redemption, Schreber was enabled to express his repressed homosexual wishes more directly and yet still under sufficient disguise that Schreber was spared the task of consciously avowing them. In short, his delusion was conceptualized as a compromise formation.

Freud's historiographical procedure in this case also illustrates the use of the comparative method (bolstering his thesis that Schreber equated the sun with God and God with his father by reference to a contemporary patient of Freud's, a hymn by Nietzsche, and cosmic myths), of psychic unity (the assumption of the generalizability of the dynamics of paranoia and of the universality of some of Schreber's symbols), and of analogical reasoning (equating the alternating reverence and rebelliousness of Schreber to the sun, to God, and to Flechsig with the typical oedipal and adolescent male ambivalence toward the father).

Another point to be made about Freud's historiographical procedure concerns his preoccupation, in both his cultural and clinical work, with elucidating the very origins of his phenomena. At times this led him into what Erikson (1975, p. 160) terms the "originological fallacy"—that is, collapsing the meanings and motives of rich and complicated present day behaviors entirely into their prehistoric or infantile beginnings. In personality development, for instance, this permitted Freud to pay relatively little attention to the latency and adolescent years—to say nothing of the vicissitudes and regularities of adult development now under investigation by

Levinson (1978) and others. In the study of religion it permitted him to focus on its putative origins in the primal parricide, totemism, and animism to the exclusion of its later history.

On the other hand, Freud was quite capable of respecting the importance of current factors in their own right (and not merely as the symbolic recapitulation of infantile ones). For instance, in the Dora case he accorded the patient's desires toward a current figure (Frau K) determinative primacy over those toward an historical one (her father in childhood); her oedipal fantasies were resurrected largely to defend against her adolescent homosexual strivings for Frau K. In *The Introductory Lectures* Freud (1915-1917, p. 364) notes that while in many cases "the whole weight of causation falls on the sexual experiences of childhood," there are others in which "the whole accent lies on the later conflicts and the emphasis we find in the analysis laid on the impressions of childhood appears entirely as the work of regression." Freud retained, to the very end, a category of psychopathology—the "actual neuroses"—caused, he believed, by purely contemporary factors (i.e., masturbation and coitus interruptus). We now recognize that behaviors possess current contextual or situational determinants, as well as intrapsychic, historical ones and that, as Buckley (1967, p. 39) says, a "complex, open system [personality or culture, for our purposes], though determinate, 'changes so [to quote Ashby] that, as time goes on, its state is characterized more [I would prefer to say 'as much'] by experiences that have come to it than [as] by its state initially.'" Freud (1901, p. 53) asserted that "In the course of years a symptom can change its chief meaning, or the leading role can pass from one meaning to another" (see also Chapter 4).

A related issue is Freud's preoccupation with the inner, as opposed to the outer, world. Initially Freud explained his neurotics' symptomatology with reference to actual traumatic events in their recent and remote history. Obsessional neurosis was posited to result from playing an active role in childhood seductions and hysteria from occupying a passive one. In *Studies on Hysteria* his patients' psychopathology was conceptualized largely as the fruit of repressed feelings about actual interactions—nursing a dying father or witnessing a detested governess' dog drinking from a glass. Nevertheless, even here Freud was not blind to the importance of the patients' fantasied elaboration upon such events or to the determinative role of prior history on their interpretations.

When Freud decided, in 1897, from the discoveries of his self analysis and further work with patients, that these were recollections of childhood fantasies rather than of actual interpersonal events, he suffered, as he (1925, p. 34) tells us, "a severe blow." It is understandable that a man reared in the mechanistic ambience of nineteenth century German science would find it difficult to accept that he was dealing with psychical, not actual, reality. Elsewhere I (1980) have argued that Freud's need to ground his neurotics' oedipal fantasies in an actual historical reality was one of the motives for the fantastic primal parricide hypothesis.

In any event, after 1897 Freud shifted his focus increasingly to the inner, as opposed to the outer, world. Although Freud always appreciated that there is an inextricable determinative interaction between psychical and actual reality, his penchant for favoring the former often caused him to pay short shrift to important features of the current and historical interpersonal context of the patient's disorder. This is evident, for example, in the Dora case, where Freud paid scant attention to the impact on his analysand of a variety of problematic figures in her present and past environment (including, in some respects, Freud himself).

The danger of course is that the outer world may come to be viewed largely as a screen upon which are projected one's prehistorically determined fantasies. Niederland (1974), for example, has demonstrated that what Freud took to be Schreber's psychotic fantasies were in part distorted recollections of actual childhood interactions with Schreber's eccentric father. Fromm-Reichmann elucidated the historical core of truth in some of Deborah Blau's hallucinations; the crux of this treatment was the discovery that the memory of an apparent actual event from the patient's childhood (attempting to murder her infant sister) was in fact the recollection of a childish fantasy (Green, 1964). Sachs (1967) graphically demonstrated the therapeutic import of distinguishing between the actual and fantasied elements in a patient's childhood remembrance of the traumatic *Anschluss*. Rosen (1955) presented a case in which it was important to determine, through the patient's confrontation of his father, that his early recollection of his mother's suicide attempt was an accurate remembrance rather than a fantasy. Whereas Freud emphasized the fantastic nature of his hysterics' seduction memories, we now appreciate the extent to which incest actually occurs.

Nevertheless, Freud never totally abandoned his quest for "actual" historical reality. For example, he continued to emphasize the "kernel of historical truth" to which interpretations should refer. Freud (1913, p. 161) asserted that "historical reality has a share in [obsessional neurosis] as well. In their childhood they had these evil impulses pure and simple, and turned them into acts as far as the impotence of childhood allowed." In many of the formulations in the Rat Man and Wolf Man case histories he claimed to be reconstructing actual reality (e.g., the castration threats in the former and the primal scene in the latter). In *The Introductory Lectures* Freud (1915–1917, p. 367) opined that in most cases recollected or reconstructed experiences from early childhood are "compounded of truth and falsehood." In "Constructions in Analysis" Freud (1937, pp. 267–268) spoke of the core of "historical truth" in many delusions and hallucinations—"in them something that has been experienced in infancy and then forgotten returns—something that the child has seen or heard at a time when he could still hardly speak." In such cases it is important to liberate "the fragment of historical truth from its distortions and its attachments to the actual present day." At several points in the Wolf Man case Freud took pains to distinguish between the elements of fantasy and of actual reality in the patient's remembrances. There Freud (1918, p. 55) also asserted that "a child, like an adult, can produce fantasies only from material which has been acquired from some source or other."

Moreover, it must be emphasized that Freud's concentration on psychical reality does not, in itself, make him ahistorical. Fantasied interactions with others are just as legitimately a part of one's history as actual ones. Indeed, we must reverse Freud's 1897 argument and suggest that his distinction between psychical and actual reality, while eminently useful, is, in some respects, actually misleading and erroneous. It is valuable insofar as it alerted the clinician to the inner face of human experience and to the role of the patient's interpretations and fantasy life. It is incorrect insofar as the distinction between psychical and actual reality is conceived as an oversharp one and insofar as psychical reality is conceptualized as somehow less "material" or less "historical" than "actual" reality.

We deal, as I said, not with pure cultures of psychical or actual reality, but with inextricable combinations of the two. Human beings, with their possession of symbolism and memory, are characterized by the fact that psychical reality—fantasies, fears, recollections, and interpretations—interpenetrates the (potentially) publicly observable, or "external," aspects of all their interactions with the world. The fantasies and interpretations will be to some degree determined by the "externals" of the situation, just as the publicly observable behaviors will be to some degree determined by the fantasies and interpretations.

Psychical reality (one's childhood fantasies and interpretations of interpersonal events) is no less material and no less historical than actual reality (the potentially publicly observable aspects of these events). Fantasies and interpretations are activities of the psychobiologically-whole-human-organism-interacting-with-an-environment as much as are publicly observable behaviors. The biological substrate and neurological processes underpinning fantasizing and interpreting are not less material and energic than those of publicly observable behaviors; the neurobiology of encoding the memory trace of a fantasy or interpretation is no less material and energic than the neurobiology of establishing the memory trace of the publicly observable aspects of an event.

In short, Freud's lifelong fear that in dealing with the patient's fantasies and interpretations he had left Brücke's materialistic path was unfounded; Freud's apprehension derived, at least in part, from confusion by the centuries old groundless equation of the psychical and immaterial ("spiritual"). Freud's contribution was the suggestion that one face of material reality is sufficiently different that we need to label it 'psychical'; he was not proposing an ontologically separate order of reality (see my comments on the patient's interpretations and historical events in Chapter 2 and on the mind-body problem in Chapters 3 and 4).

COVERING LAWS

We shall now turn to the covering law controversy, first in history and then in psychoanalysis. Hempel and his followers maintain that scientifically respectable explanations, in history or elsewhere, must invoke both particular antecedent conditions and covering laws. The explanation should be framed in such a way that the *explanandum* (i.e., phenomenon to be explained) is deducible from the *explanans* (i.e., the specific antecedent conditions operating in accordance with an explicitly stated universal law). Such a law asserts that "whenever and wherever circumstances of the kind in question occur, an event of the kind to be explained comes about" (Hempel, 1969, p. 83). Popper (1952, p. 262) concurs.

Opponents of this model, such as Dray (1969), point out that since, in practice, most historical explanations do not meet these criteria, the scholar has no use for a philosophy that inadequately reflects his procedure. Hempelians maintain that if historical explanations do not generally invoke covering laws, then so much the worse for historians. Idiographic, or historicist, writers counter that the historian is concerned with concrete and nonreplicable events, not with abstract and repetitive universals. The Hempelians riposte that the historian is interested in the concrete occurrence only insofar as it is the member of a class of events; otherwise it would be incomprehensible and irrelevant to him. Finally, there are those who point out that the notion of lawfulness, even in physics, has been modified considerably to accord with the constructs of relativity and indeterminacy. If "laws" in physics are at best probabilistic, then must not they be even more so in history? If this is granted, however, then covering law explanations lose their deductive inevitability and are hence no longer laws in the manner Hempel originally conceived them.

In practice, most historians seem to toe a middle line. For example, they often make explicit and implicit assumptions, in evaluating actions, events, and the accuracy of documents and chronicles, about how human beings (individually and in aggregate) typically behave in certian periods, cultures, and situations.[10] In no sense, however, do the majority of them believe they are searching for regularities as binding as those in the physical sciences.

------

[10]For instance, in his important monograph *The Mind of the South,* W. J. Cash (1941) attacks tbe cavalier theory of Southern history, not merely with concrete data concerning patterns of emigration from England, but by the invocation of generalizations such as the following:

Men of position and power, men who are adjusted to their environment, men who find life bearable in their accustomed place—such men do not embark on frail ships for a dismal frontier where savages prowl and slay, and living is a grim and laborious ordeal. The laborer, faced with starvation; the debtor, anxious to get out of jail; the apprentice, reckless, eager for a fling at adventure, and even more eager to escape his master; the peasant . . . . [and so forth]. But your fat and moneyed squire, your gentleman of rank and connection, your cavalier who is welcome in the drawing-rooms of London—almost never. Not even, as a rule, if there is a price on his head, for across the channel is France, and the odds are that Cromwell can't last (pp. 3–4).

The positions of Mandelbaum (1969), Scriven (1966), and Gardiner (1961) exemplify this middle ground. Mandelbaum (1969, p. 140) projects that historical research "will continue to be concerned with the analysis of the concrete nature of particular events, though it will surely continue to utilize, in ever growing measure, not only the commonsense generalizations of everyday life, but the best available generalizations which social scientists have been able to formulate on the basis of a knowledge of history."

Scriven (1966) asserts that historians utilize generalizations about what history has taught them about human nature and historical events, but emphatically denies that these amount to laws. For example, when an historian says that Francophile sentiments in the London Corresponding Society in 1792 caused alarm in that city, he does not claim that such sympathy is always cause for alarm in London. Nor is he deducing, maintains Scriven (p. 245), this explanation from a covering law to the effect that "Whenever sympathy is expressed, in certain circumstances, with a foreign power meeting certain conditions, by a group of a certain kind, alarm follows."

The historian is not claiming deductive inevitability for the events he is explaining. What he seeks is: "Merely evidence that his candidate was present, that it has on other occasions clearly demonstrated its capacity to produce an effect of the sort here under study (or there might be grounds for thinking it a possible cause rather than previous direct experience of its actual efficacy), and the absence of evidence (despite a thorough search) (a) that its *modus operandi* was inoperative here, and/or (b) that any of the other possible causes were present" (ibid, p. 250). In practice, Scriven (p. 251) believes the historian's use of such generalizations is a largely intuitive one—"a diagnostic skill . . . at identifying causes even though he does not know, let alone know how to describe, the perceptual cues he employs."

Gardiner (1961, p. 60–61) believes the historian uses "vague and open" generalizations and terms, "able to cover a vast number of events falling within an indefinitely circumscribed range;" such concepts function as "guides to understanding." Generalizations such as "economic changes in society are accompanied by religious changes" and "rulers who pursue policies detrimental to the countries over which they rule become unpopular" may provide rough and ready indications of the sorts of factors an historian will look for in his investigations of a specific set of religious changes or a particular ruler's unpopularity. But they leave open to historical investigation and analysis the "task of eliciting the specific nature of those factors on a particular occasion, and the precise manner in which the factors are causally connected to one another" (ibid., pp. 93–94). Thus deduction is only the beginning, not the end and substance, of the historian's explanation. I have argued, and shall argue again, that the same holds true for the explanations of the psychoanalytic clinician.

I believe that psychoanalysts, like historians, often implicitly invoke covering laws in their explications of specific phenomena. For example, an explanation of a particular adult sexual pattern or symptom by invoking the Oedipus complex and citing the specific fantasies, patterns of activity, and memories supporting this hypothesis, could be conceptualized as proceeding through the following covering law: "any human raised by two parenting figures will develop sexual feelings for the one of the opposite sex and aggressive feelings toward the one of the same sex." The explanation of Mrs. Jones' current depression and diminished self esteem with reference to her recent divorce and her horrific childhood might be conceptualized as proceeding through the following covering law: "rejection, deficient nurturance, and inadequate esteem by one's parents lead to self esteem problems and depression proneness in adulthood."

Consider the following passage in which Freud (1896a, pp. 154–155) asserts what amounts to a covering law regarding the connection between current symptoms, current precipitating events, and remote causes:

All the events subsequent to puberty to which an influence must be attributed upon the development of the hysterical neurosis and upon the formation of its symptoms are in fact only concurrent causes—"*agents provocateurs*". . . . These accessory agents are not subject to the strict conditions imposed on the specific causes; analysis demonstrates in an irrefutable fashion that they enjoy a pathogenic influence only owing to their faculty for awakening the unconscious psychical trace of the childhood event.

And from this generalization there follow interventions such as the following (Freud, 1896b, pp. 195–196):

If the first discovered scene is unsatisfactory, we tell our patient that this experience explains nothing, but that behind it there must be hidden a more significant, earlier experience; and we direct his attention by the same technique to the associative thread which connects the two memories—the one that has been discovered and the one that has still to be discovered.

The Rat Man case history contains invocations of such covering laws. In regard to the Rat Man's account of the specific childhood data surrounding the origin of his neurosis, Freud (1909a, p. 164) tells us:

If we apply knowledge gained elsewhere to the case of childhood neurosis, we shall not be able to avoid a suspicion that in this instance as in others (that is to say, before the child had reached his sixth year) there had been conflicts and repressions, which had themselves been overtaken by amnesia, but had left behind them the particular content of this obsessional fear.

Freud (p. 165) correctly supports his use of such generalizations (to arrive at retrodictions about his patient's early history) by reference to the empirical manner in which the generalizations were first arrived at: "To find a chronic obsessional neurosis beginning like this in early childhood, with

lascivious wishes of the sort connected with uncanny apprehensions and an inclination to the performance of defensive acts, is no new thing to me. I have come across it in a
number of other cases." (But, as Sulloway [1979] has demonstrated, there were also a priori elements in Freud's theory of
the sexual etiology of neurosis).[11]

The Dora case, as well, contains many examples of Freud's
invocation of covering laws—generally tied to many fewer
historical data than in the case of the Rat Man. For example,
from Dora's dream of flying from the burning house and her
associations that "an accident might happen in the night
. . . it might be necessary to leave the room," Freud (1901a, p.
72) inferred episodes of bedwetting in her childhood—the covering law being a posited universal connection between fire
symbolism and bedwetting. From yet another covering law—
"Bed-wetting of this kind has, to the best of my knowledge, no
more likely cause than masturbation" (ibid, p. 74)—Freud
infers the habit of self-stimulation in her childhood; Freud
then goes on to relate Dora's catarrh and gastric complaints to
conflicts over this putative behavior. From the nature of
Dora's symptoms (hysterical dyspnea and palpitations), the
knowledge that Dora's bedroom was next to her father's, and
the generalization that "dyspnoea and palpitations that occur
in hysteria and anxiety neurosis are only detached fragments
of the act of copulation" (p. 80), Freud infers a primal scene in
her childhood.

However, if psychoanalysis teaches us, as it did Sullivan
(1953), that "we are all much more simply human than otherwise," it also instructs us that no two of us are human in
precisely the same way. If psychoanalysis and history teach
us that individuals and societies often behave regularly and

---

[11]The following is another good example of Freud's (1909a, p.
181) reliance on the requirements of theory, as much as data: "According to psycho-analytic theory, I told him [the Rat Man], every
fear corresponded to a former wish which was now repressed; we
were therefore obliged to believe the exact opposite of what he asserted [i.e., that he desired, not feared, his father's death]."

predictably, they also demonstrate that they can surprise us. Indeed, the dynamic psychiatrist realizes that in even so apparently ubiquitous a phenomenon as the Oedipus complex the content of the unconscious fantasies and the mode in which they are expressed and defended against varies from person to person; moreover, one must reckon with variations such as negative complexes and the effects of cross-cultural differences in family structure and childrearing. The analyst's deductions regarding any particular individual's Oedipus complex do not obviate the need to inductively gather the data. Covering laws such as those relating the Oedipus complex to antecedent conditions and subsequent effects are, like the generalizations of the historian, approximate and open, and must be filled in with phenomenological and historical spadework concerning the concrete individual. The nexus of causes that produce adult personality structure and symptomatology is never identical in any two human beings.

In practice, psychoanalysts go back and forth between deduction and induction.[12] Retrodictive hypotheses (reconstructions) are formulated from the patient's presenting psychopathological and characterological constellation, and from what we know about regularly encountered causal linkages between specific patterns of childhood experience and adult symptomatology and character structure. Such hypotheses, while not presented prematurely to the patient, are then tested against the history and other clinical data that are subsequently obtained. The following clinical excerpts, from the treatment of two obsessive-compulsive character neurotics, exemplify what I mean.

Mr. G. was pathologically jealous of his wife and continually accused her of infidelity. No amount of reassurance on her part

---

[12]As the historian Johnson (1926, p. 168) says, "the inductive and deductive processes occur almost simultaneously in consciousness and . . . . the whole mental process under ordinary circumstances is so rapid as to elude observation."

allayed his fears and recriminations. The only ground he could produce for his anxieties was a minor flirtation early in their courtship. Mr. G. ruminated constantly about what he termed her "disillusionment" of him and the blow she dealt his masculine self esteem. He hashed and rehashed the matter in therapy, abreacting a good deal of anger each time, but with no diminution in the intensity of his feelings. From psychoanalytic theory—and prior experience with patients with similar problems—I knew that such repetitive proclamations, with no working through of the affect, usually reflect the mechanism of displacement.

In short, I hypothesized that the feelings about his wife were displaced from other individuals toward whom they were unconsciously directed. On this basis I delved more deeply into his history and uncovered information about prior disappointments with women that he had hitherto withheld. Even after abreacting feelings about these, the ruminations about his wife remained virtually unchanged in intensity. At this point, from his perennial reticence about his mother, his discomfort whenever I mentioned her, and my theoretical and clinical knowledge that recurrent problems with spouses and lovers tend to be based on prototypical ones with the parent of the opposite sex, I suggested that there must have been still earlier disappointments with women—perhaps even with his mother. A wealth of hurt and resentment emerged and over the next several weeks he became conscious of previously repressed memories of his mother's adulterous affairs and several occasions when his parents were on the brink of divorce.

Mrs. K. presented with the chief complaint of obsessive thoughts and compulsive ritualistic behaviors. The thoughts centered around fears that ill luck might befall her mother or younger sister. Immediately following these she would either phone them or engage in ritualistic behaviors designed to ensure they would not die. From theory I was aware that excessive fearfulness and oversolicitude about the well-being of another often defend against unconscious death wishes toward him. This concept was not forced upon the patient's productions; rather, it alerted me to the possibility of an unconscious constellation which I would not otherwise have considered.

Anamnesis revealed that these fears and rituals appeared when the patient was 5, shortly after the birth of the younger sister. They persisted until age 12, at which time they became relatively quiescent. At age 17, shortly after the patient's marriage, the fears about her mother and sister reasserted themselves, as did the ritualistic behaviors consciously designed to prevent their death. As it turned out, the mother was quite flirtatious with the patient's new husband. She constantly (and often successfully) competed with the patient for his attention (a repetition, it later emerged, of the patient's and mother's relationship to the father). When Mrs. K. confronted the mother about this, the latter vehemently denied this behavior; the patient's younger sister sided, as usual, with the mother. In these encounters the patient was unconscious of any hostility toward either of these family members; she was aware only of depression and disappointment. Gradually the patient's resistance to acknowledging her intense, lifelong resentment toward sister and mother diminished. She began overtly expressing this hostility in the hours—as well as her considerable guilt feelings in reaction thereto and her fears that such talking might magically kill them.

If there were no regularities in the way persons in general, or persons with certain characteristics and histories in particular, tend to behave in certain types of situations, then there would be no possibility for order and predictability in human social intercourse—much less for any science of psychology and psychotherapy. Although the psychoanalyst must learn the history, disposition, preoccupations, and pattern of compromise formations anew for each patient, if he could not safely assume some unity in the psychical processes of all people, then he would have to devise totally novel theories and therapies for every patient. Furthermore, if analysts could not presuppose some regular and lawlike aspects to human psychological functioning, what possibility could there be for empathy with their clients?[13]

Lawlike propositions such as "frustration causes (conscious or unconscious) aggression" guide the analyst's thinking in many instances. Nevertheless, in actual clinical practice, explaining the observed relationship between a particular patient's perceived frustration and his subsequent behavior may require considerable modification and qualification. A covering law adequate to Mrs. Jones' depressive response to frustrations in current relationships might read as follows:

> Current frustrations elicit unconscious aggression which will be defended against by turning against the self (leading to subsequent depression) in persons with an early history of deprivation, rejection, abuse, and parents who reacted negatively to the expression of anger.

---

[13]In the course of practice every clinician encounters powerful evidence for the unity of the psychical processes of humankind. For example, in my own work and that of my supervisees, I have encountered several patients, from divergent geographic areas and cultural backgrounds, who were preoccupied with even numbers and with symmetry (e.g., if they accidentally brushed against an object with one arm, they would brush against it with the other). These concerns, which originated in childhood, were in every case connected with the obsessional fear that if odd numbers or asymmetry were encountered a family member would die. Dreams in which a man breaks in a bedroom window are common in middle-aged spinsters and widows. Examination dreams often occur when persons are anticipating stressful situations and major changes. The list is endless. Turning to developmental psychology Piaget (1929, 1951), Kohlberg (1974), and others have garnered considerable evidence that there are transtemporally and transculturally universal and lawful aspects to cognitive and moral development. See also the evidence for psychic unity compiled by Wilson (1975, 1977, 1978) and Barash (1977).

Without primitive, explicit or implicit, law*like* generalizations there would be no possibility for reconstruction in either
history or psychoanalysis. One's knowledge could not then go
beyond what the particular chronicler or patient consciously
remembers and relates. If the analyst or historian did not
know that certain constellations tend to result from certain
antecedent conditions, then he could not begin to form a working hypothesis or to search for relevant data. If I had not
known that certain types of parent-child interactions commonly lead to deficient self esteems, preoccupations with ap-
proval by others, and depression proneness, then I would have
had no cause to doubt Mrs. Jones' initial protestations that
her childhood was halcyon. It was historical exploration motivated by my adherence to such a "covering law" that
eventually uncovered clear and conscious memories of the unfortunate aspects of her childhood.

Because historians and psychoanalysts are preoccupied
with explaining concrete, nonreplicable events and idiosyncratic constellations, many fail to see that they cannot dispense with explicit or implicit generalizations in attempting
to elucidate their phenomena.

Nevertheless, if psychoanalysts were compelled to tie every
causal explanation of any particular behavior to an explicit
and ironclad covering law, then they would often end up with
covering laws subject to so many qualifications and special
conditions that they would amount to little more than disposi-
tional statements about the patient in question.

To recapitulate, because the analyst bears in mind what he
has learned about human development and psychopathology
he does not gather his data "blind." He is engaged in pure
empiricism no more than is any other scientist or historian.
His vision is guided to the data not solely by its intrinsic
claims upon him, but by his theoretical organization of it. As
Schafer (1978, pp. 12–13) says:

[When listening to his patient the analyst uses psychoanalytic
theory in] thinking about what that person is likely to have
gone through in order to have arrived at his or her present

distinctive plight. . . . One may say that the analyst uses the general past to constitute the individualized present that is to be explained while using the present as a basis for inquiry into the individualized past. . . . [The analyst bases his interpretations] on both present communications and a general knowledge of possible and probable pasts that have yet to be established or detailed in the specific case. . . . [The psychoanalytic life historical investigation is] circular . . . the facts are what it is psychoanalytically meaningful and useful to designate, and what it is useful to designate is established by the facts; one looks for idiosyncratic versions of what has usually been found and one finds the sort of thing one is looking for. Plenty of room is left for unexpected findings and new puzzles. *Like the historian, the analyst works within this interpretive or hermeneutical circle* [my italics].

Again, in both psychoanalysis and history it is a question of balance. Let us search for such law-like, probabilistic regularities that may occur, while retaining a healthy respect for the infinite variability of human behavior.[14]

---

[14]Freud's case histories, while justifiably admired for their literary quality and their historical importance to psychoanalysis, do not, in many respects, adequately reflect either Freud's actual clinical procedure or the psychoanalytic method as currently practiced. Their synoptic, thematic character and primary intent of demonstrating theoretical principles do not give the reader an appreciation of the manifold data and day-to-day clinical interactions feeding into Freud's formulations. Moreover, psychoanalytic technique is now more historicist and empirical than in Freud's day: analyses last longer; more thorough longitudinal histories are obtained; there is a more sophisticated appreciation of the potentially distorting impact of the analyst's behavior and interventions on the patient's associations and the developing transference; premature formulations and interpretations are guarded against; and the phenomenological and interpersonal dimensions are better appreciated. Consequently, laypersons exposed only to Freud's case histories will gain a misleading impression of psychoanalytic procedure.

2 Historiography Continued

HISTORY AND PSYCHOANALYSIS AS RELATIONSHIP

Turning now to a different aspect of the psychoanalyst's and historian's procedure, I believe that their work is best understood as a relationship with their data. Dynamic psychiatrists, by the very fact that their dialogue is with living human documents, have had a keener realization of this. After the work of Sullivan (1947, 1953), Fromm-Reichmann (1950), and Searles (1965), psychodynamic therapists appreciate that their mode of investigation is one of participant, rather than detached, observation. The analyst's data do not arise in the analysand purely, but in the field of interaction between patient and therapist; the clinician is a part of the process under investigation. He knows the patient only as the latter impinges upon his psychic apparatus, with its complexes and considerations; similarly, the analyst's particular personality is constantly impinging upon the analysand and influencing his behavior. Along with this comes the, often uncomfortable, awareness of the impact of one's historically conditioned sensitivities and preconceptions on one's perception of the patient (i.e., "countertransference"). A premium is placed on the analyst's ability to empathically resonate, to transiently and partially identify with, his client. Finally, I need not belabor that dynamic therapists, like historians, insofar as is humanly possible, suspend moral evaluation in favor of understanding.

I submit the following clinical excerpt as an illustration of the interactive nature of psychodynamic data and of the manner in which the dynamic method transcends, in some respects, the subjectivist-objectivist dichotomy.

> While listening to the patient, Mr. E., the tune "Call me Mr. Wonderful" kept running through my mind. Reflecting on this, I realized that I wanted to withdraw from him. Shortly after, I became aware of the anger which the impulse to withdraw defended against. "Call me Mr. Wonderful" was a derivative of my hitherto unconscious desire that he acknowledge my importance to him. The anger was in response to my frustration at his failing to do so. It was this fantasy that first alerted me to one of his most important defensive maneuvers—keeping his distance and minimizing others' importance to him as a way of coming to terms with a number of unconscious dangers associated with intimacy and dependency.
>
> This fantasy, "Call me Mr. Wonderful," was but the first in a chain of three associations, the second being a concern with whether I was making a contribution with my clinical work, and the third a puzzling over how my deceased physician father would feel on the matter. In other words, I was alerted to Mr. E.'s defensive minimizing of my importance to him by a fantasy that was a momentary derivative of an unconscious complex about acknowledgment by my father. I had come to know the patient's behavior as it impinged upon this complex. This particular issue, though still active to some degree, was sufficiently nonthreatening that I could have conscious access to it and use it to help me understand the patient.

Of course my countertransferential response by itself was insufficient to justify my formulation. It was only because multiple lines of historical and current evidence (including similar perceptions of Mr. E. on the part of other hospital personnel, a tendency to derogate and devalue those whom he would nevertheless seek out and later admit were important to him, his accusation that his father minimized the patient's importance to him, his expression of the fear that if one allows people to become significant they will take advantage of one, and so forth) converged to support it that I considered it reliable. The patient's response to my eventual interpretation of this dynamic was confirmatory.

The treatment of Ms. X, a law student whom we shall encounter again in Chapter 3 and 4, provides yet another instance of the interactive nature of psychodynamic data:

> She had been castigating herself for failing to exercise good study habits. During this time I began experiencing an inclination to reprove her, to enjoin her to use her intelligence constructively, and to otherwise engage in paternal encouragement and admonition of her. After several more minutes of mournful self-flagellation, she looked up at me expectantly. Considering that my parental impulse might be alerting me to her preconscious and unconscious intentions, I queried, "What are you looking for right now?" She responded, "I guess I want you to tell me that I can do the work, and to shape up and cut the crap." There succeeded a chain of angry and tearful memories about her unsuccessful childhood and adolescent attempts—through episodic academically and socially self destructive behavior—to involve her detached parents in her life.

The whole idea of empathy, in history or psychoanalysis, is predicated on the assumption that our inner, "subjective" state can, when subjected to critical assessment, sometimes give us reliable information about the inner state of another. Through transient and partial identification with the analysand's nonverbally communicated affective state the analyst may "resonate" with hitherto unappreciated depression, anger, anxiety, and so forth. Through imagining how it would feel to grow up in the patient's particular environment and face the patient's particular current reality with that history behind one, the analyst is alerted to issues and questions which he would not otherwise consider.

The analytic process is distinguished by the mode of relationship—between analyst and analysand and between each and crucial aspects of his own mental experience—as much as by any methods, theorems, and information. The manner in which each comes to know the other—and himself—is as important as *what* one comes to know.

From the therapist's side, what the existentialists term "presence" is a crucial ingredient of the enterprise. Presence entails being with the patient with as much of oneself as possible, listening attentively, communicating honestly and sensitively, and attempting to grasp him in the immediacy and totality of his existence. It means *knowing* him as a fellow human being, rather than merely *knowing about* him as an object of scientific scrutiny. Indeed, since a person is always more than the sum total of the data we can garner about him, viewing him in a purely "technical" or natural science light is actually less scientific than appreciating him as a living whole. This grasp of the totality of his being is the matrix in which we obtain, and to which we relate, the historical and dynamic data.

From the patient's side, the manner in which he comes to know his therapist and, more importantly, himself is equally significant. Although he must be capable, when appropriate, of assuming an observational stance toward certain aspects of his behavior, psychopathology, and personality structure, his most important insights, as Meissner (1981, p. 286) says, will not be objectified:

> Within the psychoanalytic context, it can be said that what is of greater import to the subject analysand is not what is known but how it is known. The actual content of what is discovered through the psychoanalytic inquiry in terms of the historical account of the patient's life experience is not unimportant but it can be regarded as less important than the way in which it is known, the relationship the subject adopts toward it in the course of his psychoanalytic inquiry.

The analyst's knowing of his analysand, and the analysand's knowing of himself, is an affective knowing. Insight "is a subjectively and emotionally grasped realization and actualization within one's own experience of a basic truth about oneself" (ibid, p. 288). The therapist encourages, I would add, his patient to write a certain kind of history—not a distant and affectless report, but an "anamnesis," in the sense in which the word connotes a "reliving" of past experience.

Let us elaborate at this point on the relationship between subjectivity and objectivity in psychoanalysis—a point to which we return in the next section of this chapter.

"Subjectivity," in common parlance, is often synonymous with "bias," and means essentially that one's perception and conception is determined more by one's wishes, fears, and presuppositions than by the structure of external reality itself. Such "subjectivity" is a danger in psychoanalysis, just as in history or natural science.

My usage of "subjectivity" is different and follows from the conception that knowledge in psychoanalysis—as elsewhere—is the fruit of one's *relationship* with one's subject matter. To know someone or something is to have a relationship with him or it. Since Kant, we appreciate that all knowledge of external reality involves some contribution from the observer. Within this framework "subjectivity" refers to the impact of one's perceptual-affective-interpretive apparatus on one's picture of reality. The investigator's problem is not to eliminate such "subjectivity" since there can be no knowledge without it, but to determine, through critical self assessment and consensual validation, when his responses tell him more about his idiosyncratic mental set than about his subject matter. Enabling the analyst to make such distinctions is one of the primary objectives of the personal and didactic analyses of his training.

The personality structure of the analyst, in contrast to that of the historian, influences, not merely how the practitioner perceives and interprets his data, but the behavior of his subject matter itself. The patient's behavior is thus a vector between the patient's dynamics and stimuli issuing from the analyst hmself. In short, the analyst's appearance, demeanor, and behavioral style play a role in determining the patient's behavior. Some have used this fact to impugn the concept of objectivity in psychoanalytic treatment. Such criticisms seem based on the idea that conditions in the consulting room must either be identical to those of the controlled laboratory setting or else irremediably sloppy and meaningless. In actuality, the state of affairs is somewhere in the middle.

Although the analyst's eccentricities are not totally banished through analysis, they are considerably muted; he gains a heightened awareness of his personality traits and manner of impact on others. This, coupled with mastery of technique, minimizes the extent to which the analyst's behavior skews or distorts the manifestations of the unfolding transference and maximizes the degree to which he can treat the patient's behavior as intrapsychically determined.

> After some 30 sessions of twice weekly insight oriented psychotherapy, Professor T. commented, with a hint of impatience and irritation in his voice, that, while *he* had been copiously self revealing, I had disclosed virtually nothing about myself. When I asked him what he wanted to know, he replied, "How you feel about my problems and whether you've ever dealt with similar issues yourself." In response to my query, "What is going into this?", he paused for a few moments and said, "I guess what I really want is for you to do something my father never did—he never told me about himself or how he felt about me as his son."

It further emerged that a central motive for Professor T's diligent psychotherapeutic work was the hitherto unconscious fantasy that if he was a sufficiently "good" patient I would reward him with what he desired. My analytic stance, while it did not remove altogether my determination of his behavior, considerably increased the range of operation of the patient's unconscious motivating fantasies and the likelihood that they would come to awareness.

In asserting that the analyst's data arise from the interaction between the analysand and himself, I am not thereby denying that there is a valid distinction between subject (the analyst) and object (the analysand). The analyst uses his subjective responses to the analysand, not with the primary aim of learning about himself (though enhanced self awareness may occur), but to the end of elucidating the current and historical reality of the analysand. He studies the relationship between the patient and himself with the goal of arriving at reasonably objective knowledge about the inner world and personality structure of his client. Like Bhaskar's (1975, p. 25) natural scientist, the analyst aims for a knowledge of "real structures which operate independently of our knowledge, our experience, and the conditions which allow access to them."

Nor does the fact that the personality structure (and hence the mode of perception-interpretation of any given patient) of no two therapists is the same preclude clinicians from arriving at objective knowledge about their clients. Psychic unity and the one genus hypothesis (i.e., "we are all much more simply human than otherwise") presuppose a certain uniformity (not identity) in the reactions of clinicians to certain types of behaviors. For instance, the affect-laden imagery with which I responded to Mr. E's behavior was peculiar to myself—though the inclination to withdraw that it mediated was not. Other hospital personnel experienced the same inclination—though it was determined, in accord with their particular histories and personality structures, by fantasies and feelings differing from mine. In short, Mr. E's behavior was eliciting, *through* the dynamics of myself and the staff members, subjective responses that were alerting us to a very objective constellation in his personality—the intent to distance others.

One need not argue that, for analysis to be deemed objective, it would be necessary to demonstrate that two analysts independently analyzing the same patient would perceive and intervene identically at every step of the way. One need argue only that the analysand brings certain dynamics and historical themes to the encounter and that, in the course of treatment, both analysts should become cognizant of the central ones. They need not become aware of them in precisely the same way and as a result of precisely the same interventions.

I thus find myself diametrically opposed to Schafer (1983, pp. 39–40), who argues (in his discussion of empathy):

One must first of all disregard certain positivistic assumptions, namely that subject and object are distinct entities; that there is a single, unambiguously knowable emotional reality with which to empathize; and that empathizing may therefore be judged right or wrong on the basis of objective criteria that exist free of theoretical presuppositions and interpretive grasp of context. . . . That is to say, for the analyst the analysand is not someone who is somehow objectively knowable outside this model, whatever its nature. As an analyst, *one empathizes with one's idea of the analysand* . . . . there are numerous, perhaps countless, mental models of any one analysand that may be constructed, all more or less justified by "data" and by reports of beneficial effects on empathizing and the analytic process [my italics].

It is true that the analyst cannot have knowledge-by-direct-acquaintance of the analysand's inner world and that the former's perception of the latter is in part a function of the analyst's mental set and theoretical presuppositions. But to argue from this—which happens to be the condition appertaining to knowing in any discipline—that there is no place for the concept of objectivity in psychoanalysis is, in my opinion, a fallacy.[1]

---

[1] *"In our science as in the others the problem is the same:* behind the attributes (qualities) of the object under examination which are presented directly to our perception, we have to discover something else which is more independent of the particular receptive capacity of our sense organs and approximates more closely to what may be supposed to be the real state of affairs.

We have no hope of being able to reach the latter itself, since it is evident that everything new that we have inferred must nevertheless be translated back into the language of our perceptions from which it is simply impossible for us to free ourselves . . . . Reality will always remain 'unknowable.' The

I maintain that what I have said about the analyst's relationship with the analysand applies with little modification to the historian's encounter with his texts, monuments, periods, cultures, nations, and personalities: "historical cognition is a kind of conversation, a dialogue with the past" (Florovsky, 1969, p. 353). The historian's, like the psychoanalyst's, interaction with his subject is carried out not merely with his cognitive apparatus, but with his total personality (including his passion) as well. For example, Croce (1921, p. 13) tells us that

> When the development of the culture of my historical moment presents to me . . . . . the problem of Greek civilization or of Platonic philosophy or of a particular mode of Attic manners, that problem is related to my being in the same way as the history of a bit of business in which I am engaged, or of a love affair in which I am indulging, or of a danger that threatens me. I examine it with the same sense of unhappiness until I have succeeded in solving it.

Similarly, the historian Page Smith (1966, p. 155) asserts that good histories are "animated by the devotion of the au-

---

yield brought to light by our scientific work from our primary sense perceptions will consist in an insight into connections and dependent relations which are present in the external world, which can somehow be reliably reproduced or reflected in the internal world of our thought and a knowledge of which enables us to 'understand' something in the external world, to foresee it and possibly alter it . . . . [In psychoanalysis] We have discovered technical methods of filling up the gaps in the phenomena of our consciousness, and we make use of those methods just as a physicist makes use of experiment. *In this manner we infer a number of processes which are in themselves 'unknowable' and interpolate them in those that are conscious to us*" (Freud, 1938, pp. 196–197, my italics).

Attacking those who maintain that "being bound to the conditions of our own organization, it [scientific method] can yield noth-

thor to his subject" and are the fruit of "the deepest commitment to the people, the period, and the events about which
[the historian] is writing."

From the concept of history writing as a relationship, it
follows that the historian brings an historically determined,
conscious and unconscious, perspective and set of conflicts,
preconceptions, and preoccupations to his field of study. All
this, known or unbeknownst to him, influences his selection,
organization, evaluation, and explanation of the data. It may
even affect his choice of topic and, if he is a biographer, cause
a countertransference to his subject. "Before you study the
history, study the historian," advises Carr (1961, p. 54). As for
the mutually influential nature of the historical dialogue,
what scholar, having immersed himself in a culture, age, or
individual has not felt the impact of his subject upon him?

Of course, if the historian is aware of his historically conditioned mental-emotional set and is true to the canons of evidence, criticism, and interpretation of his craft, then his per-

---

ing else than subjective results, whilst the real nature of things
outside ourselves remains inaccessible," Freud (1927, pp. 55–56)
argued:

> In the first place, our organization—that is, our mental appa-
> ratus—has been developed precisely in the attempt to explore
> the external world, and it must therefore have realized in its
> structure some degree of expediency; in the second place, it is
> itself a constituent part of the world which we set out to inves-
> tigate, and it readily admits of such an investigation; thirdly,
> the task of science is fully covered if we limit it to showing how
> the world must appear to us in consequence of the particular
> character of our organization; fourthly, the ultimate findings
> of science, precisely because of the way in which they are ac-
> quired, are determined not only by our organization but by the
> things which have affected that organization; finally, the prob-
> lem of the nature of the world without regard to our percipient
> mental apparatus is an empty abstraction, devoid of practical
> interest.

sonality will work for, and not against, him. He will be able, like the psychoanalyst, to use his psyche, not as a well from which to project his conscious and unconscious idiosyncracies, but as an empathic instrument in his attempt to *verstehen.* Dilthey (1944), Collingwood (1946), Croce (1921), and others have expounded upon the necessity for empathy in the historian's work.

In reading an edict of Theodosius, Collingwood (1946, p. 283) tells us, the historian "must envisage the situation with which the emperor was trying to deal, and he must envisage it as that emperor envisaged it . . . he must see the possible alternatives, and the reasons for choosing one rather than another; and thus he must go through the process which the emperor went through in deciding on this particular course."

In intellectual history, that species of history (with biography) most closely resembling the psychoanalytic enterprise, the historian makes every effort to see his author's project through his author's eyes, with his author's background, and with his author's aims and procedure. He must accomplish this, and discern what it was that his subject was actually trying to say, before criticizing the form and content of his subject's work—either from a contemporary or from a present-day vantage point. If the topic is, for instance, Freud's anthropological thinking, one must feel one's way into Freud's scientific temperament, personal characteristics, cultural ambience, intellectual prehistory, theoretical biases (and their rationale), professional experience, and early exposure to anthropological writings; with this background, one must then approach Freud's task—the study of primitive beliefs and institutions—as nearly as possible in the manner in which Freud did. One must read Freud's sources and imagine how he would have read them and how his experience and creativity would have interacted with the ideas of his authors. While it is impossible to become Freud himself, as he wrote *Totem and Taboo,* it is possible, with sufficient immersion in the data and adherence to scholarly methodology, to arrive at a reasonable reconstruction of his state. The most common errors in the history of ideas result from inadequate empathy with one's author or period, from a failure to suspend disbelief sufficiently to enter into his world before criticizing him.

It is likely, for example, that Macaulay's time in Parliament enhanced his sensitivity to the political process and figures about which he wrote and that Gibbon's military service deepened his understanding of generals and maneuvers. Although the medical or science historian need not be a practitioner of the field about which he writes, there are instances in which it can be distinctly helpful—such as in the history of physics, surgery, or psychotherapy. The black historian who has himself experienced the effects of social discrimination may better appreciate the problem of slavery.

Nevertheless, empathy based upon such backgrounds is reliable only if one is sufficiently aware of the potential for bias and distortion inherent in them. Macaulay's political partisanship at times colored his view of things. Zilboorg's psychoanalytic adherence led him to an Hegelian vision of the history of psychiatry as the progressive unfolding of psychoanalysis. The black historian's experience might, if he is not careful, cause him to write a polemic, not a history, about the antebellum South.[2] One must keep in mind that, despite a certain transtemporal, transcultural unity to the psychical processes of mankind, it is possible to penetrate the modes of thought and being of our ancestors to only an approximate degree. There remains a to some extent unbridgeable gulf between a Theodosius and a Collingwood. The fruits of empathy must be subjected to the scrutiny of critical historical reason.

From the other side of the coin, the analyst's relationship with his client is in some ways elucidated by analogy with the historian's to his document. I have previously used Boisen's (1936) phrase "living human document." Ricoeur (1970),

---

[2]Even so, there are many instances in which a bait of bias has snared a carp of truth. For example, anti-royalist sentiments led certain seventeenth century English historians to reevaluate the authenticity of Arthurian legends that had hitherto been uncritically accepted.

Schafer (1978), and Lacan (1968) are among the many who compare the dynamic psychiatrist's task to the exegete's. Both analysts and historians are involved, through skilled listening and questioning, in progressively unpacking the meaning that patient or text supplies. And their exegesis, in contrast to that of the literary critic, is diachronic, as well as synchronic.

Of course there is a sense in which the analyst's text is more like a palimpsest; it has been continually rewritten and yet it bears the traces of its previous chronicles; through the analysis it will be rewritten once more. Another implication of the patient-as-text analogy is that, while there are general features and principles of construction that apply to all texts, no two texts are identical. Each is a concrete and somewhat idiosyncratic document and must be understood as such, rather than as merely another instance of some abstract notion of a universal text.

Having focused largely on methodological similarities in the two disciplines, I shall examine an apparent difference: the "presentistic," pragmatic orientation of the analyst and the antiquarian love of the past for its own sake of the historian. The dynamic psychiatrist is concerned with the patient's history from the vantage point of the latter's current symptoms and character formation; he reconstructs this history "backwards," ever mindful of what it has led up to. The dynamic therapist aims to uncover, and make the patient cognitively and affectively aware of, maladaptive patterns of behavior and the historically based conflicts and distortions in view of self and world from which they result, to the end of broadening his capacity for reality-oriented self determination. The clinician's intent, as Novey (1968, p. 13) says, "is not simply to assign cause and responsibility for events in the past but also to place them in a perspective which invites action in the present and the future." It is thus correct to say that the analyst writes history in order to make history.

Many historians, while they would concede the necessity for the analyst's present-centered perspective on his subject, would denounce such a stance in an historian as "presentism." They could then point to the legion of works that depict history as unfolding to an alleged contemporary state of perfection, that read the historian's historically, culturally, and psychologically conditioned concerns into the past, and that fail to appreciate the mode of life and thought of those under investigation. Oakeshott (1933), for example, maintains that the true historian's attitude toward the past is entirely theoretical and dispassionate. He studies the past for its own sake and not to unearth any presumed relevance to the present day. Lovejoy (1959, pp. 177, 180), while acknowledging that the historian's research is often motivated by a desire to understand the present, warns that this should not interfere with a realization that "his ancestors had ends of their own which were not solely instrumental to his ends, that the content and meaning of their existence are not exhaustively resolved into those of the existence of their posterity." It is precisely in such self-transcendence that the "mind-enlarging, liberalizing, sympathy-widening" effects of history reside. In the history of psychiatry lack of recognition of this has resulted in a plethora of presentistic writing—Zilboorg (1941) and Alexander and Selesnick (1966), for example.

Others, such as Croce (1921), Turner (1938), and Bloch (1953), feel that history writing with an eye to the present is not only permissible, but mandatory, if the result is to be relevant to the reader. When, on a trip to Stockholm with Henri Pirenne, Bloch was surprised that the great Belgian historian wanted to begin their tour with the modern town hall, the latter explained, "If I were an antiquarian, I would have eyes only for old stuff, but I am a historian. Therefore, I love life" (Bloch, p. 43). "The antiquarian strives to bring back the past for the sake of the past; the historian strives to show the present to itself by revealing its origin from the past," asserts Frederick Jackson Turner (1938). The ultimate aim of history, Carr (1961) maintains, is to throw light upon, and perhaps even transform, the present. Walsh (1969, p. 242) includes, among the historian's motives, "the need to find out what past ages were like with a view to making some assessment both of them and of our own times." For Ortega y Gasset and Dilthey history is less the reconstruction of historical occurrences than incorporating the past in the construction of the future.

In any event, most historians now appreciate that the idea of a "definitive" history of anything is misguided, that it is the task of each succeeding generation of historians to reinterpret the past from the vantage point of the interests and new knowledge of the present. Writing history with one foot in the present—or, more accurately, with a frank acknowledgment that this is the only way one *can* write it—is not the same thing as the sin of "presentism"; indeed, it may be the best protection against it. As Aron (1969, p. 260) says, "The historian does not become scientific by depersonalizing himself but by submitting his personality to the rigors of criticism and the standards of proof."

Nevertheless, while acknowledging and utilizing his current perspective, the historian must appreciate the paradox that history is more likely to be of service to the present's attempt to understand itself if that history is first reconstructed as much in its own right as possible. To return to the example of Freud's anthropological thinking, one first attempts to reconstruct the history of that thinking and to examine its contemporary ambience and critics before evaluating its impact on present day culture science.

But if the historian is more present-centered and pragmatic than commonly recognized, the good therapist is more academic than many surmise. Freud trenchantly observed that if the analyst's zeal to cure exceeds his historical curiosity, the treatment suffers. The clinician's ultimate objective is therapeutic transformation, but he knows this is achieved only through the intermediate goal of reconstructing and interpreting the patient's history.

The psychoanalyst studies his analysand's biography because of his philosophy that those who do not know history are doomed to repeat it. This repetition of the past in the present is posited to occur for at least six reasons: (1) the perennial striving of powerful unconscious fantasies originating in childhood; (2) the attempt to reanchor oneself to mental representations of a time of contentment in childhood; (3) the econ-

omy of expenditure of psychical energy in allowing one's behavior to flow along habitual and timeworn paths; (4) the
persistence of childhood modes of interpretation and expectation of self and world;[3] (5) behavior consistent with these
childhood modes often induces those in one's present environment to behave similarly to those in the past, thus ensuring
that the traumata of the past remain those of the present;
and, related to the aforementioned (6) the attempt to go back
and rewrite an improved version of the past with a variety of
parent and sibling imagoes.

IDEALISM VERSUS REALISM

Underpinning much of the discussion thus far and emerging
from our consideration of presentism is the dialectic between
idealism and realism. Let us turn to it now. In so doing we
also continue to address aspects of the subjectivism (relativism)-objectivism polarity.

Historicist writers, as we have seen, tend to emphasize the
concrete objectivity of the subject matter of history and to
adopt a "correspondence theory" of knowledge. The scholar's
task, they argue, is to arrive at hypotheses that accurately
correspond to past reality; this is accomplished by inspecting
the data without theoretical preconceptions. Some of them
write almost as if they have privileged access to the historical
occurrences themselves. Having refuted the contentions that
the historian or psychiatrist can proceed without a philosophy
of history and incipient theorization and that he can enjoy

---

[3]See Matte Blanco's (1975) insufficiently appreciated book, *The Unconscious as Infinite Sets,* where he explicates the infantile, unconscious, primary process mode (that ensures our history will repeat
itself) as a symmetrical logic which treats the world as composed of
classes rather than of particulars. In this mode "my mother is a
brunette woman" entails "a brunette woman is my mother" such
that all brunette women are perceived, unconsciously, as one's
mother.

direct access to past events, I shall focus on the idealist and subjectivist writers. In the course of this I shall reconsider the correspondence theory of historical knowledge.

Drawing on the work of Croce, Dilthey, and Collingwood, the American constitutional historian Beard succinctly outlines the idealist approach in two well known articles, "Written History as an Act of Faith" and "That Noble Dream," appearing in 1934 and 1935 respectively. In these essays Beard aims to score a number of points against the historical realists.

To begin with, he denies that the historian's subject matter is an objective reality, a *Gegenüber* standing over and against the mind of the historian. Consequently, says Beard (1935, p. 171), "The historian is not an observer of the past that lies beyond his own time. He cannot see it *objectively* as the chemist sees his test tubes and compounds [Beard's italics]." Rather, the scholar is limited to documentation in the present. Second, these traces are fragmentary; a myriad of actors and events have been lost to posterity.

Third, from this very incomplete documentation the historian makes a "partial selection or a partial reading." Fourth, because both documentation and research are "partial," it follows that the total actuality is not recapturable by the historian. "History as it actually was, as distinguished, of course, from particular facts of history, is not known or knowable, no matter how zealously is pursued the ideal of the effort for objective truth." Fifth, "The idea that there was a complete and actual structurization of events in the past, to be discovered through a partial examination of the partial documentation, is pure hypothesis" (ibid, p. 172).

Sixth, "Any overarching hypothesis or conception employed to give coherence and structure to past events in written history is an interpretation of some kind, something transcendent." Seventh, the historian does not bring to his "partial documentation" a neutral mind, but rather one colored by his time, place, culture, and personal predilections. Eighth, "Into the selection of topics, the choice and arrangement of materials, the specific historian's 'me' will enter." This choice and arrangement amounts, he (1934, p. 151) asserts, to an "act of faith"

What this comes down to is the historian's painful admission that he is "more or less a guesser in the vale of tears" (ibid, p. 143), that the most he can offer is a "version" of history (p. 173).

Collingwood, as previously mentioned, adopts much the same point of view. He ridicules the objectivist treatment of the past as tantamount to the conviction that there is "a world where Galileo's weight is still falling, where the smoke of Rome still fills the intelligible air, and where interglacial man is still laboriously learning to chip flints" (1965, p. 101). The past, declares Collingwood, is "simply nonexistent," and until the historian fully realizes this his technique is "precarious."

In thinking anticipatory of Schafer, as we shall see in a moment, Collingwood asseverates that the historian's aim is to reconstruct the present world, not the past: "he wants to be able to see this world as the living successor of an unreal, a dead and perished, past. . . . . He is trying to know the past; not the past as it was in itself . . . but the past as it appears from its traces in this present: the past of *his* world (ibid, pp. 101–102; Collingwood's italics)." Even here it is not a question of a definitive picture, but rather one sketched through an idiosyncratic lens: "each historian is a monad which mirrors the universe from a point of view that is irrevocably not any other's point of view" (p. 54). Nor does that monad faithfully reflect that limited arc of reality it subtends. The historian's position is akin to the landscape artist's: "He may fancy that he is reproducing in his own medium the actual shapes and colours of natural things; but . . . . It is the artist, and not nature, that is responsible for what goes into the picture" (Collingwood, 1946, p. 236).

With his contention that the historian must, to some degree, *create* his data, Collingwood adds a new dimension to Beard's critique of historical realism. In essence, Collingwood argues that the investigator's data depend on his prior experience and theoretical orientation, his angle of vision, his interests, and his interpretations. Beginning with an image of history as a "web of imaginative construction stretched between certain fixed points provided by the statements of authorities," he attenuates it even further: "there are for historical thought no fixed points thus given." In other words, "in history, just as there are properly speaking no authorities, so *there are properly speaking no data*" (Collingwood, 1946, pp. 242–243; my italics). The historian, he (p. 244) tells us, is just as responsible for the fixed points as for the web of imaginative construction. "Hence there is in the last analysis no distinction between his sources and his conclusions; his conclusions, as soon as he has reached them, become his sources, and all his sources are conclusions which he has reached" (Collingwood, 1965, p. 53).

Like Beard, Collingwood (ibid, p. 55) pessimistically concludes, from the fragmentary nature of the historian's evidence and the perspectivist and interpretive aspects of his work, that "The more the historian knows, the more acutely he becomes aware that he will never really know anything, and that all his so-called knowledge is to an unverifiable extent erroneous. Fact, in its reality, is unknowable." How, one wonders, does Collingwood's historian even know that he does not know?

In the philosophy of psychoanalysis Ricoeur, Schafer, and Spence carry the idealist banner. Ricoeur (1970) is concerned to differentiate between the methodology of psychoanalysis and that of the natural sciences (including behaviorist psychology). "Psychology," he (p. 359) maintains, "is an observational science dealing with the facts of behavior; psychoanalysis is an exegetical science dealing with the relationships of meaning between substitute objects and the primordial (and lost) instinctual objects." The psychoanalyst is preoccupied, he continues, not with the "facts," but with the "meaning" they assume in the life of the individual. Behavioral facts do not function as "observables," but as "signifiers" for "the history of desire": "strictly speaking, there are no 'facts' in psychoanalysis, for the analyst does not observe, he interprets" (pp. 364–365).

Schafer (1978, p. 8) conceptualizes psychoanalysis as "a method of *history-making* and world defining [my italics]." The analyst "constructs," "not *the* personal past, but *a* personal past. However convincing it may be, it remains a construction, merely a history of a certain kind [Schafer's italics]." Although Schafer acknowledges that the analyst sometimes uncovers "already established and unconsciously maintained ideas and experiences," he does not see this as a major part of the clinician's task. Rather, the psychoanalyst is engaged in *constructing* a past history and a present world of a certain kind—"through those aspects of interpretation that implement the Freudian strategy of defining significance, interrelatedness and context" (p. 15). Like Collingwood, Schafer maintains that "The point of historical inquiry is the elucidation of the present world" (p. 15). "Increasingly," says Schafer (p. 23), "the analyst and analysand proceed on the strength of the shared recognition that subjective experience itself is a *construction*. . . . They no longer think of past or present experience solely or mainly as that which is given and is to be consulted introspectively for clearer answers [Schafer's italics]." By Schafer's way of thinking, to recollect or recount any prior experience, however remote or recent, is less a recovery of it than the manufacture of a *new experience*. In his later work Schafer becomes increasingly skeptical of the notion of objective historical truth:

> there are no objective, autonomous, or pure psychoanalytic data which, as Freud was fond of saying, compel one to draw certain conclusions. Specifically, there is no single, necessary, definitive account of a life history and psychopathology . . . what have been presented as the plain empirical data and techniques of psychoanalysis are inseparable from the investigator's precritical and interrelated assumptions concerning the origins, coherence, totality, and intelligibility of per-

sonal action . . . the data of psychoanalysis [should] be
unfailingly regarded as *constituted* rather than simply encountered [my italics] (Schafer, 1980, p. 30).

One may, therefore, say of analytic interpretation that, far
from unearthing and resurrecting old and archaic experiences
as such, it constitutes and develops new, vivid, verbalizable,
and verbalized versions of those experiences . . . conventional
distinctions between subject and object, between observation
and theory, and between past and present no longer hold. From
this one may conclude that reconstruction of the infantile past
is a *temporally displaced and artificially linearized account of
the analysis in the here and now* [my italics] (Schafer, 1983, pp.
189–190, 203).

To Spence belongs the distinction of following this line of
thought to its logical conclusion. Distinguishing between
"historical" and "narrative" truth, Spence denies that the
analyst has access to the former.

On the grounds that mind is ambiguous, that every communication has many meanings, that pictorial images cannot be
adequately translated into words, that one cannot recapture
the events of the past, that clinical data is always fragmentary, that historically inaccurate interpretations may elicit
affirmative responses and therapeutic results, and that countertransferential factors and theoretical presuppositions distort the clinician's vision, Spence concludes that the analyst
must abandon all pretense to be reconstructing an accurate
picture of the past.

The importance of ambiguity in the analytic *process* has never
been properly addressed by the analytic *method*. Once we assume that meanings are multiple, we can hardly assume that
the one *we* discover is necessarily the most significant. To discover a meaning is different from discovering a lost fragment.
The ambiguity of the utterance or the symptom still remains
after we have put an interpretation on it; if we can claim, with

Searle, that there is an unlimited number of contexts that could be supplied for any utterance, we can see that interpretation is endless (Spence 1982, pp. 267–268; Spence's italics).

If an interpretation cannot be validated with reference to any putative piece of past history, then what are the criteria for a satisfactory formulation? They are, says Spence, those of "narrative," and not "historical," truth. And these standards are "aesthetic" and "pragmatic" (pp. 268, 271). One would presume to evaluate an interpretation on the grounds of its "historical truth" (i.e., its correspondence to past reality) no more than one would a painting (pp. 269–270).

By the "pragmatic" touchstone, the analyst worries about the objective truth of his statement no more than "the politician who says he is going to win next Tuesday." Just as the latter "makes the statement, not because he *knows* the outcome, but because he wishes to *influence* the outcome," so the former interprets to the end of "making something happen in the analytic space" (p. 271; Spence's italics). Nevertheless, for it to have the desired effect the analyst must "commit himself to a belief in his formulation *but not necessarily to a belief in its referent*" (p. 273; my italics).

Unfettered by shackles to unattainable historical truth, the clinician is now free to pursue the aims of beauty and instrumentality: "We no longer search for historical accuracy but consider the interpretation in terms of its aesthetic appeal . . . [interpretations] are designed to produce results rather than to document the past; they are designed primarily to bring about a change in belief" (pp. 270, 276). With this declaration it is plain that Spence has gone beyond his predecessors Ricoeur and Schafer.

The psychiatrist and philosopher of psychoanalysis Sherwood (1969) acknowledges the criteria of form, coherence, and internal consistency, while still insisting that satisfactory psychodynamic explanations must correspond to objective reality. The psychoanalyst Novey (1968), while anticipating aspects of Spence's concern with construction, internal consistency, and utility, nevertheless asserts that "some degree of correspondence must occur" (p. 34). Similarly, the historian and philosopher of history Gallie (1964, p. 71), while appreciating the affinities between the stylistic aspects of history-writing and story-telling, strenuously maintains that "to be historical a narrative must rest upon evidence . . . [and] succeed in making the subject-matter more intelligible to its readers . . . by showing its interconnections with other relevant historical evidence and results." Even Collingwood (1946, p. 246), despite his idealist tendencies and emphasis on the affinities between history and novel writing, retrenches, warning that whereas the novelist need only paint a coherent picture, the historian must construct one that is both coherent and an accurate depiction of "things as they really were and of events as they really happened." And Schafer (1983, p. 206) himself advises that, in focusing on the analyst's and analysand's ongoing revision of the latter's history, he is not arguing that "each history is a mythic creation which is exempt from the rules of verification, coherence, consistency and (for the time being) completeness."

There is not doubt that philosophers of history such as Beard and Collingwood and philosophers of psychoanalysis such as Ricoeur and Schafer have made considerable contributions to method and epistemology. It can be argued that their positions represent a necessary, if extreme, reaction to the exaggerated realism of history in the 1920's and of psychoanalysis until recently (a contention which would place the current philosophy of psychoanalysis in a situation comparable to that of the philosophy of history in the 1930's and 40's). It should be evident from earlier considerations in this monograph that I have been influenced by aspects of their point of view. Particularly important is their emphasis on the role of interpretation and their advocacy of humility in the practice of history and psychoanalysis. Nevertheless, there are dangers inherent in their positions—particularly when carried to skeptical or fideistic extremes.

To begin with, it is obvious that historical events do not enjoy continued existence in some supratemporal realm and are hence unrecapturable as actual occurrences. However, this does not vitiate the truth or utility of the idea that there *was* an objective past, a *Gegenüber* which, while it does not now exist, once did, and which we are striving to reconstruct as accurately as possible.

Although our evidence is limited to present day traces of the past, we are not concerned with such documents merely as current phenomena, but as signs pointing to a past reality in which they arose. It is as indicators of the past, not the present, that they assume their historical significance. And I hold, in contrast to Beard, that there was an inner structure to this unrecapturable *Gegenüber*—a configuration and causal nexus independent of any investigator's subsequent theorizing about it. Entailed in the thesis of historical determinism and the genetic method is the assumption that the organization of the traces bears some relationship to the structure of the historical events and that the former provides clues and pointers to the latter. This is not an empirically unwarranted proposition, for embryology and developmental psychology and the genetic sciences—history, psychoanalysis, archaeology, evolutionary biology, paleontology, and historical geology—provide considerable evidence that psychological, social, biological, and geological structures emerge in an historically continuous manner from precursors whose vestiges they continue to bear. To argue that personality structure and memory traces bear no relationship to historical events is to exempt psychological processes from the principle of historical continuity that appears to apply to the rest of the universe.

In some instances the relationship between traces and historical events is more direct than in others. Monuments and artifacts, eyewitness accounts, relatively intact hitherto repressed memories, and discrete, persistent symptoms originating in immediate response to childhood traumata approximate what the historian Renier (1950, p. 156) terms the "still perceptible termination or culmination of a sequence of events or of several sequences of events." In other cases, such as chronicles and histories penned long after the events and complicated adult symptomatic patterns appearing years after the significant episodes of childhood, the relationship is much more indirect.

The alternative—Beard's "idea that there was a complete and actual structurization of events in the past . . . is pure hypothesis" and Spence's notion that any organization of the clinical material is created by the analyst—forces historians and psychoanalysts to make history before they can write it. I believe that such denials of historical objectivity result from the conflation of a procedural proposition—that one cannot resurrect historical occurrences themselves or reconstruct them with total accuracy—with an ontological one—that the events *had* no structure other than what the practitioner imaginatively provides them.

Such a stance opens the door to either explanatory nihilism or to a cancerous proliferation of interpretations, none of which is any more accurate than the others: "there is an un-limited number of contexts that could be supplied for any utterance . . . for any given interpretation actually made there are any number of candidates that could be made and have *equal* claim on our attention" (Spence 1982, pp. 268, 287; my italics). By contrast, the principle of overdetermination has long entailed that no single interpretation ever ex-haustively addresses all the dynamics of a given behavior—without implying, however, that none of these dynamics are more central than others or that there is a limitless supply of them. In clinical case conferences we are often exposed to multiple—sometimes complementary, sometimes contradicto-ry—formulations for the same set of data. Nevertheless, the configuration of the data, and the evidential and inferential canons of psychoanalysis, ensure that the range of plausible interpretations will not be limitless, as well as providing us with grounds to choose among them. The exegesis in psycho-analysis is historical; it is not the exegesis of literary crit-icism—where the horizon of permissible interpretations often seems unending. Furthermore, the analyst's interpretation is subject to a corrective to which the textual exegete's is not—the patient's response to it.

Spence (pp. 294–295) has correctly divined the implications of his argument for psychoanalysis:

First, it makes each analyst even more alone than he is already; if there are almost no guidelines, then the risk of going wrong is sizably increased [if there are no guidelines how can one ever go wrong?] . . . the analyst, like it or not, is engaged in an *artistic struggle* with the patient and with all of his colleagues. Seen in this light, the impossible profession becomes even more so. . . . [Second] if we are shifting to a more relativistic notion of truth, then the discoveries we make in our clinical work, even though they may have direct therapeutic implications, do not necessarily generalize to other patients [my italics].

It is true that huge obstacles stand in the path of one who would reconstruct his patient's historical occurrences (behaviors, interpersonal relations, fears, fantasies, and the interaction among them).[4] Many of the contemporaneous representations of these experiences have been, as Freud himself acknowledged, repeatedly refashioned, revised, and reinterpreted over the subsequent years. Hence, the conscious recollection in the consulting room is often the trace of a trace. Other representations are so preverbal or thoroughly repressed as to be irrecoverable in any form. Although Freud generally stressed the timelessness and immutability of un-

---

[4]Much skepticism about the analyst's and historian's access to historical truth is based on a naive direct-observation theory of knowledge—i.e., 'because we cannot *see* the historical occurrences we cannot know them.' Such a criterion is not satisfied, as Atkinson (1978) points out, by much knowledge of *present*-day reality—e.g., the acceptance as veridical of a radio broadcast that it is raining in another city or that a certain state of events is transpiring across the globe. Imagine that one will accept as reliable knowledge only propositions about events that are now literally observable and one will understand the force of Atkinson's (p. 46) assertion that "most of what we consider ourselves to know about the present is indirect and a consistent skepticism about the past would lead on to a virtually total, incredible skepticism." Pause, once more, and consider how much of our everyday knowledge is *historical*—references to previous arrangements, recent conversations, a newspaper article about events in Lebanon the day before, etc.

conscious recollections, at one point he (1899, p. 322) questioned whether we ever have conscious access to these primeval memory traces or whether "memories relating to our childhood" are the most we can recapture. And Freud was quite aware of the wishful and defensive distortion to which the original memory traces can become subjected and that we are often confronting a virtually inextricable tangle of actual and psychical reality: "the childhood experiences constructed or remembered in analysis are sometimes indisputably false and sometimes equally certainly correct, and in most cases compounded of truth and falsehood" (Freud, 1915–1917, p. 367). The academic historian is in a similar predicament when confronted with the fragmentary nature of his evidence and the inevitable distortions in chroniclers' interpretations and in the transmission of documents.

Such difficulties are inherent in the subject matter of the historian and the analyst, and no amount of improvement in the technique of either will obviate them. The logical, evidential, and inferential structure of history and psychoanalysis has arisen to deal with them. The methodology of both disciplines consists largely of *rules by which one infers past reality from its present traces;* such rules are not arbitrary, but have come from the interaction of the clinical and historical greats with their data.

What does the analyst or historian assert with his formulation? In my opinion, something like the following: "This is what I believe occurred, based on the limited and in some respects distorted data at my disposal and on the rules of evidence and inference of my discipline. Although I cannot be certain that my reconstruction totally recaptures the events (including original fantasies and interpretations) as they transpired, I believe it is a reasonable approximation to them." Can the archaeologist or paleontologist claim to do more? Is there not a midpoint between denying any role to interpretation, inference, and imagination and denying any role to empiricism? That one can acknowledge the importance of interpretation and perspective, and still cleave to a concept of objectivity and historical truth is exemplified by the positions of the historians and philosophers of history Frankel

(1962), Nagel (1963, 1969), Blake (1959), Aron (1969), White (1959), Melden (1969), Mandelbaum (1938, 1963), Walsh (1958) and Hook (1963), and the psychoanalysts and philosophers of psychoanalysis Rieff (1959), Hartmann (1959), Hospers (1959), Novey (1968), Sherwood (1969), and Leavy (1980).

If the analyst abandons "historical truth" for "aesthetic" and "pragmatic" truth criteria, then how are his hypotheses to carry the ring of conviction that Spence says they must bear to produce the desired effect on the patient? How does one believe, as Spence (p. 273) advises, in one's "proposition" but not in its "referent"? Furthermore, without a concept of historical truth one of the profoundest contributions of psychoanalysis—the study of how one's historically determined desires and fears distort one's perception and interpretation of current actual reality—disappears. Bereft of a concept of historical truth how can one even determine, as Spence advocates, when a practitioner's formulation is skewed by unacknowledged countertransference or theoretical presuppositions?

Although the correspondence theory of knowledge has come under a good deal of fire and although it is hardly a valid test of the truth of all propositions (especially in the spheres of ethics, aesthetics, and mathematics), I concur with Mandelbaum (1938, p. 185) that it is accurate and useful for many aspects of the historical (and the psychoanalytic) enterprise.

When we say that a statement is true because it corresponds to the facts we do not mean, says Mandelbaum, that it is somehow a magical copy of the facts, but that the proposition expresses

> a relationship between its terms which holds between the real objects symbolized by those terms (p. 186).
>
> The word "Caesar" symbolizes the real Caesar, the word "Rubicon" symbolizes (in this context) a real river, the word "crossed" symbolizes a certain real type of action done: the whole statement "Caesar crossed the Rubicon" is true if the relation which it expresses did in fact hold of the subjects with which it is concerned, if the action which it states was done was actually done.

I believe that Mandelbaum is correct when he asserts that a correspondence theory of knowledge is implicit in the historical work of even the most ardent relativists and idealists. This is demonstrated by Spence himself, when he turns psychohistorian. The matter to be explained is Freud's imaginative interpolation of a urination episode into the Wolf Man's Grusha story. Spence asked how it is that the patient's initial recollection of being teased by a servant girl became transformed by Freud into an instance of threatened castration for micturition. Spence's (1982, pp. 190–191) answer:

> We have good reason to believe that Freud himself was troubled by bedwetting as a child. Two pieces of relevant evidence appear in *The Interpretation of Dreams,* where Freud is describing his associations to the Count Thun dream. In the first, he reports occasionally wetting his bed and, around the age of two, being reproached by his father; in the second, Freud remembers urinating in his parent's bedroom and hearing his father say, "The boy will come to nothing." "This must have been a frightful blow to my ambition," Freud writes, "for references to this scene are still constantly recurring in my dreams and are always linked with an enumeration of my achievements and successes."

From the context it appears that Spence is putting this forward, not as a narrative explanation to be judged on the grounds of its beauty or therapeutic potency, but as a reconstruction of the history of Freud's fanciful interpretation. His explanation, like dozens of everyday explanations in history and psychoanalysis, is, not certain, but plausible. It is plausible, not because it is a good story, but because it conforms, to some degree, to the canons of evidence and inference of history and psychoanalysis and with what we know about Freud himself.

Similarly, despite Schafer's emphasis on the anlysand's and analyst's current construction of historical reality, he does not seem to be able to dispense with an implicit notion of historical truth. Although it is the task of the therapist to "consciously formulate" the rules governing the patient's behavior, these "rules" are not treated as figments of the analyst's imagination, but rather as the previously existing, albeit unconscious, categories of the analysand (see Schafer, 1983, p. 185).

Finally, can we forget that one of Freud's most signal achievements was *reconstructing,* from the current preoccupations and behavior of his patients, the ubiquitous infantile sexual and aggressive fantasies and behaviors whose existence was subsequently confirmed by the direct observation of children? This is certainly one place where an objective historical (psychical and actual) reality corresponded to Freud's reconstructions.[5]

---

[5]See Hamlyn (1967, pp. 9–38), White (1967, pp. 130–133), and Prior (1967, pp. 223–232) for considerations of the history and current status of "correspondence" and "coherence" theories of truth. Acknowledgment that we do not have access to reality independently of our sensory apparatus and its extensions does not vitiate the correspondence theory of truth. Scientists still require that their formulations correspond to our sense and instrumental data—data which, we presume, are determined by the nature of the world as well as by that of our neurobiological apparatus. Furthermore, that we do not have sense or instrumental data about the ultrastructure of matter does not preclude our acquisition of reasonably objective knowledge about its macrostructure and microstructure. For example, ignorance about the anatomy of the neutron does not prevent the gross anatomist or histologist from making propositions that correspond to the structure of matter *at the level of organization with which he is concerned.*

Freud's conception of truth included—as I believe any balanced epistemology must—elements from both the correspondence and coherence theories. As for the correspondence aspects, Freud (1915–1917, p. 452) asserted that "[the patient's] conflicts will only be successfully solved and his resistances overcome if the anticipatory ideas he is given tally with what is real in him." See also Freud (1933, p. 170) where he asserted unequivocally his adherence to a correspondence theory of truth and (pp. 175–176) lashed out at the

In short, I believe that the analyst works with a correspondence, as well as a coherence, model of truth. His reconstructions aim to correspond, first and foremost, to the patient's childhood *experience* and *interpretation* of self-in-world. These experiences and interpretations, while dependent in part upon the patient's affective-conative-cognitive set at the time of the childhood occurrences, are as legitimate a part of the historical events as that which a neutral observer could have witnessed and recorded when the events transpired. Even where it is ascertained that the original interpretation was more a function of a wish or defensive trend than of the child's accurate perception of the situation, this interpretation is still an integral part of the historical event—for example, that a patient with a certain anxiety, desire, or conflict was relating to a significant other with certain characteristics behaving in a certain manner. While it is often operationally important, as remarked previously, to distinguish between "psychical" and "actual" reality, it is the to some degree inextricable intertwining of the two that constitutes the "historical event." We presume, furthermore, that the childhood interpretations of the interaction (or, more likely, of the *repetitive interactions* of a certain sort) bear some reliable approximation to the "external" (potentially public or observable, at the time) aspects of the interaction. Again, the psychoanalyst is an historiographer engaged in reconstructing the analysand's successive histories (inextricable combinations of "perception" and "interpretation").

---

intellectually nihilistic implications of radically relativist conceptions of knowledge. As to the coherence theory, Freud (1923b, p. 116) told us, by way of analogy, that "If one succeeds in arranging the confused heap of fragments, each of which bears upon it an unintelligible piece of drawing, so that the picture acquires a meaning, so that there is no gap anywhere in the design and so that the whole fits the frame—if all these conditions are fulfilled, then one knows that one has solved the puzzle and that there is no alternative solution."

This monograph contains numerous clinical examples of the manner in which evidence and inference are used to reconstruct the past. Nevertheless, it might not be amiss to give additional instances of how the Freudian psychiatrist utilizes the concept of an objective past.

> Professor T. depicted his mother as "smothering" and his father as aloof and emotionally undemonstrative. His complaints about the latter included: He was often away on evenings and weekends, never played ball with Professor T., never hugged him, refused to talk about himself with the patient, and so forth. He voiced similar dissatisfaction about his current administrator—without being consciously aware of the parallels. It was in this context that he expressed his aforementioned desire that I talk about myself and my feelings about him.
>
> Many subsequent hours were spent on Professor T's increasing awareness of the numerous occasions in the past, present, and my office when this search for the benevolent father manifested itself. As he came to terms with this issue, his behavior with his father, his employer, and myself changed considerably. He began taking the initiative in areas where he had previously been compliant or passive aggressive.

What sort of truth is this man's account of his relationship with his father? No parent or third party came into the picture to verify the accuracy of his recollection. I could not go back in time and observe the household in which he was raised. Nevertheless, what reason did I have to think (a) that the patient's recollection of events was constructed de novo at the time of therapy, (b) that it was not a reliable monument of how he experienced and interpreted his relationship with his father as a child, and (c) that his childhood interpretations (and adult reinterpretations, for that matter) did not bear some correspondence to the actual childhood interactions? My assessment was that this was a plausible chronicle and that it squared, moreover, with other aspects of his account of his father, with what I knew about his relationship with his supervisor and me, and with my knowledge of the sort of adult constellations that commonly result from such a childhood history.

In other cases, as Freud (1937b) pointed out, we may never obtain direct access to the recollections that would support or refute a particular interpretation or reconstruction. This was the case, for example, with Ms. X (who will reappear in Chapter 4).

> She experienced continual difficulty trusting others and was extraordinarily shy. Her self esteem was quite low. The patient could recall remarkably little about her parental home. From Ms. X's accounts of the dearth of intimacy between her parents and herself in adulthood and from Ms. X's style of relating to myself and others, I suggested that the paucity of childhood memories might reflect a paucity of interaction among the family members. The patient responded with tearing and more data about the unsatisfactory aspects of her adult relationship with her parents and siblings. Pertinent also were several other pieces of data that emerged: the mother had been treated for depression several times during the patient's latency and adolescent years; the father was absent at war when the patient was born and for three years thereafter; the maternal grandmother had died several months before the patient's birth; the patient's mother and maternal aunt (with whom they were living) had an altercation necessitating a move when the patient was 2; the maternal aunt recently commented upon how upset the patient's mother became whenever the mother saw a man in uniform during those years; and the mother worked part-time in a factory during the war. The patient herself presented me with the following reconstruction: "You know, I've been thinking alot about what those years must have been like—particularly in connection with what we've talked about with me and my parents, and how I don't have many early memories of them. I've been wondering how available Mama would have been during my first three years, with all that was going on. I wonder how much I got from her. I

even wonder if I was planned [she had two siblings, one and two years older respectively]". I agreed with her that, considering her mother's stressors at that time and the mother's proneness to depression, the patient may not have received much from her then. I added that this, coupled with the father's absence, may have laid the foundation for her low self esteem and negative expectations of others.

Although I could not transport myself to her childhood home or ask her mother for verification, both the patient and I believed this account was very plausible. The reconstruction was followed by a chain of thematically related associations and memories from a variety of periods in her life. We did not think we had written a novel, but rather that we had reconstructed a fair approximation of some historical occurrences.

On the other hand, there are occasions when one's reconstructions and the patient's childhood memories can be validated directly. A 21-year-old woman, whose hysterical amnesia was precipitated by her mother's recent death and her stepfather's immediately subsequent seduction attempt, was hypnotized. Under hypnosis she recounted, with considerable anxiety and in baby talk, several traumatic primal scene memories from her oedipal years. The frequency of such occurrences in her childhood home was confirmed by conversations between the social worker and the patient's aunt and older sister. With another patient a reconstruction about the nature of his early parent-child relations received strong support from his subsequent review of family photographs, slides, and movies. Serota (1964) recounted three treatments in which home movies validated reconstructions.

Spence fails to appreciate that psychoanalysts and historians, like scientists, are not searching for certainty, but for some degree of certitude. A formulation need not claim to be infallible in order to claim to be historical.[6,7]

---

[6]D. W. Hamlyn (1967, p. 38) concludes an excellent history of epistemology with the assertion that "First, there is *no* indubitable

If our aim is, as Collingwood and Schafer assert, to use the past to understand the present, then this is best accomplished by first attempting to reconstruct the past in its own right. The "objective past," while irrecoverable as actuality, is a necessary regulating principle in the labors of scholar and psychoanalyst alike. Although it is admittedly an ideal, it is an ideal that makes considerable difference in the reality of clinical and scholarly practice.

This brings us to a second point: that these writers' emphasis on the analyst's, analysand's, and historian's *current constructions* and *(re)interpretations* leads to a neglect of those representations of historical occurrences (primal memories) that are being reflected and elaborated upon. This manifests itself in Schafer's reluctance to consider the role of more or less enduring psychic contents (such as repressed memories from childhood and perennially active unconscious fantasies), in his inclination to collapse the history being reported into the current act of reportage and reinterpretation, and in his infatuation with treating every mental act as spontaneous and self originating. The patient's description of any prior mental state—even that of an instant before—is treated as the "creation" of *new* experience (Schafer, 1978, p. 91), rather than the recounting of old. In line with this, analysis is reconceptualized as the "study of itself," and the analyst and analysand as the historians of their relationship, rather than of the patient's biography (Schafer, 1983, p. 209).

---

knowledge; second, it is not necessary for the general possibility of knowledge that there should be" (my italics). Failure to appreciate this has bedeviled science and philosophy for centuries.

[7]At times, it can be argued, Freud insufficiently appreciated the limits to what can be achieved by the reconstructive enterprise. In the Wolf Man case report, for example, he claimed to have reconstructed his patient's primal scene down to the time of day and season of the year in which it occurred and to have elucidated the parents' position in intercourse, the number of times they engaged in coitus, and the father's response to the patient's voyeurism.

In short, while Schafer is indeed correct that there is a sense in which every verbalized recollection is to some degree a reinterpretation and reworking of the past and, as such, a new experience, we need to draw some distinction between the previously existing memory trace or image of the historical occurrence (the "historical fact" à la Becker) and the analysand's subsequent elaboration upon it. Although the analyst cannot recapture the actual historical occurrence, he strives to come as close as possible to the analysand's original representation and interpretation of it. Hypnotic "age regression" and Penfield's (1950) cortical stimulation studies graphically demonstrate the degree to which recollections can be preserved intact.

Furthermore, subsequent revisions and elaborations upon the primal perceptions and interpretations will bear some relationship to the original representations (i.e., there will be historical continuity in the evolution of the interpretations) and will be important historical items in themselves, reflecting the vicissitudes of the patient's intrapsychic and interpersonal equilibrium. The reinterpretations growing out of the enhanced insight and altered perspectives of the analytic experience are themselves intimately related to the primal recollections. For example, Mrs. K's eventual reinterpretation of her mother's childhood interactions with her—screaming at Mrs. K., holding the patient responsible for the mother's weight gain, accusing Mrs. K. of depressing the family and causing the mother's psychosomatic ailments, and predicting the patient would go insane—as evidence of the mother's severe psychopathology rather than of the patient's omnipotent badness resulted from an altered perspective on infantile memory traces that remained the same. In other words, the adult reinterpretation did not dissolve the infantile memory traces-interpretations; the latter were still introspectively available though their infantile significance was no longer the primary one.

To collapse memory into reporting and reinterpretation is to assist further the transformation of analysis from history-writing to story-telling. Although it is true that the analytic process transpires totally in the present (when else could it occur?), it is only through the interpretation of certain of the patient's current behaviors as traces of a past reality (i.e. as transference) that they are appreciated in their full significance. In other words, *without a concept of the past, one cannot fully encounter the present.*

In fine, the analytic process must be conceptualized as much more than simply the "study of itself". It is the study of interactions and recollections that transpire in the analytic hour—but to the end, not of constructing a solipsistic history of the analysis, but of reconstructing a reality (i.e., the patient's personality structure and pattern of interpersonal relations) that existed prior to, and that continues to exist independently of, the analytic sessions.

Third, the disinclination of Schafer, Spence, Beard, and Collingwood to separate data and interpretation allows them to speak of "creating" or "constituting" their data when it would be more accurate to speak of "criticizing and performing judgments of significance upon them." Such judgments are based upon the structure of the phenomena under investigation and upon one's philosophy of history. If this is manufacturing anything, it is *facts,* and not data. The mind of the historian or analyst does not create the data; rather, through perception, criticism, and interpretation it transforms them into "facts" (i.e., significant and causally relevant data) or else deems them irrelevant or spurious.

It is true that, insofar as the investigator's historically, culturally, and theoretically preconditioned mind-set meets any sign or symbol (e.g., monument, artifact, text, behavior, and so forth) halfway, any datum contains an element of his interpretation—just as it was already interpreted by the chronicler, archivist, artisan, or analysand who recorded or produced it. Anthropological studies demonstrate graphically the role of culture in shaping the individual's mode of perceiving even the most uncomplicated items of his nonhuman environment; the congenitally blind who become sighted in adulthood experience the world as an optical chaos until they can acquire categories of organizing and interpreting visual stimuli; and psychoanalysts know better than anyone the role of personal history in influencing one's apprehension of the world. In short, there is, as Schafer and Spence preeminently grasp, an element of interpretation or *con*ception in every *per*ception. Nevertheless, they have vitiated this insight— just as they vitiated the insight that there is an element of new experience and reinterpretation in every recollection and of construction in every reconstruction—by carrying it to the extreme.

To acknowledge that the conscious and unconscious associations and categories of interpretation of the observer contribute to any apprehension is not to deny that the object of apprehension also contributes and that there are degrees— and levels—of interpretation (as of abstraction in general). For example, it is both heuristically and epistemologically necessary to distinguish between one's apprehension of a slip and one's theoretical understanding of it. The "interpretation" involved in the latter is a different species of activity than the "interpretation" entailed in the former. Simply recognizing that a word has been misspoken is an act of apprehension that approximates what is commonsensically called "perception"; such an apprehension depends primarily on one's knowing the speaker's language and not upon allegiance to any particular theoretical system. One need not be a psychoanalyst in order to apprehend a word misspoken as a datum about an individual; if, however, this datum is to assume any particular significance for the observer (i.e. become a fact) it will do so only within the context of a theory that tells one it is significant or that alters one's angle of vision so that one can see this datum in previously unappreciated relationships to other data (recall my comments in Chapter 1 about transference as observed and interpreted).

In sum, it is operationally necessary to maintain some distinction between 'perception' and 'interpretation' or, more precisely, to differentiate among interpretations according to their level of abstraction and organization. It is essential to distinguish between a particular sense datum—the publicly observable aspects of a behavior or communication—and the overarching theoretical structure in which it takes on new meaning. It is the analyst's or historian's placing a datum into a previously unappreciated context and novel theoretical matrix that constitutes his act of interpretation, that transforms an old datum into a new fact.

Fourth, that every historian and psychoanalyst studies history from a temporal, cultural, philosophical, and psychological perspective does not commit one to a radically subjectivist conceptualization of history or psychoanalysis. The historian or psychoanalyst can work in a cultural or historical vacuum no more than his natural science counterparts. Both perceive and interpret reality through their psychodynamics and theoretical presuppositions. That one must work from a geographic, temporal, and theoretical perspective does not preclude arriving at reasonably objective knowledge about one's subject matter—historical or otherwise. Macaulay's Whig allegiance, Gibbon's anti-Christian animus, and Prescott's romanticism did not prevent their arriving at transtemporally valid insights about Stuart England, imperial Rome, and the conquest of Mexico. The historian's time and place bring with them novel issues, concerns, and methods which may lead him to reevaluate aspects of the past that were hitherto ignored and to appreciate significances that were previously missed. And we now expect good historians and psychoanalysts to become cognizant of the relativist factors in their work and to some degree transcend them. Extreme relativism undermines itself, for the concept of relativism itself becomes relative.

The so-called "Rashimon phenomenon"—that observers of the same incident (in this case a crime) generally give somewhat differing accounts of it—does not deny us, as skeptics and fideists eagerly conclude, all claim to objectivity and to a correspondence theory of truth. Jurists acknowledge the perspectivist aspects of their witness' reports while possessing procedures for testing their reliability, ferreting out the common and complementary elements in otherwise contradictory accounts, and arriving at some reasonable reconstruction of the episode in question. Although no two of us interpret reality identically, if there were not some consensually validatable (i.e., "public," for want of a better word) aspects to our interpretations, then all would be Babel. Although reality is to some extent a construction, it is a construction from something—and by individuals with some commonality in their percipient-interpretive processes.

Nor does the fact that historians and psychoanalysts approach their subjects from the vantage point of a set of problems and questions commit them to subjectivism. Although the course of investigation often alters the original questions and raises new ones, no scientist begins work without some more or less circumscribed problems in mind.

Fifth, that historians and psychoanalysts must select from the data at their disposal does not involve them, ipso facto, in a subjectivist enterprise; selectivity, as Nagel (1963, p. 78) affirms, is necessary in all science. At the outset it is necessary to distinguish between several levels of selectivity. Many idealists write as if selection occurs at the level of initial data gathering. Certain types of data, they argue, simply will not be looked for or apprehended from the outset—because they are not considered significant to the problem at hand or within the domain of the writer's theoretical orientation.

Indeed, such early selection often occurs in practice and, where it involves patently trivial matters, poses no problem. For example, the military historian will not normally concern himself with Napolean's dessert preferences or the historian of psychoanalysis with Freud's penchant for mushrooms. Other cases of selectivity may be less innocuous, however. An economic historian of the U. S. Constitution may, for instance, inattend to the ideological and sociocultural ambience because he considers it insignificant. An historian of psychiatry may ignore the cultural and economic ambience of the discipline because he considers them tangential to the development of psychiatric ideas and institutions. A psychoanalyst may ignore a client's religious history and the institutional

structure of his past and present work environments because
he considers them irrelevant to the vicissitudes of the patient's fantasy life.[8]

Although theorizing is interacting with data gathering
from the start, this does not mean that one can dispense with
a broad initial data base—in history or psychoanalysis. The
beginning phase of analysis involves a detailed anamnesis on
a variety of aspects of the patient's life—present problems,
past psychiatric problems, current life structure and social
environment, childhood and adolescence, adult development,
sexuality, education, occupation, religion, recreation, recurrent fantasies and dreams, and so forth. The analyst's aim is
to attain an overview, a dawning grasp of the patterns in the
patient's life history and experience of self-in-world. Although
he does not approach this task blind to psychoanalytic propositions, he strives to prevent his theorizing from interfering
with his appreciation of the patient's phenomenology and
history.

The historian, as well, begins by casting his net widely.
Almost certainly he already has a broad knowledge of the
context of the area he proposes to investigate. He then begins
his project with a systematic survey of primary and secondary
sources. If selectivity begins prematurely, he is in danger of
finding only what he is looking for.

Selectivity at the level of the narrative and formulation
poses less of a problem. It goes without saying that one cannot
include everything in one's monograph or case report; judgments about significance and causality must be made. However, such assessments should not be purely the product of the
clinician's or historian's personal temperament, but should
accord with the structure of the data and the logical and evi-

---

[8]The unwitting selectivity deriving from deficiencies in the analyst's recall (psychodynamically determined and otherwise) is a further complicating factor. In this regard recall that Freud's recollections of the Dora case were put to paper only after the treatment was
completed. In other cases, such as the Rat Man, Freud recorded each
session at the end of the day.

dential criteria of the discipline. To return to Collingwood's image of the landscape artist, nature, as well as the painter, should have some share in the picture.

Finally, let us turn to Spence's accusation that the analyst is suggesting what he studies and that the analysand's response is not a reliable test of the adequacy of the interpretation. Spence is correct that suggestion and the analyst's interventions can exert a powerful role on the patient's behavior. Furthermore, the empirical studies of attribution theorists document that any coherent explanation of a behavior may increase the actor's sense of understanding of and control over that behavior and, consequently, reduce his anxiety. In support of his position Spence cites the paper, "Constructions in Analysis," where Freud (1937b, p. 266) acknowledges that the analysand's "assured conviction of the truth of the construction . . . achieves the same therapeutic result as a recaptured memory;" he might also have mentioned Little Hans, where Freud (1909b, p. 104) asserts that psychoanalysis is a "therapeutic measure . . . [whose] essence is not to prove anything, but merely to alter something."

There must be countless instances where incorrect interpretations are taken up by the analysand as the real thing. In other cases, reductive explanations and partial truths are mistaken for the whole, at the expense of appreciating the richness and ambiguity of the patient's experience. We have long known about the "transference cure"—in which the patient basks in the presence of an omnipotent parent imago who gives him what amounts to a battery of new compromise formations. But that this is sometimes the case—and in supportive psychotherapy sometimes the aim—does not mean that it is always so (and especially in insight-oriented psychotherapy or psychoanalysis).

Suggestion and attribution, while they participate to some degree in every therapy, may lead to symptomatic relief but not to personality restructuring. This latter results only from facilitating the patient's awareness of his maladaptive patterns of behavior and their historical basis. In asserting the primacy of the therapeutic aims of psychoanalysis and emphasizing the importance of the patient's conviction in the analyst's constructions Freud (1937b, pp. 259, 261, 268) was not indifferent to the truth value of the formulation: "anyone who does nothing but present the patient with false combinations will neither create a very good impression on him nor carry the treatment very far . . . our construction is only effective because it recovers a fragment of lost experience . . . . What we are in search of is a picture of the patient's forgotten years that shall be alike trustworthy and in all essential respects complete."

Attribution and suggestion can become cheap and easy explanations for the analysand's response to all the analyst's interventions. If therapist-patient interactions are taken out of the context of the anamnesis and treatment as a whole, then it becomes difficult for the analyst to refute the charge of suggestion or attribution. (Of course, it is equally difficult for such charges to be substantiated).

Freud (1909b, pp. 104–105) himself acknowledged that the analyst's interpretive procedure lays him open to the charge of suggestion and elaborated upon this as follows:

> It is true that during the analysis Hans had to be told many things that he could not say himself, that he had to be presented with thoughts which he had so far shown no signs of possessing, and that his attention had to be turned in the direction from which his father was expecting something to come. This detracts from the evidential value of the analysis; but the procedure is the same in every case . . . . In a psycho-analysis the physician always gives his patient (sometimes to a greater and sometimes to a less extent) the conscious anticipatory idea by the help of which he is put in a position to recognize and to grasp the unconscious material. For there are some patients who need more of such assistance and some who need less; but there are none who get through without some of it . . . . But after all, the information which the physician gives his patient *is itself derived from analytic experience;* and indeed it is sufficiently convincing if, at the cost of this intervention by the physician, we are enabled to discover the structure of the

pathogenic material and simultaneously to dissipate it (my italics).

Although the analyst's neutrality and (relative) verbal passivity minimize his influence on the patient's productions and hence give the analytic procedure some crude approximation to a controlled experiment, the analyst cannot simply sit there silently, month after month, and expect the patient, through sheer free association, to arrive at a coherent and accurate formulation of his case. Not only could no analysand react to such a brass monkey in a natural and spontaneous way (i.e., the patient's behavior would be determined more by the analyst's unhuman demeanor than by the patient's own issues), but his experience would be chaotic without the application of some selecting and organizing principles. Furthermore, it is precisely some of his most significant and painful issues about which the patient will *not* want to talk and around which he will have erected all manner of defenses; the analyst must sensitively, though consistently, direct the analysand's attention to his defensive maneuvers, the anxieties motivating them, and the affect-laden memories and fantasies defended against. In short, it would be absurd to argue that the only way the analyst could obviate the charge of suggestion is to never interpret. At issue is *the point at which interpretation occurs.*

In practice, complete interpretations (speaking to the historically determined motives as they manifest themselves in the past, present, and transference) are delivered only after there is ample evidence for them, only after one has gleaned considerable history and encountered the same themes, patterns, and sequences many times. Complete interpretations are not hurled at the patient like bolts from the blue. Rather they have been preceded by a legion of less intrusive interventions such as reflections, questions, confrontations, clarifications, and by numerous partial interpretations—connecting current behaviors to current events and motives, current behaviors to events within the consulting room, current behaviors to historical issues, transference behaviors to historical or current issues, and historical events to still more remote historical events. During this process there is ample opportunity for the patient to correct and revise the therapist's conceptions such that the complete interpretation is in effect the fruit of collaboration between the two. Once delivered, the complete interpretation is then judged against a set of explicit criteria regarding the patient's response (see Wallace, 1983b, pp. 306–309).

The following vignette illustrates some important aspects of the suggestion controversy:

Mr. R presented (1) out of a quite conscious sense of guilt over his repetitive adulterous affairs which, however, he did not feel able to stop and (2) because of repeated occupational failures. The latter were related to his continual complaint that his talents were insufficiently appreciated by his employers. In regard to the former, he could not understand why he engaged in extramarital affairs; he considered his marriage a satisfactory one. I had been postulating, for some time, that these behaviors were caused, in part, by unresolved issues related to his father's desertion of the family (with a girl friend) when the patient was 10—i.e., that his adultery resulted from identification with his father and his occupational difficulties from displacing unconscious complaints toward the father onto his supervisors. However, I had not yet communicated this hypothesis to him. One day, well into the middle phase of therapy, he was talking about his school problems and "nervousness" in the fourth grade. Because, in previous sessions, he had begun talking more about his father and because he appeared somewhat anxious and depressed while describing the fourth grade symptoms, I inferred that his hitherto repressed awareness of the *connection* between the parents' divorce and his childhood problems was now *preconscious*, and hence addressable. Consequently, I queried, in an expectant tone of voice, "What else was going on then?" He replied, visibly stunned, "My father left home." After a long silence he remarked feeling like he had been "hit by a ton of bricks."

This excerpt points out the analytic therapist's delimma. Technique dictated, on the one hand, that I confront this man's hitherto unconscious complex when it had risen to pre-consciousness and when his resistance to dealing with it had abated sufficiently. Otherwise, a precious opportunity would have been lost. His highly charged response and the spate of associations and recollections pertaining to his father in this and subsequent sessions would seem to lend credence (not experimental proof) to the posited causal connection between the divorce and the childhood symptoms. On the other hand, critics who invoke suggestion at every turn would probably argue that my question was a leading one and that, further-more, in prior sessions I must have wittingly or unwittingly thrown out all sorts of cues about my formulation. If virtually any psychodynamic intervention is to be written off, reflex-ively, as suggestion, then there is little ground for dialogue between analytic clinicians and "suggestion" theorists.[9]

---

[9]In two lengthy essays, "Epistemological Liabilities of the Clinical Appraisal of Psychoanalytic Theory" and "Can Psychoanalytic The-ory Be Cogently Tested 'On the Couch'?", Adolf Grünbaum attacks what he (1979, p.464) terms Freud's "tally argument"—that "Only psychoanalytic interpretations that 'tally with what is real' in the patient can mediate veridical insight, *and* such insight, in turn, is causally necessary for the successful alleviation of the patient's neu-rosis" (Grünbaum's italics). He bases his criticisms primarily upon his assumptions that psychoanalytic procedure is irremediably sug-gestive and "placebogenic" and that the methods of introspection and free association cannot produce causally relevant information. Hence, he (1982, p. 393) concludes: "the seeming ineradicability of epistemic contamination in the clinical data adduced as support for the cornerstones of the psychoanalytic edifice may reasonably be presumed to doom any prospects for the cogent intraclinical testing of the major tenets espoused by Freud." Psychoanalysis is thus left in the peculiar position of being a discipline that cannot test its theorems and propositions by its own method—the very method through which the insights to be tested were arrived at! My crit-

To recapitulate, in focusing on the role of the practitioner's historical, cultural, theoretical, and psychological preconditioning I have not been arguing for untrammelled subjectivism in historical and psychiatric work. Rather, I advocate awareness of the subjective, idealist, and relativist factors in our practice because they are invariably present and so that we may master them—which means utilizing them in some cases, and checking them in others—in the furtherance of a broad and accurate view.

Though our objective reality—the "actual occurrences" and their synchronic and diachronic context—is unrecapturable in its pristine totality, we strive to reconstruct it as faithfully as possible. Though our sources never give us the whole and unvarnished truth, we do not despair of having any truth whatsoever. Furthermore, we assume, like Lovejoy (1959), that although data do not simply speak for themselves, there was an inner logic to the events under consideration, an organization and causal nexus that is not merely the product of our imagination. To hold otherwise is to divest history and psychoanalysis of all claims to be serious intellectual disciplines.

In both history and dynamic psychiatry the selection, arrangement, and interpretation of facts are not whimsical, but

---

icisms of Grünbaum's position are fourfold: (1) he does not substantiate his premise that psychoanalytic procedure is incorrigibly suggestive and "placebogenic"—rather this is accepted as virtually a self-evident given; (2) therapeutic efficacy is hardly the only (or even the primary) criterion for evaluating the validity of an interpretation and, taken by itself (in the absence of confirmatory associations, recollections, symptomatic acts, and so forth), is almost never invoked as sufficient proof of a clinical hypothesis; (3) he seems to assume that controlled experimentation is the only epistemologically respectable procedure; and (4) his work is based almost exclusively on Freud's corpus (which contains relatively little on methodology), rather than on consideration of the vast subsequent literature on analytic technique; consequently, his work evidences little appreciation of psychoanalysis as actually practiced.

rule following, behavior. Although there can be multiple vantage points on the same set of data, this does not mean that
some formulations are not broader, more explanatory, and
more internally consistent and data-connected than others.
Although each generation must refashion the history writing
of its ancestors, to accord with new knowledge, methodologies,
and concerns, this does not preclude the application of enduring criteria to the evaluation of any historian's work. Mere
passage of time does not ensure that a scholar's grasp of a
subject or period will be better than his predecessors'. There
remain methodological and epistemological standards before
whose bar each historian, like each psychoanalyst, must bow
in turn. Acknowledgment of the idealistic and relativistic factors in the historian's and analyst's work need not lead us to
skepticism or fideism.[10]

ART VERSUS SCIENCE

Before closing the section, let us examine a question that
has long bedeviled both types of historian—the academic and
the clinical: is their profession art or science? To some extent,
as Carr points out, this is a problem peculiar to the English
language, with its sharp differentiation between the "sciences" and "humanities." In Germany, Dilthey, with his distinction between the *Naturwissenschaften* and the
Geisteswissenschaften, contributed to the issue at hand.

Of course, the crux is one's definition of science. The sciences of physics and ethology, for instance, differ in subject
matter and method from one another as much as history and
psychoanalysis differ from either of them. If under the rubric
of "science" one admits only disciplines that utilize predomi-

---

[10]The trend toward radically idealistic (indeed solipsistic) conceptions of knowledge, beginning shortly after the turn of the century
and continuing to the present day, is perhaps partly a function of the
growing anomie, alienation, and narcissism about which so many
have written.

nantly experimental and mathematical methods and models, then history and psychoanalysis need not apply. By the very nature of what they study historians and analysts cannot engage in prospective, controlled experimentation nor quantification beyond a most approximate way. Nor can they channel their explanations through absolutistic laws, and their method is essentially interpretive and reconstructive. Their explanations and theorems do not carry the predictive power of the natural scientist's. The historian and psychoanalyst cannot attain the same degree of observational detachment as the scientist. Finally, historical and psychoanalytic perspectives are to some degree time and culture bound.[11]

Nevertheless, none of these objections closes the case. To begin with, not all natural sciences are experimental; some, such as paleontology, operate with a methodology that is broadly historical and reconstructive[12] and others, such as ethology, with naturalistic observation. Second, not all sci-

---

[11]The cultural relativity of psychoanalytic theory and therapy has been overstated in many respects. For example, it is often argued that the sexual repression theory of psychopathology applied to the puritanical Victorian epoch, but not to today's sexually liberated culture. This is incorrect on two counts. First of all, fin-de-siècle Vienna was less prudish than is popularly supposed. When Freud began work the interdicts had already begun to break down. Second, incestuous fantasies remain very nearly as unconscious as before; it is, rather, their *derivatives* that are less likely to be repressed, and more likely to be consciously entertained or acted out, than before.

[12]The well known Harvard scientist S. J. Gould (1982, pp. 27-28) tells us: "As a paleontologist and evolutionary biologist, my trade is the *reconstruction* of history. History is unique and complex. It cannot be reproduced in a flask. Scientists who study history, particularly an ancient and unobservable history not recorded in human or geological chronicles, must use *inferential rather than experimental methods*. They must examine the *modern results* of historical processes and try to reconstruct the path leading from ancestral to contemporary words, organisms, or landforms" (first two italics mine; third italics Gould's).

ences make equal use of mathematics. Furthermore, if, as I believe, much of what history and psychoanalysis study is nonquantifiable anyway, then to quantify is to lose, not gain, in scientific precision. Third, since Heisenberg and Einstein we appreciate the probabilistic nature of all statements about the behavior of reality. Fourth, psychoanalysts and historians often engage in successful *retro*diction. The former can, at times, make low level *pre*dictions—e.g., transferential behaviors, based upon the individual's history, that are likely to occur in the course of treatment; the assessment, based upon past history and current environment and mental status, of suicidal or homicidal tendencies. In any event, since the advent of quantum theory much of physical science is concerned, not with predicting individual events or the behaviors of discrete entities, but with calculating the probabilities of patterns of events and the behaviors of entities in aggregate. Finally, as the physicist Bridgman (1961) notes, all science is to some degree interpretive, and no scientist can now ignore the impact of his mental-perceptual set and methodology on the behavior of his subject matter; and Kuhn (1970) has argued persuasively that there are historically and culturally relative aspects of the scientific endeavor.

An apparent difference, elaborated upon by Ranke, Dilthey, and many others—that science deals with the general and recurrent, and history with the unique and particular—is incorrect in principle, correct in practice. It is the former because historians and psychoanalysts, like all scientists, cannot dispense wth generalizations and classes. It is the latter in that the analyst or historian, insofar as he is a practitioner and not a theoretician, is preeminently concerned to explain the development and configuration of the spatio-temporally concrete phenomenon (individual or culture) under consideration; his use of general theorems and universal schemata is subordinated to this task.

If by "science" one means a discipline that rigorously and systematically investigates its phenomena, is radically self conscious of its methodology and its relationship to its subject matter, weighs and sifts the data according to coherent and

internally consistent theories and canons of evidence, and attempts to arrive at rational explanations of reality, then history and psychoanalysis are sciences. But they are not physics, nor chemistry, nor biology. Historians and psychoanalysts
adopt methods and models—including empathy and introspection—appropriate to the peculiar nature of what they
study, rather than slavishly aping those of the natural scientists. This is also true for their concept of causation, which we
shall examine momentarily. And the sharp subject-object dichotomy of the natural sciences does no justice to the interactional nature of historical and psychoanalytic work.

Since the psychoanalyst's subject matter—the interaction
between analyst and analysand—is not amenable to quantification or controlled experimentation, his method must, by
necessity, be a clinico-historical one. His evidence is, consequently, *clinico-historical,* and not experimental or mathematical. This, in my opinion, should be the analyst's reply to
the criticisms of statistician and experimentalist. Clinical evidence includes: historical and current themes (including enduring preoccupations, desires, and fears); recurring sequences of situations and behaviors; characterological
patterns and styles of verbal & nonverbal communication;
current and historical contexts of behaviors; patterns of parapraxes, inhibitions, and symptomatic acts within the session;
associations and patterns of associating; dreams; transference; the analysand's responses to the analyst's interventions and interpretations; and, last but hardly least, the analyst's affective, cognitive, and mnemonic responses to the
patient, including the clinician's fantasies and imagery.[13]

---

[13]In this regard Spence (1982, pp. 215–262) is correct to point out
the significance of the analyst's "subjective" responses to the analysand. They are part of what he terms the "privileged competence"
that only the treating analyst, as he sits in the immediate presence
of the patient, can have. Participants at case conferences and audi-
tors of taped interviews have, by contrast, only "normative competence." That is to say, lacking access to what transpired in the therapist's mind and to subtle nonverbal messages lost to even the most

From the multiplication, convergence, and intertwining of these and other lines of evidence, the clinician obtains considerable empirical warrant for his hypothesizing.

Nor can it be denied that, despite their scientific aspect, both history and psychoanalysis have strong affinities to the arts. Both concern themselves with form, feeling, and imagination, and their endeavor is to some degree an intuitive one. Neither practitioner can be devoid—in his discernment or in his written organization of it—of the more artistic aspects of creativity. Their subject matter generally permits more latitude for alternative interpretations—complementary or contradictory—than that in the natural sciences. The psychoanalysts Reik (1949) and Noy (1969) have written persuasively about the artistic side of psychoanalysis, and Ranke (1973, p. 34) himself asserted that in its tasks of "re-creation" and "portrayal," "history must be science and art at the same time."

THE MUTUAL CONTRIBUTIONS OF HISTORY AND PSYCHOANALYSIS

These have been obscured from the side of dynamic psychiatrists by apparent unawareness of the critical philosophy of history and its relevance to psychodynamic theory and practice and, from the side of historians, by a tendency to adopt an all or none attitude toward the utility of psychoanalysis. For example, Schafer, who reinterprets analysis as a "life historical discipline," makes no reference to authors like Walsh, Dray, Collingwood, and Becker even though the issues they address are essentially identical to his. Some historians take

---

accurate audiovisual recording procedures, they are not privy to much of the process by which the clinician arrived at his particular understanding. Consequently, it becomes necessary, as Spence advocates, that the presenter "naturalize" his text—gloss it with his associations and affective responses to the patient's material (much as I attempted to do in the "Call me Mr. Wonderful" vignette).

it on faith that the methodology of psychoanalysis can be transplanted, root and branch, to the historical enterprise, while others, such as Stannard (1980), attack psychoanalysis with the same ahistoricism and lack of moderation of which they accuse psycho-historians.

To the psychoanalyst, history offers: (1) a brake on extravagant assumptions of psychic unity—by pointing up the relativity of much of human character and culture over time; (2) a restraint on the potential for nomothetic excesses inherent in the conception of fixed and universal developmental stages—by emphasizing an idiographic approach; (3) a greater comprehension of the role of socio-cultural factors in individual psychology; (4) a heightened awareness of one's own place in history and, consequently, a richer appreciation of what is brought to one's encounter with the patient; (5) another perspective, from the philosophy of history, on vital methodological and epistemological issues with which the analyst is concerned; and (6) a more thorough comprehension, through studying the history of his profession, of its place in contemporary culture and its current issues. This last can have the beneficial result of minimizing something that is all too common in the psychoanalytic and psychotherapeutic literature—reinvention of the wheel and the repetition of the errors of one's ancestors. It can also assist the fledgling psychoanalyst or psychotherapist in consolidating a professional identity and sense of continuity with a clinical and intellectual tradition.

The contributions of psychoanalysis to history are less clear-cut, but substantial as well. The biggest obstacles to the historian's appreciation of them are the speculative excesses of so-called "psychohistorians." These include analyzing whole cultures and epochs as if they are personalities, making deep interpretations about the motives of dead persons notoriously resistant to furnishing their associations, ignoring all factors but the psychological ones, and abandoning the evidential and critical canons to which any good historian cleaves. Many scholars gratefully take such excesses, which any college sophomore could recognize, as sufficient excuse to be done with psychoanalysis once and for all. I believe that here, as elsewhere, there is room for a middle way.

To begin with, one must appreciate that psychoanalysis is a clinical method, applicable to one situation alone—the ongoing interaction between therapist and patient in the consulting room. It is only here that one can listen to the train of associations; frame the questions, confrontations, and clarifications through which one garners so much of his information; observe the unfolding transference; and test one's clinical hypotheses (i.e., interpretations) against the patient's subsequent recollections and behavior. It is important to appreciate that when psychoanalysis is applied to history, what is transferred are *insights* about human nature originally arrived at by the psychoanalytic method, but not the *method* itself. Such insights applied to history cannot be treated with the same assurance as the clinically based propositions of psychoanalytic therapy.

If, however, the historian recognizes this, I see no reason he cannot use psychoanalytic theory to draw limited inferences about the personalities of his subjects. Indeed, when he uses economics and social science in his work it is generally their theory and insights which he is transplanting rather than their methods themselves. I believe the historian has a rough and ready concept of individual motivation anyhow, which can be considerably enriched by psychoanalytically informed systematization and appreciation of the role of unconscious motives, defensive processes, and intrapsychic conflicts in human affairs. However, psychoanalytically informed inferences can be used only with personages about whom one has a wealth of reliable information in the form of diaries, letters, reports of contemporaries, and perhaps even (as with Freud and Osler) accounts of their dreams. Their usage with whole cultures is much more problematic and has been treated elsewhere (Wallace, 1983c).[14] And psychodynamic factors

---

[14]An important question concerns the degree to which the mechanisms of individual psychology can be used to elucidate group behavior. While it is in no sense correct to speak of a mass mind with

must be placed within the context of all other factors. Because of this I feel there is no justification for a subspecialty such as "psychohistory"; history is simply history and will make use of any insights at its disposal—psychoanalytic ones included.

Greater than the aforementioned, however, is the role psychoanalysis can play in the historian's refining and monitoring of his best instrument—himself. To the extent that he becomes cognizant of his own historical conditioning, and the conscious and unconscious issues and affects deriving therefrom, then to that degree will he approach that unrealizable ideal of objectivity. Finally, psychoanalysis makes the same contribution to the historian's appreciation of his methodological and epistemological issues that history does to the psychoanalyst's comprehension of his.

SUMMARY

Having concentrated largely on the similarities between history and psychoanalysis, I do not wish to give the impression that there are not considerable differences as well—deriving primarily from the fact that the analyst's subject is alive and

---

structures homologous to those in the individual, it seems that the idea that whole nations or cultures may repress troublesome aspects of their history, recapitulate the past in the present, attempt to actively master passively experienced historical traumata, and perennially attempt to fulfill ancient, but not fully articulated, strivings is suggestive at the very least. Erik Erikson's (1958) "great man in history" model and Robert Lifton's "shared themes" approach constitute considerable improvements on the standard Freudian approach to history. (For an attempt to integrate psychodynamic and traditional historical explanations in the history of ideas see Wallace, 1980a; for a criticism of criticisms of psychohistory see Wallace, 1983e.) The idea that whole cultures and periods can institutionalize certain aspects of psychological function—such as defensive maneuvers or primary process modes—is also an interesting one.

reacting to him, while the historian's is generally not. The analyst's aim remains that of therapeutic transformation; the analysand's current psychopathology is foremost in his mind; and his history writing hence has a presentistic slant that could not be tolerated in an academic historian. The psycho-analyst is an ongoing participant in the history he studies in a way that the historian is not. The metaphor of the patient as document is only approximate. Finally, like the sociologist and unlike the historian, the analyst must reckon with the current contextual determinants of his subject's behavior— i.e., the influence of present-day institutions and persons (in-cluding the analyst himself).

Nevertheless, I believe the similarities outweigh the dif-ferences. I have attempted to dissect out the former and elabo-rate upon them along a number of parameters. Crucial to both practitioners is adherence to a middle way that avoids equally the Scylla of idealism and positivism and the Charybdis of realism and historicism.

In the second part of this study I focus much more on meth-odology and epistemology in psychoanalysis than in history, though I maintain that the psychoanalyst works with the same concept of determinism on the microscopic level that the historian uses on the macroscopic. In short, my treatment of psychoanalytic causation is founded upon the premise that psychoanalysis is the preeminently historical psychology.

II
CAUSATION

The concept of psychic causality is in a peculiar position in psychoanalytic theory and practice. On the one hand it is considered, as Arlow and Brenner (1964) maintain, one of the core concepts of the discipline. On the other hand, the basic textbooks and theoretical treatises, while invariably referring to "psychic causality or determinism," rarely unpack or explicate the meaning of these terms (see, for example, Fenichel, 1945; Alexander, 1963; Menninger, 1958; Glover, 1955; Kubie, 1950; and Greenson, 1967). It is generally taken for granted that the reader will understand what the author means by the concept or that causation in psychoanalysis and natural science are pretty much one and the same.

Fortunately, recent years have witnessed increasing reexamination and reevaluation of the psychoanalytic concept of cause. The work of Robert Waelder (1963), Paul Ricoeur (1970), George Klein (1976), Robert Holt (1976), and the existentialist philosophers and psychiatrists springs immediately to mind. There are numerous epistemological and methodological problems surrounding the concepts of psychic causality and historical determinism, and I shall examine some of these. This involves an historical and logical analysis of Freud's thinking on determinism. My focus on contemporary criticism pivots round the work of Roy Schafer (1976, 1978) and his sources, since they address many of the issues involved. The final subsection touches briefly on the free will-determinism controversy.

3 The Historical Background

CAUSATION[1] IN SCIENCE AND PHILOSOPHY

There is a sense in which it can be argued that a primitive notion of psychic causality was the *first* conception of causality. The animistic cosmogony explains natural events as the effects of the occult operation of so many souls, spirits, or wills.[2] The pre-Socratic concept of causation was, in large part, a projection of the psychological, moral, and juridical concept of human responsibility onto nature. Anaximander, for example, refers to the actions of one element upon the others as "injustices," for which each makes reparation to the other: "the warm elements committing an injustice in summer and the cold in winter" (Copleston, 1962, p. 41).

Aristotle broached the first scientifically systematic concept of causality—his use of the words *aitia, aiton,* continuing to carry, however, the connotation of legal responsibility. Aristotle propounded four causes: material, formal, efficient,

---

[1]In this discussion I shall, like most authors, use the terms "causation" or "causality" and "determinism" interchangeably. Some writers, by contrast (e.g., Reiner, 1932, pp. 711–714), distinguish between the two.

[2]See Frankfort, Frankfort, Wilson, and Jacobson (1967, especially pp. 23–29) for an excellent discussion of ancient near eastern concepts of causation.

117

and final. His paradigm was that of human agency (e.g., the relationship of the sculptor or builder to his material) and of biological reproduction and development. A. E. Taylor (1955, p. 51) explicates Aristotle's four causes in the case of an oak tree:

> There must have been (1) a germ from which the oak has grown, and this germ must have had the latent tendencies toward development which are characteristic of oaks [material cause] . . . (2) This germ must . . . have had a tendency to grow in the way characteristic of oaks and to develop the structure of an oak [formal cause] . . . (3) Also the germ of the oak . . . grew on a parent oak [efficient cause] (4) And there must be a final stage [the adult oak] to which the whole process is relative [final cause].

Science in the Middle Ages generally limited itself to explanations in terms of Aristotle's efficient and final causes. Sixteenth and seventeenth century physical science ceased to concern itself with final causes and became preoccupied with efficient causes and causal laws. By the nineteenth century life science, as well, had largely abandoned the search for final causes, although teleological causation has reemerged in certain areas of twentieth century biology and although it has never been entirely absent from psychology.

In any event, since Aristotle, to explain why has generally been considered to state the cause or causes of the phenomenon under consideration. The philosopher Richard Taylor (1967, p. 63) defines cause, most generally, as "that set of conditions, among all the conditions that occurred, each of which is necessary and the totality of which was sufficient for the occurrence of the event in question."

The cause-effect relationship seems so embedded in reality, and in logical and everyday discourse, that it is surprising to discover it has been controversial for centuries. Ancient skeptics, such as Carneades, contended that we can never form more than probable cognitions about external events and their connections. Islamic philosophers such as Al-Ghazali and medieval Christians such as Autrecourt denied to finite bodies the power of effecting changes in one another, tracing all causality directly to God. Malebranche and the seventeenth century occasionalists argued that observation reveals only succession, not causation.

In a similar vein, Hume, the first formidable modern critic of causality, argued that we apprehend regularities in the succession of events, from which we develop "felt expectations" which we then project onto the objects under consideration. In other words, a mental connection is taken for one in reality. "One event follows another, but we can never observe any tie between them. They seem *conjoined,* but never *connected*" (Hume, 1777a, p. 98). Hume thus maintains that we possess no way of divining the precise nature of that succession of events or activities that we refer to as the cause-effect relationship. Causation thus becomes a heuristic device, "cause" being defined purely operationally as "an object precedent to and contiguous with some other object and such that objects like the former stand in similar relations of precedence and contiguity to objects like the latter" or, even more skeptically, as "an object precedent and contiguous to another, and so united with it in the imagination, that the idea of one determines the mind to form the idea of the other, and the impression of the one to form a more lively idea of the other" (Hume 1777b, p. 215). Hume's argument has received its strongest criticism on the grounds that it fails to distinguish between meaningful and coincidental correlations and that it does not account for apparent cause-effect relationships where the objects and events are not contiguous. Moreover, Searle (1983, p. 123) argues, it does not appreciate the common sense fact that "we directly experience this [cause and effect] relationship in many cases where we make something happen or something else makes something happen to us" and that, by extrapolating from our experience as causal agents, we come to relatively direct apprehension of certain cause-effect relationships in the environment.

For Kant, causality is a structural principle of the human mind. It receives its warrant from the apparent fact that we can construe the linkages between events, as we apprehend them through our senses, in no other way. Maine de Biran, Whitehead, and others contend that our only instance of direct insight into the nature of causal efficacy is when we experience ourselves as the causal agent of some change in our surroundings.

Comte, the founder of positivism, eschewed causal language and advocated a search for the laws connecting singular phenomena with superordinate regularities and general facts. Many positivists continue to hold that an important gauge of the level of sophistication of any science is the degree to which its explanations dispense with a concept of cause.

Bertrand Russell (1929) viewed causality as a metaphysical construct "inextricably bound up with misleading associations" and advocated its "complete extrusion from the philosophical vocabulary." Wittgenstein called causation "superstitious," and many subatomic physicists have embraced indeterminacy. The physical scientist and philosopher Reiner (1932, pp. 709–710) charges that causation is an anthropomorphic concept that, with the advent of relativity theory, "ceases to exist in physics."[3] General systems theory arose largely from a recognition of the inadequacy of unilinear, Newtonian cause and effect schemes to explain the complicated and interactive phenomena of the universe. Like Reiner, Morris Cohen (1931, p. 224) derides the concept of causation as "anthropomorphic" and asserts that "technical

---

[3]Rado (1932, pp. 683–700) concurs that causality is anthropomorphic and animistic—i.e., that it is a projection onto the physical world of the concept of human will—and that, as such, its usage in the natural sciences is anachronistic and fallacious. Nevertheless, he draws the fascinating conclusion that human behavior may be the only arena in which causal principles do apply!: "I should not be surprised were psychoanalysis to succeed in attaining a complete understanding of our mental life with its deterministic manner of viewing things. Determinism has, to be sure, proved to be a truly anthropomorphic postulate. However, our mental life is an exquisitely anthropomorphic object of research; it is *anthropos* himself" (p. 700).

and mathematical language . . . is surely, if slowly, replacing expressions of causal relations with mathematical functions or equations." Gardiner (1961), Hart and Honoré (1959), and Collingwood (1940) point out that what is denominated the "cause" or "causes" of a given phenomenon is often determined by the subjective and pragmatic considerations of the investigator.

While most philosophers and scientists continue to cleave to some concept of causation (Hume [1777b] himself terming it the "cement of the universe"), there is general agreement that there is no means of conclusively validating it or discerning its nature. For example, Ernest Nagel (1969, p. 349), a thoroughgoing determinist and antiHeisenbergian, confesses that "I do not believe that determinism is a demonstrable thesis, and I think that if it is construed as a statement about a categorical feature of everything whatsoever it may even be false." For Arthur Pap (1962, p. 311) the idea of universal determinism "is not analytic, nor is it an inductive generalization that could be refuted by contrary instances. It is best described as a *guiding principle* [Pap's italics]." Richard Taylor (1967, p. 57) concurs that "there is no logical, scientific, or empirical way to prove either the universality or the non-universality of causation." Von Wright (1972, p. 136) asserts that "only for *fragments* of the world *can* determinism ever become established. It is part of the logic of things here that the validity of the deterministic thesis for the *whole* world must remain an *open* question [Von Wright's italics]." Popper (1965, p. 61) retains causality as a methodological rule, while excluding the ontological principle of causation, which he regards as metaphysical, from the realm of logico-empirical investigation. Mario Bunge (1979, p. 352) concludes that "nothing warrants the presumption that we shall ever attain more than a *hypothetical* (but improvable) knowledge of causes, effects, and their links (whether causal or not)." Indeed, he (ibid) admonishes,

> Reality is much too rich to be compressible once and for all into a framework of (causal) categories elaborated during an early stage of rational knowledge, which consequently cannot ac-

count for the whole variety of types of determination, the number of which is being increased by scientific research and by
philosophical reflections upon it.

There is by no means unanimity, among philosophers and
scientists, on the nature of the cause-effect relationship.
Bunge enumerates a number of different types of causal and
noncausal explanations. A number of questions remain unanswered. Does causality have ontological, or merely explanatory, status? Exactly how is it that one state of affairs can be
said to effect another? In what sense do causes necessitate
their effects—or do they? Where is the locus of cause in the
cause-effect relationship; does it reside in one object or event
or the other, or in the interface between them? At what point
in the temporal succession of events does one designate the
cause, and where the effect? Must causes always lie prior to
the effects; are there not cases where the temporal relationship seems one of simultaneity rather than succession or
where the cause appears to accompany the effect throughout
the duration of the latter? Does determinism always imply
predictability; does it imply inevitability? Must we posit one
uniform concept of causation for all sciences; are, for example,
physicists' concepts of causality identical to biologists'? Are
there teleological facets to causality? Must causal explanations, to be valid, include reference to laws? Are laws causal
propositions? The list is endless.

In short, the concept of causation is not simple and self-
evident and those who treat it as such give us cause to doubt
their familiarity with the problems.

CAUSATION IN HISTORY

From the concept in science and general philosophy, let us
turn to it in history and the philosophy of history. Having
previously demonstrated similarities in the methodology and
epistemology of these disciplines and that of psychoanalysis, I
believe that a consideration of causation in history is relevant

to the matter at hand—particularly in the light of Schafer's criticism that psychoanalysis is involved in historical, not causal, explanation, an argument that presupposes an antithesis between the two. Consequently, I recapitulate the various historical positions before proceeding to a discussion of psychic causality itself.

Leopold von Ranke (1973, p. 40) enunciated the task of history as "penetration of the causal nexus." Langlois and Seignebos, in their 1898 classic on historical method, assert that "the notion of cause . . . is indispensable for the purpose of formulating events and constructing periods." Edward Carr (1961, p. 113), in his popular book, defines history as "a study of causes." Though he acknowledges that there must be some differences between mechanical, biological, psychological, and historical causation, as a working historian he does not see much importance in pursuing them. (Is not this the attitude of many clinicians as well?) For Carr (pp. 121–122), historical determinism is "the belief that everything that happens has a cause or causes, and could not have happened differently unless something in the cause or causes had also been different"; at the same time he (p. 142) approvingly quotes Huizinga that "Historical thinking is always teleological." Carr (p. 135) views causal explanations as products of the interaction between theory and data: "The causes determine [the historian's] interpretation of the historical process, and his interpretation determines his selection and marshalling of the causes."

In his primer on methodology, the historian Gottschalk (1950), like Carr, accepts the viability of causal explanations in history. Distinguishing between the "immediate cause or occasion" and the "remote or underlying causes" of historical events, he places primacy with the latter: " the immediate cause is not really a cause; it is merely the point in a chain of events, trends, influences, and forces at which the effect becomes visible" (p. 210). Clearly this is similar to the psychoanalyst's distinction between the precipitating, and predisposing or historical, causes of a symptomatic behavior. Even more than Carr, Gottschalk (p. 211) emphasizes the influence of the scholar's theoretical presuppositions on his causal analyses: "the causal explanations of events rest upon philosophies of history; and of philosophies of history there is no end." The Committee on Historiography of the Social Science Research Council plainly endorsed the concept of causation in history: "The concept of causality has entered into narrative to such an extent that the writing of history might become mere cataloguing or chronology without it" (McMurtrie et al., 1946, p. 137).

Ernest Nagel (1963, p. 85) defines the historian's task as the explication of "various features of particular happenings by exhibiting these factors as causally related to other particular occurrences." Like Hempel, he believes that, in performing this task, the historian invokes covering laws. While placing less emphasis on covering laws, Mandelbaum (1938, p. 265, 1969, p. 134) concurs that "causal analysis" is the historian's task.

Many historians adopt a usage of causality that is strikingly similar to the psychoanalyst's. Indeed, it can be contended that psychic causality is among the earliest of all concepts of causation in history (recall Thucydides' emphasis on character and motive as the mainsprings of history) and that, with the possible exception of theological determinism, it has always been the most prevalent. Ranke (1973, p. 17) himself maintained that the "psychological forces of multiple, intermeshing human abilities, emotions, inclinations, and passions . . . concern the historian as the most direct mainsprings of action and the most immediate causes of the events resulting from action." Marc Bloch (1953, p. 194), in his classic, *The Historian's Craft*, asserts that "Historical facts are, in essence, psychological facts. Normally, therefore, they find their antecedents in other psychological facts." Collingwood (1946, p. 214), following his teacher Croce, looks for the *idea* behind the action. It is on this ground that he distinguishes between causation in history and in natural science: "When a scientist asks 'why did that piece of litmus paper turn pink?' he means 'on what kind of occasions do pieces of litmus paper turn pink?' When a historian asks 'why did Brutus stab

Caesar?' he means 'what did Brutus think that made him decide to stab Caesar?'" Collingwood makes it plain that it is the actor's thought that is the causal principle. Collingwood's concept of motivation is, however, all too rational, conscious, and affectless.

The philosopher of history Walsh (1969, p. 66) and the historian Hughes (1964, p. 42) explicitly acknowledge the likeness between the causality of history and that of psychoanalysis. The former says: "And it can be contended with fair plausibility that the historian, in studying impulsive acts and seeking to uncover the thoughts behind them, has a task which compares at some point with that of the psychoanalyst, whose success in revealing carefully worked out plans behind apparently irrational actions is surely relevant to the subject we are considering." Because of the peculiar nature of the subject matter of historians and psychoanalysts Walsh (p. 68) believes, like Meyerhoff (1959, p. 21), that their concept of causation includes teleological facets: "The series of actions in question forms a whole of which it is true to say not only that the later members are determined by the earlier, but also that determination is reciprocal, the earlier members themselves being affected by the fact that the later ones were envisaged." This is of course not to assert that the reciprocity is temporal, or that the effect in any way precedes the cause! It is simply to say that the effect was envisioned in the cause. In a moment we shall see that Freud's concept of causation included a teleological dimension. Walsh (p. 67) denominated the process by which the historian delineates causes as "colligation," and it sounds virtually identical to what the analyst does: "the procedure of explaining an event by tracing its intrinsic relations to other events and locating it in its historical context."

Dray and Oakeshott espouse explanatory principles that are, as we shall see, in many respects hyperrational anticipations of those of Schafer. For the former (1969, p. 109), what the historian seeks is "information about what the agent believed to be the facts of his situation, including the likely results of taking various courses of action open to him, and what he wanted to accomplish. . . . Understanding is achieved when the historian can see the reasonableness of a man's doing what the agent did, given the beliefs and motives referred to. . . ."

Oakeshott (1933, p. 140) opposes cause and effect explanations in history on the grounds that they create an "arbitrary arrest or disjunction in the flow of events . . . [and an] arbitrary distinction in the character of events." To it he opposes his own concept of the "unity of history." For him (ibid, p. 142), historical explanation (like psychoanalytic explanation for Schafer) is not causal analysis, but rather redescription. The historian's task is to give "a complete account of change" in which it is appreciated that all events are contributory: "*'pour savoir les choses il faut savoir le detail'* . . . [history is] the narration of the course of events which, in so far as it is without serious interruptions, explains itself."

Oakeshott then congratulates himself that he has obviated the need to invoke hypothetical causes. But is not this in many ways a regression to a naive Rankian notion of the facts, unhindered by theory, assembling and explaining themselves? Is it not similar to the existentialist conceit that the patient's phenomenology will simply explain itself, without the intervention of the investigator's organizing principles? Are not Oakeshott's descriptions conditioned by presuppositions and theoretical constructs as much as explicitly causal propositions? What historian (or psychoanalyst) is ever in the position to give a "complete account of change?" Is not one's very selection of which aspects of a course of events to focus on and describe determined by an implicit or explicit assumption about the causal connections among them? Does not Oakeshott (pp. 136–137) himself say, "No course of historical events exists until it has been constructed by historical thought, and it cannot be constructed without some presuppositions about the character of the relation between events."?

Beard (1936) and Marrou (1966) are other historians chary of causal explanations. The historian Zinn (1964, p. 147) derides causation as "one of those metaphysical conundrums created by our own disposition to set verbal obstacles between ourselves and reality"—a proposition which is itself, I believe, a causal one.

By contrast, the historians Elton (1970, p. 101) and Fischer (1970, p. 165) view historical explanations as causal and remark on the euphemisms for cause in ostensibly noncausal formulations—"factors," "influences," "roots," "foundations," "undercurrents," "bases," "elements," and so on. Fischer (ibid, p. 166) asserts "I have never read an extended historical intrepretation which does not include causal statements, or cryptocausal statements, in at least a peripheral way." The philosopher of history Scriven (1966, p. 241) concurs that "In merely describing the course of a war or a reign the historian is constantly choosing language which implicitly identifies some phenomenon or aspect of a phenomenon as a cause and some other as an effect." In an analysis of a single page of an *Encyclopedia Brittanica* article on English history he counted thirty causal claims, although the word "cause" was used but twice! The historians Barzun and Graff (1970) and the philosophers of history Stover (1967), Frankel (1962), and Murphy (1973) concur that historical explanations are causal.

For Demos, Nagel, and Berlin the concept of causation hinges on the question of inevitability. Demos (1969, p. 280) maintains that "motives, aims, and decisions" are the "sources of human actions." He belongs to that school, however, that wants to draw a sharp distinction between "causes" and "reasons" (a topic we return to in Chapter 4). For Demos, reasons incline, but do not necessitate: "Brutus assassinated Caesar because he feared that Caesar might make himself a tyrant. Here we have an action issuing from a decision, in turn issuing from a reason. To give a reason is to explain why he did it without implying he had to do it." Of course, such a proposition presupposes that Brutus' explicit reason was his only motive and—what is unlikely—that unconscious, historical determinants did not participate.[4]

---

[4]Similarly, Hart and Honore' (1959) and Gardiner (1961) distinguish between "causes" and "reasons." The former (pp. 48–49) differentiate between "interpersonal transactions" in which one

Isaiah Berlin's equation of determinism and inevitability was the ground on which he rejected the former. From this equation he (1954, p. 26) concluded that determinism entails the elimination of personal responsibility: "If I extend this category without limit, then whatever is, is necessary and inevitable. . . . [Consequently] To blame and praise, consider possible alternative courses of action, damn or congratulate historical figures for acting as they do or did, becomes an absurd activity. Admiration or contempt for this or that individual may indeed continue but it becomes akin to aesthetic judgement."

Nagel, in contrast to Berlin, does not believe that the doctrine of historical determinism is wedded to any notion of inevitability. That there are "ascertainable limits to human power" does not, he (1969, p. 320) asserts, negate the fact of individual choice and effort. For Nagel deterministic propositions in history always proceed backward, that is, they attempt only to account for that which has already transpired with reference to its history; they entail no retroactive predictions of inevitability: "[historical determinism is the proposition that] if a deterministic system is in a definite state at a given time, the occurrence of that state at that time is determined—in the sense that the necessary and sufficient condition for the occurrence of that state at that time is that the system was in a certain state at a previous time" (ibid, p. 323). Bunge (1979, p. 103) concurs that *causality does not entail inevitability* [Bunge's italics]."

I agree with Nagel and Bunge. Historical determinism and psychic causality assert only that all behaviors are caused by the actor, with his conscious and unconscious history, decisions, fears, and interpretations. The inevitability question is forever unanswerable. What is important is that an action or

---

party can be said to threaten or coerce another into action ("causes") and those in which one party can be said only to advise, tempt, or entreat behavior in another ("reasons"). Other authors, such as Sherwood (1969), deny the validity of such a demarcation.

event *has occurred* and must be explained *in retrospect.* Any thesis for or against inevitability lies in the *post hoc explanation,* not in the unrecapturable events themselves (see the free will-determinism and inevitability discussions in the next chapter).

Nor is psychic and historical determinism conjoined to predictability. It does not imply, whether in principle or practice, that human behavior is predictable in more than a highly approximate and probabilistic manner. It merely says that "whatever results is determined by the prior history and antecedent personality structure of the agent." While accurate *retro*diction is often possible, absolute *pre*diction is impossible for at least two reasons: (1) we are never aware of all the relevant antecedent conditions—either within the person or in his environment; and (2) because the human capacity for creative synthesis (of the components of his psychological structure and function), while itself determined, can allow for novel and surprising responses. One can, like Lowes (1927) for example, deterministically explain Coleridge's writing of *Kubla Khan* with reference to Coleridge's prior reading and experience; but could one have predicted, from a knowledge of the poet a moment before the creative act, the precise manner in which he would select, fuse, and transform the elements at his disposal? As Barrett (1961, p. 53) says, "the unconscious, when it is truly creative, is far more unpredictable than the conscious mind."

The notion of "chance" or "accident" in history neither negates, nor is negated by, the concept of determinism. "Chance" events such as the sudden eruption of a hero upon the scene, a plague which decimates a defending army, a drought, a leader's infatuation with a beautiful woman, and the death of a king from a pet monkey's bite may indeed play a role in turning the course of history. But such "accidents" do not escape the causal nexus. They were the effects of prior, albeit perhaps unforeseen and unforeseeable, causes, just as they enter history by becoming causes themselves. As Carr (1961, p. 129) says, by "accidents" in history we mean "a sequence of cause and effect interrupting—and, so to speak, clashing with—the sequence which the historian is primarily concerned to investigate"; he (ibid) quotes approvingly Bury's definition of accidents as the "collision of two independent causal chains." In line with this, Carr correctly points out that chance or accident usually exerts its effect as a necessary, but not sufficient, cause. In short, if for the want of a nail the battle was lost and the nation destroyed, the question becomes, 'what were the antecedent conditions such that the battle was fought, crucial materiel was missing, and that the state collapsed from but a single event?' Similar points apply to the accidents that precipitate the disorders that the psychiatrist treats.

From a consideration of inevitability, predictability, and chance let me turn to a special feature of deterministic explanations in history—their elliptical character; as we see in the next section, this applies to causal propositions in psychoanalysis as well. For example, what does it mean to say that a change in the mode of production "causes" a change in political structure and ideology? Does not this seemingly simple, unilinear cause and effect statement subsume an infinite number of interlocking determinants (people, ideas, technology, physical environment, economics, and so forth) feeding back upon one another in a bewildering manner? It should not be forgotten that it is people who determine the changes in mode of production, to which they then respond by recognizing the inadequacy of former political structures and ideologies to the new situations with which they have confronted themselves.

Unilinear cause and effect chains, with sharp delineations between causal agents and their effects, do not do justice to social or psychological historical phenomena. Intellectual historians, as they investigate the role of educational, empirical, psychological, sociocultural, and creative factors in their figures and movements, appreciate this as well as anyone.

There is no better example of this subtle interaction of ideas and influences than in Freud's discovery and formulation of the Oedipus complex. This was previously thought to have been largely the fruit of his self-analysis, but it is now appreciated that it had more complex origins. Freud had certainly read the Oedipus story in his youth. Contemporary plays and novels, the sexological literature, and Fiess's ideas had sensitized him to the role of infantile sexuality and the possibility of incestuous longings. Then Breuer's work, the writings of Nietzsche and others, and his own clinical work led him to the conviction that important constellations of ideas and affects can remain unconscious. His own Oedipus complex, particularly in the years immediately preceding and following his father's death, was clamoring for attention. Patients were recounting incestuous stories to him which Freud first treated as the product of real seductions; as John Gach (personal communication) suggests, these patients' demands very likely stimulated Freud's own unconscious wishes that they, as mother imagoes, seduce—or be seduced by—him. In the midst of this, Freud became aware of his own oedipal strivings, which further sensitized him to such longings in his patients, and contributed to his abandonment of the seduction hypothesis. In generalizing from data uncovered in himself and a few patients to the entire human race, Freud was invoking the principle of psychic unity, with which he was thoroughly familiar from his reading of the cultural evolutionists. In then returning to the Oedipus legend to "confirm" (Freud's own word) the universality, across time and space, of the complex he had discovered in Vienna, Freud was borrowing another principle from nineteenth-century anthropologists—the comparative method. This complicated interaction of ideas can be illustrated in many other areas of Freud's thinking as well, particularly in his sociocultural work (see Wallace, 1983c). This is illustrated in the next section with reference to the history of Freud's concept of psychic causation itself.

From this synopsis it is apparent that most historians work with a notion of causation, that it includes teleological elements, and that it is strikingly similar to the psychoanalyst's concept of causation. Others, however, adopt a position similar to Schafer's and argue for the extrusion of causation from historical explanations.[5]

PREHISTORY OF PSYCHIC CAUSALITY AND HISTORICAL DETERMINISM

Medicine has long possessed a primitive concept of psychic causality—of the influence of ideas and emotions on health and disease. Consider, for example, the following case history from Galen—which must count as one of the earliest explicitly psychodynamic formulations:

> She was suffering from one of two things: either from a melancholy dependent on black bile, or else trouble about something she was unwilling to confess . . . . After I had diagnosed that there was no bodily trouble and that the woman was suffering from some mental uneasiness . . . somebody came from the theatre and said that he had seen Pylades dancing; then both her expression and the color of her face changed . . . and I noticed that the pulse had suddenly become extremely irregular . . . Thus I found out that the woman was in love with Pylades, and by careful watch on the succeeding days my discovery was confirmed [by testing her pulse on occasions when Pylades was mentioned as compared with occasions on which

---

[5]Historians differ on the degree to which they consider the individual and his psychology as a causal factor in the historical process. Contrasting viewpoints are those of Hook (1950), who places great stress on the "hero in history," and Engels (in Hook, 1950, p. 79) who emphasizes the broader social and economic currents and asserts "That Napolean—this particular Corsician—should have been the military dictator made necessary by the exhausting wars of the French Republic—that was a matter of chance. But in default of a Napolean another would have filled his place, that is established by the fact that whenever a man was necessary, he has always been found: Caesar, Augustus, Cromwell." I believe that the best historians are those who integrate both points of view.

other topics or other dancers were being discussed] (Galen, in Siegel, 1973, p. 208).

Let us shift now to the nature of causation in psychoanalysis. What is the history and prehistory of the idea and how did Freud understand the concept?

Any discussion of the determinants of Freud's idea of psychic causality must take account of the interactional nature of determinism which I have just discussed. Freud's idea was neither a priori nor a posteriori; there was a complicated interaction between prior reading, clinical experience, and creative synthesis.

To begin with, Freud cut his intellectual teeth on the mechanistic determinism of his teacher and mentor, Ernst Brucke. He adopted wholeheartedly the self-confident oath of Brücke and DuBois-Reymond.

> No other forces than the common physical-chemical ones are active within the organism. In those cases which cannot at this time be explained by these forces one has either to find the specific way or form of their action by means of the physical-mathematical method or to assume new forces equal in dignity to the chemical-physical forces inherent in matter, reducible to the force of attraction and repulsion (in Jones, 1953, pp. 40–41).

But Freud was also a student of philosophy, history, and anthropology. Each of these fields furnished Freud with a concept of causality in the psychical sphere.

Freud took three semesters of philosophy under Franz Brentano at the University of Vienna, and even considered following his M.D. with a Ph.D. in that subject. Brentano may well have influenced, as Gach (personal communication) suggests, Freud's inclusion of intentionality in his concept of cause. The major works of Hobbes, Hume, Locke, Mill, and Kant sat on his shelves (Trosman & Simmons, 1973). Locke's *Essay on Human Understanding,* Hume's *Essays Literary, Moral, and Political,* and Kant's *Critique of Pure Reason* are signed and dated by Freud respectively 1883, 1879, and 1882. While still a student, Freud translated a volume of Mill's essays. He would have been exposed to Herbart and Schopenhauer in Brentano's lectures; the former was cited in *The Interpretation of Dreams* and Freud owned works by Schopenhauer. Each of these philosophers, as we shall see, furnished Freud with various concepts of psychic determinism.

Thomas Hobbes was one of the most staunch and consistent determinists who ever lived.

> When a man thinketh on any thing whatsoever, his next thought after is not altogether so casual as it seems to be. . . . All fancies are motions within us, relics of those made in the sense: and those motions that immediately succeeded one another in the sense, continue also together after sense: insomuch as the former coming again to take place, and be predominant, the latter followeth, by coherence of the matter moved, in such manner, as water upon a plane table is drawn which way one part of it is guided by the finger (Hobbes, 1651, p. 28).

Like Freud, Hobbes (p. 29) made a point of demonstrating the relevance of this principle to even the "wild ranging of the mind." By way of example he offered the following explanation of a seemingly nonsensical question—"What was the value of a Roman penny?"—posed by an individual during a discussion of the English civil war.

> For the thought of the war, introduced the thought of the delivering up the king to his enemies; the thought of that, brought in the thought of the delivering up of Christ; and that again the thought of the thirty pence, which was the price of that treason; and thence followed that malicious question, and all in a moment of time; for thought is quick (ibid).

Hobbes also spoke of trains of thought directed by desire. His example of this, mentation governed by the desire to recover a lost object, is an excellent instance of free association. "Sometimes a man seeks what he hath lost; and from that place, and time, wherein he misses it, his mind runs back, from place to place, and time to time, to find where and when he had it" (ibid).

Just as Freud conceived of symptoms, parapraxes, and other observable behaviors as the effects of antecedent mental acts, so Hobbes (p. 47) asserted that *"imagination is the first internal beginning of all voluntary motion* [my italics]." These acts of imagination were termed "endeavors" and subdivided into "appetites or desires" and "aversions." "Will" is defined as "In deliberation, the last appetite, or aversion, immediately adhering to the action, or the omission thereof" (ibid, p. 54).

On the free will-determinism issue he was a convinced determinist.

> Liberty and necessity are consistent, as in the water, that hath not only liberty, but a necessity of descending by the channel; so likewise in the actions which men voluntarily do: which, because they proceed from their will, proceed from liberty; and yet, because every act of man's will, and every desire, and inclination proceedeth from some cause, and that from another cause, in a continual chain, whose first link is in the hand of God, the first of all causes, proceed from necessity (ibid, p. 160).

Locke (1690) emphasized the determining role of the passions in human behavior. He propounded a notion of their driving power not unlike that of Freud's pleasure-unpleasure and constancy principles: "The motive for continuing in the same state or action, is only the present *satisfaction* in it; the motive to change is always some *uneasiness:* nothing setting us upon the change of state, or upon any new action, but some uneasiness . . . which for shortness' sake we call determining of the will" (p. 49). This "present uneasiness" is equated with desire.

Hume (1777a) provided Freud with both a causal explanation of the association of ideas and of the determination of the will. "Even in our wildest and most wandering reveries, nay,

even in our very dreams," says Hume (p. 57), there is a meaningful connection between the various ideas.

> Were the loosest and freest conversation to be transcribed,
> there would immediately be observed something which con-
> nected it in all its transitions. Or where this is wanting, the
> person who broke the thread of discourse might still inform
> you that there had secretly resolved in his mind a succession of
> thought which had gradually led him from the subject of con-
> versation (ibid).

Hume (p. 108) saw the conjunction between motives and
voluntary actions as being "as regular and uniform as that
between the cause and effect in any part of nature." Thus the
concept of universal causation in human behavior is inferred
in the same way as that in the physical world—from observed
regularities in the temporal sequence and correlation of
events.

Hume's concept of psychic determinism seems wedded to a
notion of predictability in principle: "however we may imagine we feel a liberty within ourselves, a spectator can commonly infer our actions from our motives and character; and
even where he cannot, he concludes in general that he might,
were he perfectly acquainted with every circumstance of our
situation and temper, and the most secret springs of our compulsion and disposition."

Although Freud neither cited nor owned (so far as we know)
works of Hume's Scottish contemporary, Thomas Reid, it is
probable that Freud had direct or indirect acquaintance with
him—especially given his infatuation with British thinkers
and his statement to Martha Bernays (in Jones, 1955, p. 179)
that all his real teachers were either "English or Scotch." In
any event, Reid deserves mention as a forerunner of the psychoanalytic concept of psychic causality.

Reid (1813–1815, p. 63) maintained that "in all determina-
tions of the mind that are of any importance, there must be
something in the preceding state of mind" and that "every
action, or change of action, in an intelligent being, is propor-

tional to the force of motives impressed, and in the direction of that force" (p. 284). Even so, Reid's principle was not universal; it allowed for exceptions in the case of "trifling" behaviors, which were conceived to be without motive; furthermore, he explicitly rejected the possibility of unconscious motives (p. 285).

Immanuel Kant postulated a realm of freedom of the will in the noumenal sphere—largely on moral grounds. Nevertheless, in the empirical realm of phenomena, where man lives out his day-to-day life and the psychiatrist works, he cleaved to determinism. Insofar as man is part of nature and the space-time continuum Kant held him to be determined by antecedent causes. Besides Hume, Reid, and Kant, a host of other enlightenment philosophers—such as Voltaire and Holbach—were preaching behavioral determinism and may have influenced Freud as well.[6]

Herbart, the philosopher-psychiatrist whose *Psychologie als Wissenschaft* (1824) and other pedagogical and psychological works strongly influenced nineteenth century German thought, is the most remarkable anticipator of dynamic psychiatry. The parallels between his ideas and Freud's, as Maria Dorer pointed out in 1932, are too numerous to be coincidental—the unconscious, conflict, mental forces, constancy principle, repression, and the economic point of view. Herbart's causal principle was that of mental representations, each possessing a certain charge and rising and falling from consciousness in accordance with its intensity.

---

[6]"Our volitions and our desires are never in our power. You think yourself free, because you do what you will; but are you free to will or not to will; to desire or not to desire?" (Holbach, in Edwards, 1961, p. 121). And Voltaire (ibid, p. 120), evidencing that belief in determinism does not in itself necessitate personal humility, tells us: "Everything happens through immutable laws . . . everything is necessary. . . . I necessarily have the passion for writing this, and you have the passion for condemning me; both of us are equally fools, equally the toy of destiny. Your nature is to do harm, mine is to love truth, and to make it public in spite of you."

Schopenhauer is another philosopher whose ideas furnish, as Freud himself acknowledged, striking parallels to Freud's. Schopenhauer espoused a determinism in the psychological sphere identical to that in the physical, and the following passage could well serve as that philosopher's credo (1960):

> Every man, being what he is and placed in the circumstances which for the moment obtain, but which on their part also arise by strict necessity, can absolutely never do anything else than just what at that moment he does do. Accordingly, the whole course of a man's life, in all its incidents great and small, is as necessarily predetermined as the course of a clock.

Essentially, his line of reasoning was: character determines our motives and motives our behavior; since we do not freely choose our characters, our behaviors are wholly determined. In line with this, he preached a fatalistic resignation to the facts of one's character since they were, in his view, unalterable—in stark contrast to Freud, who took psychic determinism as grounds for therapeutic optimism! Like Hume (and Freud, as we shall see), he subscribed to the notion that human behavior is predictable in principle, but not in practice—because we never possess knowledge of all the relevant antecedent conditions.

John Stuart Mill subscribed to a causal view of human nature and the following is characteristic of passages which would have influenced Freud in his view of psychic causality and the psychic unity of mankind:

> Human beings do not all feel and act alike in the same circumstances; but it is possible to determine what makes one person, in a given position, feel or act in one way, another in another; how any given mode of feeling or conduct, compatible with the general laws (physical and mental) of human nature, has been, or may be, formed. In other words, mankind have not one universal character, but there exist universal laws of the Formation of Character (Mill, 1969, p. 14).

Mill (1874, 272–290) saw the will as wholly determined by our desires and aversions. He also had a concept of multiple causality that may well have influenced Freud's idea of overdetermination.

Two other Englishmen whose ideas must be counted among the a priori determinants of Freud's concept of psychic causality are the historian Henry Thomas Buckle, whom Freud (1873–1939, p. 379) tells us he read in adolescence, and the cultural evolutionist Edward Tylor, whom Freud respectfully cites in 1899 and 1913. In a passage reminiscent of Hume and Schopenhauer, Buckle (1862, p. 14) asserts:

> That when we perform an action we perform it in consequence of some motive or motives; that these motives are the result of some antecedents; and that, therefore, if we were acquainted with the whole of the antecedents, and with all the laws of their movements, we could with unerring certainty predict the whole of their immediate results.

Freud (1920b, p. 168) too would account for our inability to predict future behavior with reference to our inadequate access to knowledge of the determining factors and their strength relative to one another.

Tylor (1874, Vol. I, p. 2), who became a powerful influence on Freud's view of culture, maintained that "human thoughts, wills, and actions accord with laws as definite as those which govern the motion of waves, the combination of acids and bases, and the growth of plants and animals." Tylor's concept of psychic causality seems wedded, like Mill's, to an implicit notion of covering laws. Similarly, Herbert Spencer and other cultural evolutionists Freud read propounded doctrines of psychological and sociological determinism.

Turning now from psychical causality to the related principle of historical determinism, the strongest a priori factors appear to be Freud's exposure to Darwin and the cultural evolutionists. Darwin's influence on Freud is by now widely known and was frequently acknowledged by Freud himself. By the end of medical school Freud had acquired Darwin's major books; indeed, Freud (1925, p. 8) had counted Darwin's work as one of his reasons for choosing a medical career. In

The Expression of the Emotions Darwin applied the principle of atavism to the explanation of human behaviors, group and individual. Emotional expressions were conceptualized as ontogenetic and phylogenetic survivals—explained, in other words, by reference to the history of the individual and the race. Freud too would come to view neurosis as (ontogenetic *and* phylogenetic) atavism and he (Breuer & Freud, 1895, p. 181) explicitly cited Darwin in support of his own journey into the patient's past to discern the meaning of the apparently senseless current neurotic symptom.

In previous works (1980b, 1983c) I have documented the extraordinary impact of cultural evolutionism on Freud's psychological and anthropological thinking. As we have seen, Freud adopted their basic principles—psychic unity, the comparative method, the biogenetic law and Lamarckism, the equation of contemporary primitive with primeval man, the idea that cultures can be rated along an evolutionary scale, and the doctrine of survivals. Like Spencer (1898) and Morgan (1907), the evolutionists believed that cultures were determined by their antecedent conditions and that their development proceeded lawfully through fixed and immutable stages.

The doctrine of survivals was a clear parallel, in the cultural sphere, to Freud's historical, atavistic explanation of neurosis in the psychological. Tylor (1874, p. 16) defines survivals as "processes, customs, opinions, and so forth, which have been carried on by force of habit into a new state of society different from that in which they had their original home, and . . . [they] thus remain as proofs and exemplars of an older condition out of which a newer has evolved." In short, both Darwin and the cultural evolutionists looked to history to explain contemporary biological, psychological, and sociological phenomena.

The empirical determinants of Freud's theorems of psychic causality and historical determinism are well known to every psychoanalyst. They include: his conversations with Breuer about Anna O., his experiences with Charcot and the French hypnotists, the impotence of his somatic treatments of neurosis, and his early psychotherapeutic investigation and self-analysis.

I wish to make it clear that I am arguing neither for purely a priori nor purely empirical determinants of Freud's concepts. Rather, I see them as growing out of an inextricable interaction between the two. His early exposure to theorists of psychic causality and historical determinism left him with a certain mental set which then interacted with his clinical data. *A priori conviction in the causality, hence meaningfulness, of human behavior led him to look for order in behaviors his psychiatric contemporaries saw as the chaotic and senseless manifestations of brain lesions or "hereditary neuropathic taint"; to one receptive to the data, the themes, patterns, configurations, and regularities of sequence would become apparent enough.* In short, Freud's theoretical preconceptions did not impose themselves on the data. Rather, the psychoanalytic theories of psychical causality and historical determinism emerged from the *interaction* between a prepared mind and its data. Furthermore, there were important differences, as we shall see in a moment, between Freud's concept of causation and that of his predecessors. With the exception of Schopenhauer and Herbart, none of his precursors had a developed conception of unconscious motives. Furthermore, their causal concepts were too mechanistic to do justice to a purposeful organism. Freud's genius lay in synthesizing a therapeutically operational concept of unconscious and purposeful causation from his reading and experience.

CAUSATION IN FREUD

Let us shift now to the nature of causation in psychoanalysis. How did Freud understand it?

Freud had three concepts of the causation of human behavior that operated simultaneously, with varying degrees of intensity, throughout his career: biogenetic, instinctual, and purposeful. There is considerable overlap between the first two, since instincts were taken to be phylogenetic survivals from man's biological prehistory (Freud, 1915–1917, p. 354). Two other notions of causality—the "repetition compulsion" and "external associations"—never played more than a peripheral role in Freud's explanatory schemata. All five are discussed in turn.

Biogenetic Causality

Biogenetic causality manifested itself in passages such as Freud's formulation of the etiology of the Wolf Man's castration anxiety:

> At this point the boy had to fit into a phylogenetic pattern, and he did so, *although his personal experiences may not have agreed with it.* Although the threats or hints of castration which had come his way had emanated from women, this could not hold up the final result for long. In spite of everything it was his father from whom in the end he came to fear castration. In this respect *heredity triumphed over accidental experience;* in man's prehistory it was undoubtedly the father who practiced castration as a punishment and who later softened it down to circumcision (Freud, 1918, p. 85, my italics).

Freud (1905a, p. 241) asserted that the order in which the component instincts emerge is biogenetically determined. The repression of sexuality in the latency period was also posited to be biogenetically based (ibid, pp. 177–178). He (1930) even speculated that crucial characteristics of the superego are ontogenetic recapitulations of phylogeny. The biogenetic current runs strong in Freud's (1913) theory of culture—i.e., primitive behavior as phylogenetically archaic and the primal parricide hypothesis.

Nevertheless, despite the pervasiveness of the biogenetic strain in certain aspects of Freud's theorizing, in his clinical formulations he pays little attention to phylogenetic factors and, where he invokes them, usually brings forth ontogenetic explanations that do not require the phylogeny to sustain them. Freud (1918, p. 97) even chided Jung for putting phylogenetic factors ahead of ontogenetic ones.

Instinctual Determinism

Holt (1976) has written trenchantly on Freud's instinctual determinism which he, like myself, views as distinct from and, in practice, subordinate to his clinical concept of purposeful determinism. The *Project* is Freud's earliest expression of instinctual determinism. The central nervous system is conceptualized as "receiv[ing] stimuli from the somatic element itself—endogenous stimuli—which have equally to be discharged. These have their origin in the cells of the body and give rise to the major needs: hunger, respiration, sexuality" (1895a, p. 317). Coitus, for example, is caused by "an endogenous tension . . . noticed when it reaches a certain threshold. It is only above this threshold that it is turned to account psychically, that it enters into relation with certain groups of ideas, which thereupon set about producing the specific remedies." Clearly the deterministic concept in *The Project* is closely associated with the concept of tension and the "principle of inertia" (i.e., the tendency of neurons to divest themselves of excitation). It is discomfort associated with the sensation of increased tension that motivates the organism to a variety of discharge-oriented maneuvers. The organism's aim to maintain its state of internal excitation at a minimal level would become known as the "constancy" or "pleasure principle."

This model, and the one subsequently developed in *The Interpretation of Dreams*, draw heavily upon a stimulus-response, reflex arc model of causation: "All our psychical activity starts from stimuli (whether internal or external) and ends in innervations . . . Reflex processes remain the model of every psychical function" (Freud, 1900, pp. 537–538).

Three Essays on the Theory of Sexuality (1905a) and *Two Principles of Mental Functioning* (1911a) continue to propound instinctivist theories of motivation. The causal role of sexual tensions, resulting from "special chemical substances produced in the interstitial portions of the sex-glands," is emphasized (Freud, 1905a, p. 215). In the same vein, the neuroses are compared to the "phenomena of intoxication and abstinence that arise from the habitual use of toxic, pleasure-producing substances (alkaloids)" (ibid, p. 216).

In *Instincts and Their Vicissitudes* Freud (1915, p, 120) contrasted sharply the nature of the stimulus in the case of instincts with that in the case of objects and forces impinging upon the organism from the outside world:

> the nervous system is an apparatus which has the function of getting rid of the stimuli that reach it, or of reducing them to the lowest possible level . . . we then see how greatly the simple pattern of the physiological reflex is complicated by the introduction of instincts. External stimuli impose only the single task of withdrawing from them; this is accomplished by muscular movements, one of which eventually achieves that aim . . . Instinctual stimuli, which originate from within the organism, cannot be dealt with by this mechanism. Thus they make far higher demands on the nervous system and cause it to undertake involved and interconnected activities by which the external world is so changed as to afford satisfaction to the internal source of stimulation.

Instinct theory and the emphasis on constitutional factors remained strong in Freud's metapsychology. In *New Introductory Lectures on Psycho-Analysis* Freud (1933, pp. 153–154) was concerned to remind us that:

> [the neuroses are] in fact severe, constitutionally fixed illnesses . . . Our analytic experience that they can be extensively influenced, if the historical precipitating causes and accidental factors of the illness can be dealt with, has led us to neglect the constitutional factor in our therapeutic practice, and in any case we can do nothing about it; but in theory we ought always to bear it in mind.

Nevertheless, Freud never ignored, in even his most instinctivist and phylogenetic moments, the role of external reality. For example, in *Three Essays on the Theory of Sexuality* Freud (1905a, p. 190) tells us that the recrudescence of sexual activity at the close of the latency period is "determined by internal causes and external contingencies." "Though it was necessary [in the study of the perversions] to place in the foreground the importance of the variations in the original disposition, a cooperative and not an opposing relation was to be assumed as existing between them and the influences of actual life" (1905a, p. 231). And again, in an especially sophisticated elaboration upon the matter, appended to the text in 1915, we read (1905a, p. 239):

> It is not easy to estimate the relative efficacy of the constitutional and accidental factors [in the course of sexual development]. In theory one is always inclined to overestimate the former; therapeutic practice emphasizes the importance of the latter. It should, however, on no account be forgotten that the relation between the two is a cooperative and not a mutually exclusive one. The constitutional factor must await experiences before it can make itself felt; the accidental factor must have a constitutional basis in order to come into operation.

This line of thought culminates in *The Introductory Lectures* where Freud (1915–1917, p. 362) introduces the "aetiological equation." Adult neuroses are posited to result from the interaction between a disposition due to the infantile fixation of libido and the accidental traumatic experiences of adulthood. The infantile fixations themselves were determined by the interaction between "sexual constitution" and "infantile experience."

The dynamic culturalists would carry this much farther, arguing that there is no hard and fast line between biological and social dynamisms. Objecting to Freud's tendency to view the environment as important primarily insofar as it stimulated, gratified, or opposed the instinctual drives and their derivatives (which were considered the prepotent motor of human behavior), they argued that social factors are just as determinative of human behavior as are biological needs.

Bartlett (1939, p. 73) and Kardiner (1939, p. 133) exemplify this point of view. The former says, "It is not a question of the conflict between biological impulse and social blockage. The driving forces are quite as much social products as the social barriers which block them." As Kardiner put it, we are not confronted directly by biological forces within the individual, but with "the finished products of the interaction of biological forces and external realities . . . Man is not an animal whose *needs* and behaviors are all phylogenetically fixed . . . Variations in social structure will change some needs, or create new ones" (Kardiner's italics). Indeed, they are correct that, at the level of psychoanalytic discourse, it is impossible to neatly dissect the factors in human motivation and identify some as purely biological and others as purely social. Human biology interacts with the pressures and opportunities of its environment from the outset. Consequently, the individual's patterns of motivation are as much a function of prior socialization as of biology; the psychoanalyst confronts, I argue later in this chapter, affect laden motivating fantasies that are end products of the interaction between the two.

The Repetition Compulsion

Before turning to Freud's psychological concept of causation, let us touch briefly on the repetition compulsion. With a prehistory in Freud's thinking from at least 1905 (e.g., *Jokes*)— and probably much earlier (i.e., exposure to Nietzsche's idea of the "eternal recurrence of the same")–the concept was fleshed out in 1920. This superordinated regulatory principle was broached to explain certain unpleasurable repetitive phenomena—post traumatic dreams, the fate and transference neuroses, and various children's games—that Freud felt disobeyed the pleasure principle.

> The fulfillment of wishes is, as we know, brought about in an hallucinatory manner by dreams, and under the dominance of the pleasure principle this has become their function. But it is

not in the service of that principle that the dreams of patients suffering from traumatic neuroses lead them back with such regularity to the situation in which the traumas occurred. . . . They arise, rather, in obedience to the compulsion to repeat . . . (1920a, p. 32).

Freud also dealt extensively with the fate and transference neuroses, his second example: "In the case of a person in analysis, on the contrary, the compulsion to repeat the events of his childhood in the transference evidently disregards the pleasure principle in every way."

The fate neurosis is more or less the transference neurosis writ large. The last example, children's play (such as the repetitive reel and peek-a-boo games), was the one Freud was least sure of since it was an alloy of both "the compulsion to repeat and instinctual satisfaction which is immediately pleasurable" (1920a, p. 23). In fact, Freud (1905b) had clearly said that the repetitiveness of jokes and children's play is pleasurable in and of itself—because of the "economy in psychical expenditure."

We must admit that Freud, the intrepid observer, has correctly divined the repetitive nature of all these phenomena. However, on the firm foundation of observation he builds a shaky edifice indeed. Freud (1920, p. 24) himself concedes that "what follows is speculation, often far-fetched speculation, which the reader will consider or dismiss according to his individual predilection. It is further an attempt to follow out an idea consistently, out of curiosity to see where it will lead." From the building blocks of a repetition compulsion, "overriding the pleasure principle," Freud proceeds to fashion a new theory of instincts:

At this point we cannot escape a suspicion that we may have come upon the track of a universal attribute [the repetition compulsion] of instincts and perhaps of organic life in general which has not hitherto been clearly recognized or at least not explicitly stressed. *It seems, then, that an instinct is an urge inherent in organic life to restore an earlier state of things* . . . the expression of the inertia inherent in organic life (1920a, p. 36; Freud's italics).

Ignoring misgivings that pursuing this line of reasoning may "give an impression of mysticism or of sham profundity," Freud continues on the inexorable path to the death instinct.

It is possible to specify this final goal of all organic striving. It would be in contradiction to the conservative nature of the instincts if the goal of life were a state of things which had never yet been attained. On the contrary, it must be an old state of things, an initial state from which it is striving to return by the circuitous path along which its development leads. If we are to take it as a truth that knows no exception that everything dies for *internal* reasons—becomes inorganic once again—then we shall be compelled to say that *"the aim of all life is death"* (1920, pp. 37–38; Freud's italics).

Thanatos is the culmination of the emotionally determined chain of reasoning that produced the repetition compulsion (Wallace, 1983d). Schur (1969, p. 169) opines that "we cannot escape the conclusion that Freud had already arrived at his hypothesis of the death instinct and was using various aspects of unpleasurable repetitiveness to confirm it." In *Moses and Monotheism* Freud would raise the repetition compulsion to the world-historical plane. Much of Jewish and Christian history was explained as the symbolic repetition of the primal parricide and the attempt at absolution for this deed (this representing a point of convergence between the repetition compulsion and Freud's biogenetic-Lamarckian determinism).

What is so interesting about the reasoning that led to (or justified) the repetition compulsion and Thanatos is not only its many fallacies, but the fact that Freud did not see that explanations for unpleasurable repetitive phenomena were already at hand in psychoanalytic theory.

Schur has written extensively about the weaknesses of Freud's argument, one of the most conspicuous being Freud's failure to adequately distinguish between pleasure as an affect and pleasure as an economic concept. For example, merely because the patient experiences his transference neurosis as unpleasurable does not mean that its repetitive behaviors are in violation of the regulatory function of the pleasure principle. Freud (1920a, p. 11) himself knew that "most of the unpleasure that we experience is *perceptual* unpleasure." He even asserted that "*all* [italics added] neurotic unpleasure is of that kind—pleasure that cannot be felt as such . . . unpleasure for one system and simultaneously satisfaction for the other" (p. 14).

Nevertheless, Freud (1920a, p. 20) tried to make this line of thought seem insufficient by smuggling in the notion that many transference phenomena are based on experiences that could never, "even long ago, have brought satisfaction." But this position is vitiated by his statement that unpleasant transference experiences "are of course the activities of instincts intended to lead to satisfaction" (p. 21). That "no lesson has been learnt from the old experience of these activities having led instead only to unpleasure" does not justify the invocation of a repetition compulsion; it is unreasonable to expect unconscious strivings to learn anything. And in this same work Freud reiterated the idea that "unconscious mental processes are in themselves timeless. This means in the first place that they are not ordered temporally, that time does not change them in any way and that the idea of time cannot be applied to them" (p. 28).

Herein we are approaching what appears to be the correct explanation of the repetitive phenomena of the fate and transference neuroses. From the early days of psychoanalysis Freud (1900, p. 553) emphasized that unconscious wishes "share this character of indestructibility with all other mental acts which are truly unconsious. . . . These are paths which have been laid down once and for all, which never fall into disuse and which, whenever an unconscious excitation recathects them, are always ready to conduct the excitatory process to discharge." The concept of fixation further develops this line of thought: "early impressions of sexual life are char-

acterized by an increased pertinacity or susceptibility to fixation in persons who are later to become neurotics or perverts";
in neurotics they "tend in a compulsive manner toward repetition" (Freud, 1905a). In 1915(a) Freud used the phrase
"compulsion to repeat" to characterize this eternal pressure of
the repressed desire for expression. It is this *incessant striving*
(entirely compatible with the pleasure principle) that is the
major explanation for the recurrent phenomena of the fate
and the transference neuroses. On this point Schur (1969) and
Kubie (1939) agree.

Freud's characterization of these unpleasurable, repetitive
phenomena as "daemonic," only to be explained by the repetition compulsion, resulted, as Schur (1969) points out, from
fallacious reasoning: since unpleasure perennially results,
then there must be a force whose aim is to achieve this tragic
goal. In actuality the only goal is that of the repressed fantasy
for satiation. The affect of unpleasure results, not because this
is the intention, but because the striving for expression is
opposed by other forces so that the final result is not always
consonant with the tendency toward pleasure. Schur feels
that the other phenomena Freud considered—post traumatic
dreams and children's play—can also be explained by the
pleasure principle. In sum, the repetition compulsion, like
Freud's concept of Lamarckian and biogenetic determinism, is
a fallacious and superfluous attempt to explain what is adequately subsumed under the pleasure principle and the psychological concept of causation we are about to consider.[7]

---

[7] I have previously suggested (Wallace, 1983d) that the concept of
the repetition compulsion had strong noncognitive determinants—
foremost of which was Freud's discomfort with certain unpleasura-
bly repetitive phenomena in his own life: recurrent difficulties with
male friends with whom Freud had previously had close and dependent relationships (Breuer, Fliess, Jung, and others); *Todesangst*
and recurrent superstitions; and anniversary reactions. There I argued that these phenomena were largely determined by Freud's
father conflict.

Psychological Causality

Interestingly enough, Freud's *earliest* conception of causality is psychological, not biological. In this discussion I argue, like Holt (1976), that Freud's psychological concept of motivation—as purpose, wish, intention—was in fact his dominant one, and that Freud's difficulty acknowledging this was a function of his excessively mechanistic conception of science (recall Brücke's credo) and of his jealousy for the scientific status of psychoanalysis.

As early as 1892, in "A Case of Hypnotic Treatment," Freud had formulated a primitive conception of his later ideas. Here an hysteric's (Frau Emmy von N.) symptoms were conceptualized as caused by a "counter-will":

> (Firstly,) in accordance with the tendency to a *dissociation of consciousness* in hysteria, the distressing antithetic idea, which seems to be inhibited, is removed from association with the intention and continues to exist as a disconnected idea, often unconsciously to the patient himself. (Secondly,) it is supremely characteristic of hysteria that, when it comes to the carrying out of the intention, the inhibited antithetic idea can put itself into effect by innervation of the body just as easily as does a volitional idea in normal circumstances. The antithetic idea establishes itself, so to speak as a *"counter-will,"* while the patient is aware with astonishment of having a will which is resolute but powerless [all italics Freud's] (Freud, 1892–1893, p. 122).

Studies on Hysteria and the immediately subsequent paper, "The Aetiology of Hysteria," develop such ideas into a systematic theory of the psychologic causation of neurosis, a phenomenon considered by most of Freud's contemporaries to be the result of "hereditary neuropathic taint" or cerebral degeneration. Freud made a point of distinguishing the causal principle in hysteria from that in the purely somatic processes with which the physician is confronted. He differentiated, for

example, between the erythema occurring "whenever an affect arises" and that which emerges when the skin is stroked
or irritated. The former is "determined by *ideas* [my italics]"
and the latter by purely mechanical and physiological factors
(Breuer and Freud, 1895, p. 188). (Of course Freud was aware
that in hysterical erythema "an abnormal excitability of the
vasomotors" must also be present.) It was their "determin[a-
tion] by ideas" that allowed Freud (1896b, p. 193) to speak of
neurotic symptoms as meaningful, as "mnemic symbols." In
the *Project* itself Freud (1895a, p. 347) asserted that "hysterical patients are subject to a *compulsion* which is exercised by
excessively intense ideas [Freud's italics]."

Ideas, often associated with traumatic interpersonal events,
were repressed, whence they (and the "strangulated" affect
associated with them) manifested themselves as symptoms.
The repression itself was caused by the patient's *intention* to
"repudiate" the "incompatible idea":

> The splitting of consciousness in these cases of acquired hys-
> teria is accordingly a *deliberate* and *intentional* one. At least it
> is often introduced by an act of volition; for the actual outcome
> is something different from what the subject intended. What
> he wanted was to do away with an idea, as though it had never
> appeared, but all he succeeds in doing is to isolate it psychi-
> cally (Breuer and Freud, 1895, p. 123; my italics).

From an initially somewhat mechanical emphasis on the
causal role of the external environment, Freud would soon
shift his focus to the determinative role of intrapsychic factors. In short, he came increasingly to believe that it was not
so much the actual events per se that were traumatic as the
fantasies associated with them: "between the symptoms and
the childish impressions there were inserted the patient's
phantasies" (Freud, 1906, p. 274; my italics). Nevertheless,
Freud never lost sight of the current and historical interpersonal matrix of the patient's desiring and fearing. From an
early preoccupation with the symptom's current precipitating
causes, Freud would soon move to a concern with the pre-

disposing, historical ones. Already, in *Studies on Hysteria,* Freud had grasped the principle of overdetermination (pp. 173, 287–290)—that each symptom or behavior is caused by several (at times many) conscious and unconscious tendencies.

In an 1895(b) paper on anxiety neurosis Freud (pp. 135–136) engaged in a sophisticated analysis of the multiple causation concept propounded in *Studies on Hysteria.* His categories are "preconditions," and "specific," "concurrent," and "precipitating," or "releasing," causes. If the effect is to occur, all of these factors must participate:

> We may characterize as the *precipitating* or releasing cause the one which makes its appearance last in the equation, so that it immediately precedes the effect.
>
> *preconditions* are those in whose absence the effect would never come about, but which are incapable of producing the effect by themselves alone. . . . For the specific cause is still lacking.
>
> The *specific cause* is the one which is never missing in any case in which the effect takes place, and which moreover suffices, if present in the sufficient quantity or intensity, provided only that the preconditions are also fulfilled.
>
> As *concurrent causes* we may regard such factors as are not necessarily present every time, nor able, whatever their amount, to produce the effect by themselves alone, but which operate alongside of the preconditions and the specific cause in satisfying the etiological equation.

This remains the framework most clinicians use today. Freud's case histories illustrate brilliantly the relationship between the current traumatic, or precipitating, event (Herr K's proposition to Dora, Little Hans' witnessing a horse fall down, and the mother's marital arrangement for the Rat Man) and the patient's past history and dynamics. At times Freud would seem to accord the initiative to the precipitating event itself—i.e., in awakening from dormancy an unconscious intention or complex—and at times to the underlying

motives themselves—i.e., as actively reaching out and grasping, so to speak, the "precipitant."

The correspondence with Fliess in 1897 documents Freud's
growing conviction in the importance of psychical, as opposed
to somatic, causes of psychopathology. Freud's (1887–1902, p.
212) analysis of his writing block in that relationship (that it
was "aimed at hindering our intercourse"), his interpretation
of his paralysis in a dream as the "fulfillment of an exhibi-
tionistic wish" (ibid, p. 206–207), and his (ibid, p. 209) for-
mula that "symptoms are *fulfillments of wishes*" (Freud's italics) are in line with his increasing emphasis on the
determinative role of purposive ideas in human behavior. In a
draft of 1897 (ibid, p. 204) Freud invoked fantasy, not instinct,
as the causal factor: "If now the intensity of such a phantasy
increases to a point at which it would be bound to force its way
into consciousness, it is repressed and a symptom is generated
through a backward impetus from the fantasy to its constitu-
ent memories." In another draft of the same year Freud (ibid,
pp. 207–208) spoke of the etiological role of unconscious death
wishes in psychopathology. In an 1898 paper Freud (p. 297)
explained his forgetting an address as the result of an "unconscious . . . intention" to forego visiting the household in question (so that he might be on his way to a prearranged holiday
with a friend). The mnemonic falsifications and distortions in
screen memories were said to be "tendentious—that is, they
serve the purposes of the repression and replacement of objec-
tionable or disagreeable impressions" (Freud, 1899, p. 322).

In *The Interpretation of Dreams* the phrase "purposive
ideas" appears repeatedly in Freud's explication of psychical
causality. The ordering of ideas in a chain of associations was
seen, for example, as occurring under the influence of overriding "purposive ideas" (Freud, 1900, p. 530–531). More than to
anything else, this book is dedicated to demonstrating that
dreams are determined by the interplay between unconscious
"wishes."

In *The Psychopathology of Everyday Life* Freud (1901b, p.
240) defined psychic determinism as the idea that "our psychical functioning [is to] be explained by *purposive ideas* [my

italics]": "*Certain shortcomings in our psychical functioning . . . and certain seemingly unintentional performances
prove, if psycho-analytic methods of investigation are applied
to them, to have valid motives and to be determined by motives
unknown to consciousness*" (ibid, p. 239, Freud's italics). The
prime aim of this book was to demonstrate that this principle
extended even to behaviors that were apparently trivial, nonsensical, arbitrary, or "accidental": "there is a *sense* and *purpose* behind the minor functional disturbances in the daily life
of healthy people" (ibid, p. 162; my italics). For example,
Freud (ibid, p. 141) explained a patient's misplacing his keys
on the day before Freud's fee was due as a "symptomatic act—
that is, something he had done *intentionally* [my italics]." The
Austrian minister's declaration that the session of the Lower
House was "closed," when he meant to say "opened," was
determined by what he "secretly wished" (ibid, p. 59). Freud's
seemingly arbitrary choice of the number "2467," in a letter
to Fliess about the dream book, was determined by Freud's
"wish" to have 24 more years of productive work and to tri-
umph over Colonel M. (p. 243).

In the 1912 edition of *The Psychopathology of Everyday
Life,* Freud (ibid, pp. 248–249) borrowed a vignette from
Jones to illustrate the methodology by which one arrives at
the ideas and preoccupations determining seemingly trivial
and arbitrary activities. A young acquaintance of Jones' spontaneously produced the number "986" and challenged Jones
to give a causal explanation of it. The friend's associations
began with his recollection of a newspaper misprint—the
day's atmospheric temperature was reported as '986°F' rather
than '98.6°F'. Noting that he often laughed uproariously over
this seemingly jejune incident, the visitor went on to remark
on the intense heat of the fire in Jones' room and reflected
that it was probably this which had stimulated his dormant
memory of the misprint. Next the man reflected that the concept of heat had always impressed him; he considered it "the
most important thing in the universe," "the source of all life,"
and so on. Finally, he thought of the smokestack opposite his
bedroom window. He commented that he often watched the

flame and smoke billowing from it, while deploring the chimney's waste of energy. From such associations ("heat, fire, the source of life, the waste of vital energy from an upright tube") Jones surmised that the young man was preoccupied with masturbation—an hypothesis that the visitor himself subsequently confirmed.

Much of this book concerns itself with disturbances of memory: "when the reproducing function fails or goes astray, the occurrence points, far more frequently than we suspect, to interference by a tendentious factor—that is, by a *purpose* which favours one memory while striving to work against another" (ibid, p. 45; Freud's italics). The classic example of this is Freud's substitution of the names "Botticelli" and "Boltraffio" for "Signorelli."

Freud was sharing a coach with a stranger and the flow of conversation moved from the reverence of the Turks in Bosnia and Herzegovina for their physicians and these people's resignation to their fate, to the painter at Orvieto (Signorelli) whose name Freud could not recall. In the interval between talking about the Turks and talking about Orvieto, Freud had (quite consciously) suppressed the desire to tell the stranger about these same Turks' utter despair in the face of sexual disorders, calamities which they view as worse than death itself. Reflecting on this Freud recognized that his train of thought was leading him to a painful recollection—that Freud's impotent patient had recently suicided at a resort called "Trafio." It was, in short, a (momentarily unconscious) "motive" (p. 4) that led Freud to substitute "Botticelli" and "Boltraffio" for "Signorelli": "What I *wanted* [my italics] to forget was not, it is true, the name of the artist at Orvieto but something else—something, however, which contrived to place itself in an associative connection with his name, so that my act of will missed its target and I forgot *the one thing against my will;* while I wanted to forget *the other thing intentionally*" (Freud's italics, ibid, p. 6). "Bot*ti*celli" and "Bol*traffio*" were hence compromise formations between the repressed material—Signor*elli* and *Trafio*—and the forces opposing its recollection.

Freud's explanation of why the seemingly neutral name "Signorelli" was drawn into the repressed complex regarding his patient and the topics of death and sexuality invokes the concept of "external associations," the fifth causal principle to which I earlier alluded.

> The name Signorelli has undergone a division into two pieces. One of the pairs of syllables (*elli*) recurs without alteration in one of the substitute names; while the other, by means of the translation of *Signor* into *Herr,* has acquired a numerous and miscellaneous set of relations to the names contained in the repressed topics [presumably also the patient's], but for this reason is not available for [conscious] reproduction. The substitute for it [for *Signor*] has been arrived at in a way that suggests that a displacement along the connected names of "*Her*zegovina and *Bos*nia" had taken place, without consideration for the sense or for the acoustic demarcation of the syllable. Thus the names have been treated in this process like the pictograms in a sentence which has had to be converted into a picture-puzzle (or rebus) (ibid, pp. 4–5).

Freud's subsequent work—the case histories of "Dora," "Little Hans," and the "Rat Man," for example—continues to invoke the idea of "external associations." For example, Little Hans' phobia extended from horses to vehicles (*Wagen*) by means of his stereotypical use of the word "because" (wegen): "Hans was accustomed to pronounce the word [Wagen], and hear it pronounced, Wägen [exactly like *wegen*]" (Freud, 1909b, p. 59). A much more intricate linkage is posited for the words "*Raten—Ratten—Spielratte*" in the Rat Man report. Such words are termed "linking words" or "verbal bridges."

Freud (1901b, p. 6) would question, however, whether external associations such as these are sufficient to bring the neutral material into repression or symptomatic expression along with that of the complex or "whether some more intimate connection [than verbal or tonal similarity or temporal contiguity] between the two topics is not required." "On close enquiry," Freud (ibid) concludes, "one finds more and more frequently that the two elements which are joined by an external association (the repressed element and the new one) possess in addition some connection of content [as in the Signorelli example]."

It would thus seem that the relationship between the external association and the repressed content is similar to that of the day residue and the latent dream thoughts, and to that between the unconscious motives and the facilitating conditions (inebriation, fatigue, etc.) of a parapraxis. The repressed strivings utilize the verbal bridge or linking word to express themselves in a compromise formation. Expressed metaphorically, the relationship of the external associations to the unconscious complex seems that of the iron filings to the magnet.

Returning now to Freud's purposive concept of causation, in the Dora case Freud (1905, p. 42) conceptualized his patient's hysterical symptomatology as "actuated by motives" and "tendentious"—"the *aim* could be none other than to detach her father from Frau K" [my italics]. The "cause" of Dora's first dream is an "intention" to flee the house where she felt her virginity threatened—this aim itself determined by a still more unconscious intention (pp. 67, 85). "Illnesses of this [Dora's] kind are the result of intention. . . . An attempt must first be made by the roundabout methods of analysis to convince the patient herself of the existence in her of an *intention to be ill*" (my italics, ibid, p. 45). The Dora case is chock full of explanations of psychopathology in terms of wish, intention, and purpose. Her hallucination of smoke, for example, was determined by her unconscious longing for a kiss from Freud, a smoker like Herr K. and her father (p. 74). Her unconscious *fantasy* of defloration was cited as a key determinant of her second dream (p. 100).

In this case Freud also considers the role of "secondary" or "epinosic" gain. This brings both the current interpersonal environment and the concept of *"function"* (p. 43) [my italics] into Freud's notion of causality. Such "motives" (p. 42) arise after the fact of the symptom itself, but may come to contribute to its maintenance as strongly as the more purely historical and intrapsychic determinants.

A little girl in her greed for love does not enjoy having to share the affection of her parents with her brothers and sisters; and she notices that the whole of their affection is lavished on her once more whenever she arouses their anxiety by falling ill. She has now discovered a means of enticing out her parents' love, and will make use of that means as soon as she has the necessary psychical material at her disposal for producing an illness. When such a child has grown up to be a woman she may find all the demands she used to make in her childhood countered owing to her marriage with an inconsiderate husband, who may subjugate her will, mercilessly exploit her capacity for work, and lavish neither his affection nor his money upon her. In that case ill-health will be her one weapon for maintaining her position. It will procure her the care she longs for; it will force her husband to make pecuniary sacrifices for her and to show her consideration, as he would never have done while she was well; and it would compel him to treat her with solicitude if she recovers, for otherwise a relapse will threaten (ibid, p. 44).

Indeed, throughout Freud's case histories explanations in terms of *purpose, aim, goal, wish, function,* and (as we shall see) *meaning* far outnumber those in terms of instincts.

In *Five Lectures on Psycho-Analysis* Freud (1909c, p. 38) uses the words "motive" and "cause" interchangeably:

Psycho-analysts are marked by a particularly strict belief in the determination of mental life. For them there is nothing trivial, nothing abritrary or haphazard. They expect in every case to find sufficient *motives* where, as a rule, no such expectation is raised. Indeed, they are prepared to find several *motives* for one and the same mental occurrence, whereas what seems to be our innate craving for *causality* declares itself satisfied with a single psychical *cause* [my italics].

Freud (1909a, pp. 235–236) conceptualized the Rat Man's fears that harm would come to his father in the next world as "a *compensation* for these death-wishes which he had felt against his father . . . it was *designed* in defiance of reality,

and in deference to the *wish* which had previously been showing itself in fantasies of every kind—to undo the fact of his
father's death [my italics]." Here, plainly, is a causal construction that incorporates the concepts of function, design,
and wish. In the Schreber case Freud (1911b, p. 47) argued
that "the exciting *cause* of the illness was the appearance in
him of a feminine (that is, a passive homosexual) *wishful
phantasy,* which took as its object the figure of his doctor" [my
italics].

In *The Introductory Lectures* Freud (1915–1917, p. 36)
makes it his explicit aim, in his investigation of parapraxes,
"to leave all physiological or psychophysiological factors on
one side and devote ourselves to purely psychological investigations into the sense—that is the meaning or purpose—of
parapraxes." Again, the "sense of a psychical process" is defined as "the *intention* it serves and its position in a psychical
continuity. *In most of our researches we can replace sense by
intention or purpose* [my italics]." There the "dynamic view" is
characterized by its goal, "not merely to describe and classify
phenomena, but to understand them as signs of the interplay
of forces in the mind, as a manifestation of *purposeful intentions* working concurrently or in mutual opposition" (ibid, p.
67; my italics). Consonant with this aim, parapraxes are conceptualized as "serious mental acts" which arise from two
mutually opposing "intentions" (p. 44). Continuing to elabo-
rate upon causation in *The Introductory Lectures* Freud (pp.
61, 107) uses words such as *"purpose," "meaning," "motive,"*
and *"goal"* [my italics]. In a moment we shall examine more
fully the relationship between "purpose" and "meaning."
"Unconscious day-dreams" are defined as "imaginary" and
are declared to be "the source not only of night-dreams but
also of neurotic symptoms" (ibid, pp. 372–373).

The inversion of the patient in "A Case of Homosexuality in
a Woman" was motivated by her desire for revenge against
her father whom she felt had rejected her. Her dreams were
determined by "the *intention* to mislead me [and] . . . the
wish to win my favour [my italics]" (Freud, 1920b, p. 165).
The Wolf Man's attraction to servant girls was determined, in

part, by "an intention of debasing his sister and of putting an end to her intellectual superiority" (Freud, 1918, p. 22).

From this it is clear that Freud's working concept of causation was more teleological than mechanistic. Freud's genius, as Ricoeur (1970, p. 361) correctly maintains, "consists in maintaining that the strange phenomena which had previously been left to physiology are explainable in terms of *intentional ideas* [my italics]." Unfortunately, as previously mentioned, Freud was never fully comfortable with his purposive and meaningful conception of cause. He was plagued by the nagging suspicion, expressed in the self-dissection dream and elsewhere, that he had strayed from the revered Brücke's strict materialistic path. This was doubtless one of the factors that made it difficult for him, at first, to accept the fantasy elements in his patient's recollections.

Nevertheless, loyal to Brücke's mechanism as he was, Freud was too good a clinician not to recognize that, however much he longed to theorize in terms of biological tensions, excitations, and drives, in the consulting room he dealt with mental experience and human communication: "it [is] a certainty that the patients whom we described [in *Studies on Hysteria*] as neurotic were in some sense suffering from *mental* disturbances and ought therefore to be treated by psychological methods" (Freud, 1932, p. 219; Freud italics). He (1915d, p. 123) acknowledged that "An exact knowledge of an instinct is not invariably necessary for purposes of psychological investigation. . . . Although instincts are wholly determined by their origin in a somatic source, in mental life *we know them only by their aims* [my italics]." His partial resolution of this tension—between his nineteenth century scientific ego ideal and his appreciation of reality—was to work clinically with a teleological concept of psychical causation, while paying lip service to mechanistic concepts. For example, even in the *Project* he recognized the necessity to talk in terms of the "will"—though he reassured himself that it is ultimately a "derivative of the instincts" (1895a, p. 317). In *The Introductory Lectures* he (1915–1917, p. 373) asserted the "importance of the part played by phantasy in the formation of symptoms," while speaking of the libido that cathects it. He apologetically justified his clinical procedure as a psycho-therapeutic Brest-Litovsk, a temporarily necessary conces-sion to psychology of activities that would ultimately be expli-cable and treatable 'somatically'.

Similarly, his hydraulic model of the etiological role of trauma, fixation, and regression in neurosis concealed funda-mentally psychological concepts. That what is being fixated are mental, not purely biophysical, activities is evident in the following explication of fixation and regression (Freud, 1917, p. 276).

> A perfect model of an *affective* fixation to something that is past is provided by mourning, which actually involves the most complete alienation from the present and the future. . . . It may happen, too, that a person is brought so completely to a stop by a traumatic event which shatters the foundation of his life that he abandons all *interest* in the present and future and remains permanently absorbed in *mental concentration* upon the past [my italics].

Freud had, in any event, never clarified how one gets from a substantive, (theoretically) quantifiable libido, ebbing and flowing in its hypothetical "channels" (ibid, p. 170), to the meaningful behaviors in which fixation and regression man-ifest themselves and to the fantasies, feelings, and recollec-tions which are all one ultimately encounters when one ana-lyzes them.

Freud's inability to accept the extent to which his psycho-logical truth had cracked its biophysical mold left him, as Holt (1976) suggests, with two concepts of causation—a mech-anistic, biological and a purposive, meaningful one. His meta-psychological commitment to biological reductionism had two unfortunate consequences: (1) it committed psychoanalysis to confusion and ambiguity, as Freud was painfully aware, on one of its basic theoretical concepts—instinct; (2) it committed him to a mind-body dualism (Freud, 1915–1917, pp. 121–122). Moreover, it left him with a core theoretical concept whose reputed referents were not accessible to empirical study by psychoanalytic technique. Freud (1933, p, 95) was left with the uncomfortable admission that "The theory of the instincts is so to say our mythology. Instincts are mythical entities, magnificent in their indefiniteness . . . we are never certain that we are seeing them clearly."[8]

Let me make it plain that I am not arguing here that constitutional factors play no determinative role in psychopathology, character structure or personality type, fantasy formation, and human motivation in general! We have long known that organic disorders such as pellagra and paresis can lead to

---

[8]Freud's writing is ambiguous on the concept of instinct. Although in places Freud used the term to refer to something purely biological (1915b, pp. 147–152) or non-psychical (1915c, p. 177), he generally regarded it as "a concept on the frontier between the mental and the somatic, as the psychical representative of the stimuli originating from within the organism and reaching the mind, as a measure of the demand upon the mind for work in consequence of its connection with the body" (1915d, pp. 121–122; my italics; see also Freud, 1911b, p. 74, and Freud, 1905a, p. 168). What is never clarified is the relationship between the biological substrate of the instinctual drive and its psychical representative. At times he (ibid) seems to be equating instinct with the latter, at times (Freud, 1915c, p. 177) with the former. Nor was Freud clear on the relationship between the instincts and the environment. While acknowledging that the behavior of significant others can affect the time of awakening of libidinal impulses, he was ambiguous on whether external stimuli can influence the underlying intensity of the drive. Recent ethological studies suggest that the concept of instinct must be made considerably more complicated than originally conceived and that it must accord to environmental stimuli and experience a much larger determinative role (see Campbell & Misanin, 1969 and Lifton, 1979, p. 41). The entire issue is of course complicated by Strachey's unfortunate rendering of Freud's "*Trieb*" (urge or drive) as "instinct"; *Trieb* carried a much less purely biologistic connotation than "instinct." Freud reserved the term "*Instinkt*" for reference to animal behavior.

profound psychological changes. Many medical and neurological diseases and genetic biochemical lesions produce striking behavioral abnormalities. The evidence for biologically heritable and constitutional factors in, not only the major psychoses, but neuroses and character types as well is strong (see, for example, Buss and Plomin [1975], Loehlin and Nichols [1976], Schwarz [1979], and Floderus-Myrhed et al., [1980]). Sociobiology and ethology are garnering impressive evidence for the biological facets of human motivation (Wilson, 1977, 1978, Barash, 1977). Structuralist (e.g., Lévi-Strauss, 1963, Chomsky, 1968) and Piagetian evidence for the transcultural and transtemporal unity of important aspects of human behavior and psychological development suggest that there are powerful hereditary-constitutional factors in culture and personality. Nor do I maintain that there are not constitutional determinants of sexual and aggressive behavior and of the regular developmental unfolding of the different modes of infantile organ pleasure (see Wallace, 1983b, pp. 44–47). Rather, I am arguing that our motive fantasies are the epiphenomena of neither purely biological nor purely societal elements, but of the *interaction* between them. In any event, at the level of clinical discourse the analyst is concerned with symbolically mediated and meaningful human behaviors. He is limited to the data of human communication; since he has no direct access to the putative instincts, any statements about them are unprovable and irrefutable.

One need do no more than pick up any current psychoanalytic textbook or case report to see that the analyst's working concept of causality is psychological and purposive—the affect laden fantasy or wish. Greenson (1967, p. 23), for example, equates the causal "forces" in the mind with "purposeful intentions" and Brenner (1973, p. 3) with "wish or intent." Similarly, the concept of "psychic energy" is, as Brenner (ibid, p. 20) asserts, a psychological, not a physical, one: "It can be defined only in psychological terms . . . We must resign ourselves to the limitations imposed by our present state of knowledge, and avoid making a meaningless equation between the psychic and the physical." In the same breath in which he opined that "all our provisional ideas in psychology will presumably someday be based on an organic substructure" Freud (1914, pp. 78–79) asserted that his present theorizing "tr[ies] in general to keep psychology clear from everything that is different in nature from it, *even biological lines of thought* [my italics]."

Acknowledging that the psychoanalytic concept of causation is psychological does not commit one to an ontological mind-body, spirit-matter, split. What we term "mind" is an abstraction that refers to the organization of those properties which emerge from the interaction between two species of *matter*—the human body and its environment. Psychic causality, like psychological concepts in general, has arisen to explain the psychologically emergent aspects of this interaction. To address these symbolic phenomena psychologically is not to deny their physiological facets, but rather to acknowledge that these functions are not presently explicable biologically. In short, the psychology-biology dichotomy is an *explanatory,* not an ontological, split; *psychical causality is not immaterial causality.*[9]

The extent to which the cognitive-conative-affective dimension of human behavior will be comprehended physiologically and the extent to which it will continue to require psychological categories of explanation remains to be seen. Although the analyst is largely uninformed—pending the discoveries of neurobiology and endocrinology—about the biological substrate of human personality structure and motivation, he is hardly indifferent to it. To learn, for example, that there are heredi-

---

[9]Correlatively, psychotherapy is no less material and energic (i.e., 'somatic') a treatment than pharmacotherapy. Through analysis there occurs a shift in the patient's *total pattern of functioning*— some aspects of which must be understood psychologically (as a transformation in the pattern of compromise formations and interpretations) and others physiologically (alteration in the balance of endocrine and neurobiological functioning).

tary-constitutional nuclei for certain character types and syndromes, genetically determined preferences for particular styles of compromise formation and defense, and biochemical factors in aggressiveness, passivity, and other traits could have clinical, as well as theoretical, implications; such findings have already revolutionized our approach to the major affective disorders and to certain categories of schizophrenia.[10]

_____

[10]However much biological models may replace their psychological counterparts, it is difficult to imagine a viable explanation of human behavior that could ignore the current and historical environment. Twentieth century biologists grasp that their unit of study is, not the hypothetical isolated organism, but the organism-in-continual-interaction-with-its-milieu. If the behavior of the simplest animal cannot be understood without reference to its environment, then how can that of the human being, who is interacting with an environment that includes a symbolic dimension as well. Neuropsychiatrists appreciate that the behavior of the most organically disturbed patient cannot be sufficiently comprehended without reference to his current and historical environment (its impact on the specific content of his hallucinations and delusions, for example); similarly, neurological disturbances such as Huntington's chorea—like "organic" diseases in general—assume, after the fact of their emergence, conscious and unconscious meaning within the context of the patient's history and personality structure.

It may be that aspects of symbolically mediated human behavior will forever defy reduction to biological explanatory models, just as aspects of biological (and even chemical) systems appear to resist subsumption to the models of physics. (Popper [Popper and Eccles, 1981, p. 18] asserts that "the often referred to reduction of chemistry to physics, important as it is, is so far incomplete, and very possibly incompletable." Indeed, within the field of physics itself he (ibid) cites the reduction of Young and Fresnel's optics to Maxwell's electromagnetic field theory as perhaps the only example of a "successful and complete reduction"!) If, for example, we arrive at the point where we can exhaustively explain the neurophysiological facets of a particular individual's oedipal fantasy or self-world view, will that

Nor does admitting teleology into our causal concept make us unscientific, as Freud feared. The belief that it does so fails to take account of at least two factors: (1) that one's explanatory framework should be adjusted to one's subject matter (and not vice-versa) and if that subject behaves purposefully, then one needs concepts that reflect this; (2) science no longer considers teleology as acausal or ipso facto unscientific. Teleological explanations, for example, have reentered twentieth century biology. In regard to teleology, let me quote Bunge, the historian of causality (1979, p. 304):

> It is even likely that teleological laws will not be replaced but will be explained by other laws, that, for example, they will be shown to have emerged in the course of the evolution of organisms and associations of living beings. . . . Teleological laws will perhaps be explained as a new mode of behavior of material systems, resulting from a long past process of trials and errors in the adventure of adaptation, and stabilized by the mechanisms of heredity. Scientific philosophy does not require the extrusion of teleological explanations in connection with

mean that we can then dispense with any attempt to appreciate the fantasy and *Weltanschauung*? And if we do dispense with them, then how are we to interpret the act of dispensation itself—neurophysiologically or logically and symbolically (or will we be able to speak of 'interpreting' at all?)? To elucidate the physiological underpinnings of man's psychologically emergent properties is not to prove the latter nonexistent or to deny their causal efficacy in the world. What would we say about a biologist who denied the homeostatic and integrative activities of the organism because these activities must themselves be undergirded by subatomic, atomic, and molecular interactions? It is fascinating that that aspect of humanity—the symbolic dimension—that most differentiates us from the rest of the animal kingdom has proved so embarrassing to many theorists that they either refuse to address, or explain away, that with which the theorists themselves are most intimately familiar—human sentience! (See also my comments on the "ghost in the machine" in Chapter 4.)

the higher integrative levels; it demands merely the avoidance of the obscurantist interpretations of teleological patterns in terms of immaterial and unintelligible entelechies.

Consider also, in this light, the words of Hartmann (1927, pp. 402–403):

> The principle of causality is not limited to causal equations. The kind of 'teleological' interpretation which is often used in psychoanalysis, and above all, in Adler's individual psychology, in which mental processes are understood in terms of their goals which may either be set consciously, or are unconscious—all this does not contradict a causal explanation. To view a process within a teleological framework can generally in biology be a valuable methodological framework.

A prime reason for scientific antipathy to teleological explanations is the misconception that they violate the fundamental tenet that causes must lie temporally prior to their effects. In other words, it is charged that explications in terms of purpose or goal involve the illogical assumption that the future (the effect) can somehow determine the present (the cause). This accusation, as Hempel (1965, p. 254) points out, is unfounded:

> When the action of a person is motivated, say, by the desire to reach a certain objective, then it is not the as yet, unrealized future event of attaining the goal which can be said to determine his present behavior, for indeed the goal may never be actually reached; rather—to put it in crude terms—it is a) his desire, present before the action, to attain that particular objective, and b) his belief, likewise present before the action, that such and such a course of action is most likely to have the desired effect. The determining motives and beliefs, therefore, have to be classified among the antecedent conditions of a motivational explanation, and there is no formal difference on this account between motivational and causal explanation.

Braithwaite (1966, p. 32) concurs that teleological formulations of human behavior are understood as causal explanations, with intentions as causes. See also Mackie's (1980, pp. 270–296) conceptualization of teleology as a subspecies of efficient causation.

In addition to the dimension of purposiveness, Freud's clinical concept of causation includes, as we have seen, one of *meaningfulness.* The cause of Frau Emmy von N's stammering and clacking—the "conflict between her intention and the antithetic idea (the counter-will)"—was also termed the "meaning" of the symptomatology (Breuer & Freud, 1895, pp. 92–93). In *The Interpretation of Dreams,* for instance, he shifts back and forth between speaking of the "causes" and the "meaning" of the dream. Dreams were conceptualized both as the effects of underlying causes—i.e., wishes—and as disguised communications (see also Freud, 1915–1917, pp. 100–101). The dreamer's associations were conceptualized as both leading one to the antecedent causal fantasies and as revealing the meaning of the dream (Freud liked to compare dream interpretation to the decipherment of ancient scripts). Much of the theoretical portion of the book was devoted to elucidating the lexical rules by which the grammar of the latent content is transformed into that of the manifest content. To interpret a dream is both to elucidate its meaning and to assign it a place in a causal nexus: "for 'interpreting' a dream implies assigning a 'meaning' to it—that is by replacing it by something which fits into the chain of our mental acts as a link having a validity and importance equal to the rest" (Freud, 1900, p. 96). Again, in the same work, the concept of "wish fulfillment" is introduced in Freud's explication of the meaning of the dream (ibid, p. 122).

In the Dora case, Freud (1901a, p. 15) continues to use, interchangeably, the concept of the "causes" and the "meaning" of the dream:

after the work of interpretation has been completed they [the dreams] can be replaced by perfectly correctly constructed

thoughts which can be assigned a recognizable position in the
chain of mental events . . . dreams seemed to call for insertion
in the long thread of connections which spun itself out between
a symptom of the disease and a pathogenic idea. At that time I
learnt to translate the language of dreams into the forms of
expression of our own thought language.

In his case histories Freud often goes back and forth between analyses in terms of cause and meaning. For example,
he (1909a, p. 217) speaks of "translat[ing]" the "meaning" of
the Rat Man's obsessional idea—the meaning in this case
being equivalent to the cause (i.e., the unconscious patricidal
fantasy). In the Dora case, Freud (1901a, pp. 18, 47) asserts
that "a symptom has more than one meaning and serves to
represent several unconscious processes simultaneously
. . . the practical aim of the treatment is to remove all possible
symptoms and to replace them by conscious thoughts. . . . *One*
of the meanings of a symptom is the representation of a sexual
phantasy," Freud (ibid, p. 47) continues [Freud's italics].
Dora's catarrh, for instance, "express[ed] her regret at [Herr
K's] absence and her wish to make him a better wife" (ibid, p.
83).

Even *Three Essays,* the manifesto of instinctivism, acknowledges the dimension of meaning in psychopathology
and the consequently exegetical elements in the analyst's
task.

> symptoms are substitutes—*transcriptions* as it were—for a
> number of emotionally cathected mental processes, wishes,
> and desires, which, by the operation of a special psychic pro-
> cedure (repression) have been prevented from obtaining dis-
> charge in psychical activity that is admissable in conscious-
> ness . . . [the treatment consists in] systematically turning
> these symptoms back [retranslating] . . . into emotionally
> cathected ideas—ideas that will now become conscious [my
> italics] (Freud, 1905a, p. 164).

In *The Introductory Lectures* Freud (1915–1917, p. 284) elucidated the "meaning" of the symptom with reference to "its

'*whence*' and its '*whither*' or '*what for*'—that is, the *impressions* and *experiences from which it arose* and the *intentions* which it serves [my italics]." "Symptoms have a sense and are related to the patient's experiences," he (p. 257) continues. This is exemplified in the case of the obsessional woman whose repetitive ritualistic behavior—showing her maid a stain on a tablecloth and running into the bedroom and sending the maid on a trivial errand—was a "representation" of the wedding night trauma of her husband's impotence, his continual returning to her bed to try unsuccessfully, and his clumsy attempt to cover up his embarrassment vis-à-vis the maid by pouring red ink on the sheets (p. 262). It expressed, furthermore, the patient's "intention" to undo the past mishap and to deny her discontent with her husband (pp. 262–263). In his 1927 paper on fetishism Freud (p. 152) discoursed on the meaning and purpose of the perversion. In 1932 he (p. 219) spoke, in one breath, of the necessity to understand the "meaning" and the "causes" of psychopathology.

Freud was correct to consider the facet of meaning, as well as of purpose, in his explication of psychic causality. It is man's possession of language, the fact that his behavior is symbolically mediated, that forces one to do so. Meaning is determined by the conscious and unconscious, current and historical interpersonal context of our desiring and fearing. To restate this more precisely, raw sexual and aggressive drives do not sit about waiting to attach themselves to, or be pulled out by, any object that presents itself; rather, our sexual and aggressive impulsions are directed, from the outset, to the internal representations of important persons in the environment. The original objects of these impulsions were, of course, the central figures from childhood, and these desires remain bound, to a significant degree, to representations of these prototypical objects. We humans cannot help but desire in an object-directed fashion; nor, since important aspects of our superego and defensive functioning are the fruit of identifications, can we check our desires in other than an object-related mode.

That which causes our behaviors—affect-laden fantasies—are both *purposive* and *meaningful*. Each behavior is simultaneously caused and is a compromised communication.[11] Meaning and causation are simply two different facets of the same thing. Freud's idea of psychic causality was thus an assertion that *(1) all observable or (potentially) self reportable behaviors are the result of antecedent mental events; (2) these events are purposive strivings; (3) they are meaningful communications; and (4) they serve some function within the individual's mental economy and current interpersonal environment.* The theorem of psychic causality is simultaneously the theory of psychic meaningfulness, purposefulness, and functionalism. The idea that a human behavior could be meaningless or serve no purpose troubled Freud quite as much as the idea that it could be uncaused. The words "motive" and "meaning" often occur in tandem with one another and are used synonymously (see Freud, 1909a, p. 186).[12]

---

[11]The communicative aspect of "drives" and symptoms was grasped by Freud as early as the mid-1890's. In *The Project,* for example, he (1895a, p. 318) notes that "At first the human organism is incapable of bringing about the specific action [designed to discharge the tension of the drives]. It takes place by *extraneous help,* when the attention of an experienced person is drawn to the child's state by discharge along the path of internal change. In this way this path of discharge acquires a secondary function of the highest importance, that of *communication* [Freud's italics]." In a letter to Fliess in December, 1896, Freud (1888–1902), p. 239) asserts that "[hysterical] attacks of giddiness and fits of weeping" are all "aimed at *another person*—but mostly at the prehistoric, unforgettable other person who is never equalled by any one later" [Freud's italics]. Years later, in "Mourning and Melancholia," Freud (1917, p. 248) writes of the disguised communicative value of the patient's self reproaches—veiled reproaches toward current and historical others.

[12]In the Standard Edition *Ursache* is generally translated as "cause," *Motive* as "motive," *Determinismus* as "determinism," *Absicht* as "intention," *Tendenz* as "purpose," *Ziel* as "aim" or "goal," and *Sinn* as "meaning" or "sense." In German, as in English, there is ambiguity and overlap in the usages of "cause," "reason," and

The affinity between Freud's concept of causality and that of most historians is obvious—the major distinction being that the latter is all too likely to take insufficient account of unconscious and affective factors. Historians, as much as analysts, assume their subjects' behaviors are explicable in terms of their ideas, desires, fears, and so forth. Even though historians are more concerned with the behaviors of whole groups, periods, and cultures, and more interested in economic and institutional factors than in personal fantasies, they cannot dispense with a concept of individual motivation. Cultural forces, if they are to be effective, must become established as motives within personalities.

There are similarities and differences between the concept of causality in psychoanalysis and history on the one hand, and that in the physical and biological sciences on the other. Among the similarities are the idea that our fantasies *precede* and *effect* the phenomena under consideration, and the implicit assumption that mental acts or symbolically mediated behaviors do not occur by accident or chance. Among the most important differences are that the conscious and unconscious affect-laden fantasies that lead to all human behaviors (excepting the grossly neurological) are not simply blind mechanical forces but *strivings* to bring about a longed-for *future* state of affairs. In other words, our fantasizing, conscious and unconscious, is *goal-directed* and *purposeful*. It is also—at least potentially—communicative. Therefore, when we ask what "causes" a particular behavior we are asking a question about antecedent conditions that include its purpose and meaning. As Toulmin (1954), Flew (1954), and Ricoeur (1970) suggest, "motive" is perhaps the term that best captures the peculiar nature of psychic causes—that they push from behind, look ahead, and communicate. If one wishes to use the word "reasons" in this sense, then I have no quarrel with him—though in the next chapter I propose a more circumscribed use for the term.

"motive" (See, for example, the *Oxford English Dictionary* and Langenscheidt's German-English Dictionary).

Furthermore, I concur with Ricoeur (1974, p. 160) that Freud's intermingling of the concepts of "meaning" and "force"—for which Schafer and others have vociferously criticized him—is appropriate to the reality under consideration. There is an energic, as well as a meaningful, aspect to our determining affect-laden fantasies. That we cannot elucidate the precise nature of this energic or, as many psychoanalysts term it, "instinctual" or "cathectic," face of mental life does not permit us to dispense with it. Whatever their relations to the biophysical, the related concepts of *mental* force, energy, and tension accurately correspond to vital aspects of the phenomenology of human desiring and goal-seeking behavior. Psychic force or energy and meaning converge in the concept of the "wish" or, as Ricoeur (1970, 1974) terms it, of "desire." Unfulfilled longings and intrapsychic conflicts carry with them states of tension or dysphoria which, in their capacity to impel us to action, constitute their "energics"; they carry with them a current and historical interpersonal and symbolic nexus that contributes their meaning. *Jokes and Their Relation to the Unconscious* is the best demonstration of the utility of this mixed discourse of meaning and energy in the elucidation of human phenomena.

From this analysis it follows that interpreting in history and psychoanalysis is, as in the rest of science, causal hypothesizing.[13] Where psychoanalytic and historical hypotheses differ from those in the natural sciences is (1) in the necessity for the former to take account of the symbolic and teleological, as well as the purely antecedent and efficacious, aspects of causation in human behavior, and (2) in the limitation of the

---

[13]I am of course using the term "interpretation" in the narrow and formal sense of a clinical hypothesis that unites historically-constitutionally based determinants to current and transferential behaviors. I do not mean for "interpretation" to stand for "understanding" in general. A good deal of understanding in noncausal categories—grasping the patient's world-view and phenomenology—is prerequisite to any causal explanation.

former to retrospective inferences from patterns, as explicated in Chapter One.

The vignette of the previously encountered Ms. X illustrates the purposive, meaningful, and antecedent aspects of causation in human behavior.

> Ms. X, a first year law student, presented with an inability to study. Frantically, she had been turning to all of her professors for advice, tutorials, and study sessions. Her past history revealed parents who were physically present, but emotionally absent, who never bothered themselves about her school work or early career interests, and who stifled her expressions of affection and other feelings. Consequently, the patient developed a low opinion of herself and a conviction that others would be no more receptive to her needs than were her parents. After a dozen sessions it came to her while jogging, in a flash, that she was actually sabotaging her academic success—and as a surreptitious way of getting attention from the professors and me (whom she also begged for advice). In other words, her study problems were *caused* by her unconscious desire for attention and her equally unconscious assumption (based on childhood experience) that she must seek this attention indirectly lest she be rejected.

The principle of psychic causality asserts that behaviors which follow immediately upon certain events in the environment, and actions or statements which occur in temporal contiguity with one another, are meaningfully and causally connected (often via an unconscious linch pin) to one another. This is the theoretical ground upon which the analyst attends to the sequence of his patient's associations and to the analysand's responses to the therapist's interventions. For example:

> During the early evaluation and therapeutic sessions with Mrs. F, I noticed that every time I broached anything having to do with sexuality she shifted in her chair, averted her eyes,

and coughed nervously. She did so, for example, when I questioned her about menarche, masturbation, sexual fantasies, early relations with boys, and her current sexual relationship with her husband. From this I hypothesized that there was a cause-effect relationship between my questions and her agitation. When I knew her better, it became clear that my questions had impinged upon anxiety-laden unconscious conflicts over sexuality, stemming from her origin in a family that was preoccupied, negatively, with sex.

This vignette also illustrates that dynamic therapists do not generally infer cause-effect relationships from only one concatenation of events, but from recurrent linkages or patterns of them (see Chapter 4).

Without a concept of psychic causality much that transpires within the therapeutic sessions would seem meaningless. For example, a patient with a lifelong history of extreme discomfort with anger, stemming from his upbringing in a home where expressions of anger were taboo and brought ostracism, gingerly expressed a bit of irritation to me. He then closed his eyes and silently looked down. After several minutes he opened them and looked up out of the fleeting fantasy (fear) that I had left the room. I had to do no more than point out the connection between the two behaviors—expressing anger and fearing I had left the room—for him to divine the intrapsychic danger and causal connection. On another occasion I informed this man of my impending summer vacation. This was followed by silence and, eventually, a glance at the air conditioner: "I hate that damn thing. It's too cold in here. Will you cut it off?" At that moment he was unconscious of the connection between my announcement and his reaction, though he gradually became able to acknowledge his hurt and anger at my leaving.

In 1926 Freud posited that the interaction (conflict) between opposing unconscious intentions leads to the apprehension of an imminent danger situation, to which the ego responds with the generation of anxiety. This anxiety itself becomes an important causal factor in Freud's reconceptualization of symptom formation. Anxiety is the motive for the individual's construction of a variety of defensive and compromise formations.

It is important to appreciate that Freud is here discarding the last vestiges of his mechanistic theory of causality. Anxiety is no longer conceptualized as an automatic, reflex-like response to the damming up of libido, but as the result of intentional and meaningful activities: "whereas I formerly beleived that anxiety invariably arose automatically by an economic process, my present conception of anxiety as a *signal* given by the ego *in order to affect the pleasure-unpleasure agency* does away with the necessity of considering the economic factor" (p. 140, my italics); this reproduction of anxiety is explicitly declared an "intentional" one (p. 138). The concept of interpretation is also incorporated more fully into Freud's notion of causality. In other words, anxiety is generated because of the individual's historically-constitutionally determined unconscious interpretation of his impulse and situation as a dangerous one.

From 1920–1923 onward the development of ego psychology accorded to ego ideal and superego functions an increasingly important determinative role in human behavior. Since Freud conceptualized these structures as largely the fruit of identifications (the precipitants of abandoned object cathexes), he was opening the door to increased consideration of the place of societal factors in motivation.

HISTORICAL DETERMINISM

Historical determinism is the handmaiden of psychic causality. Although the two concepts are not identical, there is a circular relationship between them. By this I mean that the idea of psychic causality is the rationale for taking a history, and yet the operation of psychic causality is revealed primarily by taking that history. By "historical determinism" in psychoanalysis I mean that: *the present day configuration of any personality has arisen out of previously existing ones, that any individual's current (conscious and unconscious) in-*

terpretations of self and world, and present desires, fears, inhibitions, and behavior patterns are causally related to the history of his actual and fantasied interpersonal relations. By "history" we mean the course of the *interaction* between the individual's constitution-personality structure and his environment.

When we assert that the individual's history lives on in his present we do not mean that mental life is "four dimensional"—that there is one aspect of it where the pristine historical *occurrences* are still alive. All aspects of the psyche are equally current, all behaviors are motivated by present day wishes and anxieties. When we say that a behavior is determined by "historical," rather than "current," factors, what we mean is that it is determined by present-day (conscious and unconscious) attitudes, desires, fears, and expectations originating in certain historical conditions and which continue to be bound to the living *representations* of these conditions.

The psychoanalytic theory of psychopathology as a maladaptive way of dealing with unconscious intrapsychic conflict is of course founded squarely upon the bedrock of historical determinism. Both the conflict and the maladaptive means of handling it arise from the interaction between one's biological endowment and nascent personality structure on the one side and the environment on the other. The symptomatic and characterological modes of coping with conflict are special cases of atavism—the persistence of once adaptive, historically determined modes of behavior into the present, where they are no longer necessary and useful. Our "task," as Freud (1915–1917, p. 270) said, "is then simply to discover in respect to a senseless idea and a pointless action, the past situation in which the idea was justified and the action served a purpose." Adult neuroses and character styles are thus conceptualized as the effects of historically conditioned conflicts, behaviors, and misinterpretations of reality.

The case of Ms. H with issues somewhat similar to those of Ms. X, exemplifies this:

As a small child, Ms. H was rejected by her busy and alcoholic father. Still she loved and longed for him and, when she reached out to him, his rebuffs brought pain, humiliation, and impotent rage. To avoid the pain of future rebuffs and the attendant anger (which was itself conflictual for her since she was enjoined against even feeling, much less expressing, such things), she eventually withdrew from her father and repressed her needs for him. One must admit that, under the circumstances, there was a certain adaptiveness in this. However, such expectations of, and behavior toward, the first important male in her life became so ingrained in her that, when she left home, she transferred them to men in general, particularly those who might in some way be significant to her. She would do one of two things: either withdraw and be coldly aloof from men who unconsciously interested her or else, by identifying with her father, let them briefly into her life and then actively reject them before they could reject her. By so doing, she ensured that men ended up being as cold and indifferent to her as her father was—the famous neurotic self-fulfilling prophecy. Thus, a behavior pattern, appropriate to an admittedly inappropriate situation in childhood, continued into adulthood where it was no longer adaptive. Before long she began treating me similarly. She was late for and cancelled sessions, expressed boredom during the meetings, accused me on several occasions of being inattentive and uncaring, derogated the value of the treatment, and contemplated terminating. She was, in other words, acting out, rather than consciously remembering and talking about, the complex of feelings and expectations associated with her father's rejection of her. When I translated her behavior into words, her tardiness and withdrawal ceased and she began working in therapy.

Anniversary reactions, such as those in the family described below, are particularly powerful demonstrations of the principle of historical determinism:

Mrs. E, a 34-year-old woman with hysterical back pain and depression, presented after a suicide gesture precipitated by a chance meeting with her former husband. After her first suicide attempt at age 16, she was admitted to a psychiatric hospital. This followed an elopement with her boyfriend who soon mistreated, disappointed, and rejected her. A few years later she married a man whose father had deserted his family when he was eight years old, leaving his mother with himself and two brothers. When the patient and her husband had three children, one of them a boy eight years of age, the husband deserted the family, quickly remarried and, like his own father, established a new family and had no further contact with the first one. Lifelong problems between the patient and her daughter intensified after the divorce. When the daughter was 16, she ran away with a boy of whom her mother (my patient) disapproved, took an overdose of the *mother's* medication, and ended up in the hospital where her mother was first admitted!

This woman raised her daughter in the aloof yet authoritarian way in which her own mother reared her, sought out a man similar to her distant and womanizing father, and nagged and rebuffed him so that he became even more so. The daughter in turn was unconsciously identifying with the mother and learning from her how to "cope" with distress. The ex-husband was merely behaving as his father had taught him a father was supposed to behave. The presence of three children, one of whom was a *boy of eight,* was sufficiently similar to the situation when his own father left him that it functioned as the stimulus for what he would probably have done sooner or later anyway.

The therapist gains an intense appreciation that each person is the product of the history of the mutual interaction between himself and his environment, that he perceives himself and others through a filter of conscious and unconscious historically based preoccupations, wishes, fears, and expectations, and that he acts and reacts on this basis.

As mentioned in Chapter One, Freud emphasized the determinative role of the individual's earliest history. He believed that the traumata of early life played a neurotigenic role out of all proportion to their apparent significance.

It seems that neuroses are acquired only in early childhood (up to the age of six), even though their symptoms may not make their appearance till much later. The childhood neurosis may become manifest for a short time or may even be overlooked. . . . There is no difficulty in accounting for this aetiological preference for the first period of childhood. The neuroses are, as we know, disorders of the ego; and it is not to be wondered at if the ego, so long as it is feeble, immature and incapable of resistance, fails to deal with tasks with which it could cope with later on with the utmost ease. In these circumstances, instinctual demands from within, no less than excitations from the external world, operate as "traumas," particularly if they are met halfway by certain innate dispositions. . . . The damage inflicted on the ego by its first experiences gives us the appearance of being disproportionately great; but we have only to take as an analogy the differences in the results produced by the prick of a needle into a mass of cells in the act of cell division (as in Roux's experiments) and into the fully grown animal which eventually develops out of them (Freud, 1938, pp. 184–185; my italics).

As previously mentioned, trauma leads to the *fixation* of a certain amount of psychical energy (fantasies, fears, and feelings, for all practical purposes) to the mental representations of experiences from the psychosexual stage at which the trauma occurred. Hereafter one's development may move forward but there remains a weak spot related to the point of trauma. Stressors in adulthood, sufficiently similar to those in childhood, can lead to a regression to modes of mentation and behavior characteristic of the phase of fixation or of the phase anterior to it.

For example, the obsessive compulsive behaviors of the aforementioned Mrs. K, begun at age 5 in reaction to her oedipal and sibling rivalry, manifested themselves again at age 17 when she was confronted with adult traumata resembling the infantile ones. Quiescent for a time, they resurfaced following her discovery that her second husband was romantically involved with one of the patient's friends. Apropos the role of the immaturity of the ego in childhood traumata, Mrs. K, an attractive and highly intelligent person, lived in constant fear that she would turn out like her deaf and schizophrenic aunt, as her mother repeatedly predicted to her. In short, as a small child she did not possess the critical capacity to recognize the absurdity of the mother's sadistic prognostications. As an adult, the patient intellectually recognized the ridiculousness of the mother's prognoses, but was unable to emotionally free herself from them.

There is considerable evidence that, as Freud thought, the nature and timing of early traumata are specifically related to the form of psychopathology in adulthood—e.g., that oral trauma is important in schizophrenia, anal trauma in obsessive-compulsive disorder, and oedipal trauma in hysteria (Mrs. K, for instance, exhibited many hysterical features in addition to her obsessive-compulsive ones). Nevertheless, psychoanalysts today think in terms of the child's *development as a whole* rather than searching for a singular trauma from the oral, anal, or phallic periods that polarized the patient once and for all toward psychopathology. Although the earliest years have a determinative importance quite out of proportion to their duration, the foundation for adult character and psychopathology is laid, not by events in any given period of two or three years, but by the *total pattern* of experiences in childhood and adolescence (see, for example, Hartmann & Kris, 1945). In short, it is the *style of interaction* between the child and his parents (and significant others) throughout all the periods that is determinative. Indeed, Erikson, Levinson, and others have demonstrated that personality continues to be shaped by life history subsequent to adolescence. (If it did not, how could psychotherapy itself stand any chance of working?) Freud (1915–1917, p. 364) himself acknowledged that though "There are cases in which the whole weight of causation falls on the sexual experiences of childhood," there are other instances in which "the whole accent lies on the later conflicts and the emphasis we find in the analysis laid on the impressions of childhood appears entirely as the work of regression."

Such a concept of historical determinism is compatible with explanations that proceed backwards in short steps rather than with formulations that leap directly from, say, effects in a 40 year old to causes in a toddler. In his actual clinical work Freud more often then not proceeded in the former fashion though he was capable of speculative leaps and of the theoretical insistence upon the importance of the "deferred effect" of childhood experience.

In actuality, there is always *continuity* between the causes of childhood and their adult effects. The causes of childhood are significant because (1) of their repetitiveness throughout childhood, (2) because of the unconscious persistence of images of them and of the associated feelings and fantasies striving for expression, (3) because the environment serendipitously presents the person with current traumata resembling the infantile ones, and especially, (4) because of a sort of vicious circle (or escalation) in which the historically determined mind-set leads the individual to act in ways that elicit similar "causes" from the current environment. The thesis of historical determinism is thus a proposition of ongoing causality.

The aims and methodology of psychoanalytic treatment follow logically from the conception of psychopathology as an atavistic mode of dealing with unconscious, historically determined intrapsychic conflict. The analyst's neutrality, lack of self-disclosure, and verbal inactivity are all designed to permit the maximum possible historical, intrapsychic determination of the associations, inhibitions in associating, feelings, fantasies, parapraxes, remembering, forgetting, silences, reporting of dreams, and other behaviors that are the substance of analysis. By influencing the nature of the analysand's fears and fantasies as little as possible, the analyst allows him not merely to recollect, but to act out a truer picture of his past in the present. The patient transfers, in other words, his neurosis from the past and present outside world to the therapist's office.

The more the analyst is simply a benign and understanding listener and facilitator, the greater is the contrast between the analysand's historically grounded expectations of him and their lack of justification by the analyst's actual behavior. Being struck by this contrast, the analysand slowly becomes aware that he is living atavistically, in the past not the present. This living awareness that he has been unconsciously imposing historically determined categories of interpretation upon himself and those in his environment—that his fears and fantasies are more appropriate to a child of 3, 5, or 10 than to an adult of 30, 40, or 50—is the most transformative aspect of psychodynamic treatment.

If the balance of forces within the patient's mind has truly shifted, if his neurotically distorted view of self and world has truly been altered, then he will change as a matter of course, without any prodding or exhortation on the therapist's part. The analysand will change simply because he *no longer needs* his old unsatisfactory ways of seeking and avoiding (often simultaneously) gratification. This is because *the old dangers are no longer there* now that he is no longer living in the same reality. In other words, since all behaviors (psychopathological ones included) exist for some adaptive advantage (either within the context of the internal or external worlds, or of both), then when the intrapsychic and current realities to which they are adaptive change, then the behaviors will too. For example, when Ms. H realized that the danger she feared from intimacy with men was an historical, currently unrealistic one, then her aloof and rejecting behavior was no longer adaptive within the context of psychic reality. She no longer *had* to withdraw from men, but had increased her conscious options tremendously. When she began exercising these options her behavior no longer induced men to act toward her as she feared. Since men started responding to her differently, her old, neurotic pattern was no longer adaptive within the context of external reality as well. Her changed view of self and world resulted in changed behaviors which led to different reactions to her; these reactions in turn made it easier for her to change still further. A beneficent circle was set in motion.

The analyst and analysand are involved in studying the patient's successive interpretations of his history in order to arrive at novel perspectives and reinterpretations that will themselves influence the subsequent direction of that history; "the way one's past is seen cannot be overestimated as a force in determining the course of future events" (Novey, 1968, p. 149).

4 Critique of Psychoanalytic Causation

CRITIQUE OF PSYCHIC CAUSALITY AND HISTORICAL DETERMINISM

There are numerous epistemological and methodological issues surrounding the concepts of psychic causality and historical determinism. Since Schafer (1976, 1978) has treated many of these, my discussion pivots round a critique of his ideas.

Schafer has mounted what is far and away the most organized and telling attack on psychic causality and historical determinism. His ideas, among the most original since those of Hartmann, Kris, and Loewenstein, have stimulated some of the most vitriolic and ad hominem rhetoric in psychoanalysis. Many react to him as if he is asking them to exchange the idea of causality for that of chaos, that of intelligibility for arbitrariness and nonsense, that of behavior as impelled and constrained by unconscious and historical factors for an exaggerated pre-Freudian notion of consciousness and free will, and especially, as if he is asking psychoanalysis to abandon all pretensions to scientific status.

Although I disagree with Schafer on many points, I believe such fears of action language are, by and large, unfounded. He is asking us to substitute one set of explanatory principles for another. Indeed, he makes the remarkable claim that, unbeknownst to ourselves, we are already subscribing to his system! At the outset it must be appreciated that we are addressing the claims of two different languages, two models of conceptualizing the nature of the psychoanalytic interaction and of explaining the data derived therefrom. I can conceive of no rigorous empirical test that could rule for or against one or the other. Rather, they must be judged on logical grounds, as well as by the ineluctably personal, conscious and unconscious, standards of each of us. The criteria include internal consistency, explanatory power, parsimony, the extent to which empirically unwarranted assumptions are required, correlation with clinical methodology, and compatibility with personal and clinical experience.

Furthermore, I believe that there are few clinical implications of the matter at hand. Although Schafer writes at times as if his explanatory language does have some impact on one's mode of talking with patients—particularly in the use of verbs, adverbs, and the active voice—he generally puts forward his system as a manner of *thinking* about patients, rather than of *talking* with them. (Indeed, one must remember that Schafer argues that the analyst is already doing what action language says he should do.) I do not believe that any analyst would take issue with Schafer's (1978, p. 180) enunciation of the aims of psychoanalytic treatment: "the analysand progressively recognizes, accepts, revises, refines, and lives in terms of the idea of the self as agent."

I first enumerate the grounds of Schafer's criticisms of psychic causality before considering each of them in turn.

To begin with, he (1978, p. 74; 1976, p. 232) charges that psychic determinism is a "mechanistic" and "subhumanizing" or "dehumanizing" language of "impersonal forces": "It sets the motive or desire *apart* from the person, establishes it as the true agency of the deed, and reduces the person to being merely its vehicle or executive apparatus [my italics]" (ibid, p. 94). "By definition, the impersonal forces of psychodynamics would have to remain forever beyond the human analysand's reach; indeed, the idea of these forces establishes a world in which there could never be an analysand" (Schafer, 1976, p.

21). For motivational explications Schafer substitutes explanations in terms of the actor's (conscious or unconscious) *definition of the situation*. The agent is conceived of as always acting *in accord with* his interpretations of the world.

Second, and in tandem with this, causal locutions—such as "the thought occurred to me" and "resentment led me to do it"—promote the patient's "disavowal" of his authorship of the fantasies and feelings under consideration. Parapraxes, for example, become interpreted as "saboteurs of speech . . . themselves impersonal" (ibid, p. 43). Third, the concept of psychic causality requires us to view every behavior as somehow prepared by a prior fantasy and hence ensnares us in an infinite regress of causal explanations—looking for the fantasy behind the fantasy behind the fantasy. For Schafer, by contrast, each behavior is spontaneous and self originated. The explanatory task is not to relate them causally to one another, but to discover the rules and definition of the situation that they imply. Fourth, lacking access to controlled experimentation and mathematical precision, analysts cannot claim to identify causes in any "rigorous and nontrivial sense of the word" (Schafer, 1976, p. 205).

Fifth, he claims that causal language reflects neither the discourse of clinical work nor that of everyday life—which is one of intentionality, reasons, aims, goals, and meaning. Sixth, and related to this, he avers that deterministic language does not reflect the historical and hermeneutic nature of the psychoanalytic enterprise. The therapist is involved, not in divining causes, but in placing actions within a broader historical and unconscious context which renders them more intelligible. In this light, he (1978, p. 42) approvingly quotes Wittgenstein, "When a dream is interpreted, we might say it is fitted into a context in which it ceases to be puzzling." Clearly, Schafer, in contradistinction to Freud, is drawing a sharp distinction between motive and meaning. In the philosophical debate on reasons and causes one would have to place Schafer squarely in the camp that distinguishes sharply between the two and that disallows causal explanations of human behaviors. By this way of thinking a reason might be defined as 'a proposition in accord with which a behavior makes sense.'

Is Causal Language Mechanistic?

Let us begin by examining Schafer's contention that causal language is impersonal and treats the agent as an epiphenomenon of mechanistic forces. It should be clear from my citations of Freud that the causes of which psychoanalysis speaks are not mechanistic forces, but the agent's mental activities or purposive ideas. Such causes can be construed as impersonal only if one redefines them as such, only if one mechanizes the concept of *mental* force. Schafer assumes that the metapsychologist does mechanize this concept.

I believe that Schafer's charge that metapsychological causes are mechanistic is predicated, in part, on the errors of two of his sources—the philosophers A. I. Melden (1961) and Gilbert Ryle (1949). It is plain that Melden (1961, pp. 114–128) accepts but one definition of cause—the Humean, in which the cause must be logically independent of its effect, in the sense that the cause must be describable without reference to any aspect of its effect: "[alleged causes of an action] cannot serve further to characterize the action" (ibid, p. 88). Since motivational locutions involve reference to the effect— e.g., "desire *for*, wanting to bring about *such and such*"—they are "not genuine causes" (p. 128). "Blind," mechanistic, Humean causes, on the other hand, can only explain "happenings" (i.e., purely physical or physiological events) rather than meaningful human behaviors (ibid). The fallacy here is the acceptance of only one kind of causality—mechanistic. Melden has not refuted the principle of causation in human affairs; he has simply defined it away—by disallowing purposive or teleological features in any conception of cause.

Ryle (1949, p. 63) charges that motivational explanations of human behavior commit us to a "ghost in the machine" or mind-body ontological split—the assumption that there are "mental states and processes enjoying one sort of existence and bodily states and processes enjoying another."

> So, to say that a person pulled the trigger intentionally is to express at best a conjunctive proposition, asserting the occurrence of one act on the physical stage and another on the mental stage; and, according to most versions of the [ghost in the machine] myth, it is to express a causal proposition, asserting that the bodily act of pulling the trigger was the effect of a mental act of willing to pull the trigger (ibid).

I believe that two fallacies are committed here. First, Ryle assumes that because we speak of certain acts as mental (e.g., intentions) and others as physiological (e.g., neuromuscular innervation) we are committing outselves to a mind-body dualism at the level of ontology. He is confusing description and conceptualization of experience and behavior with statements about the ultimate nature of reality. No psychiatrist, any more than Freud himself, would deny that all that is termed "mental" arises, in some as yet inexplicable way, from the interaction between body and world. One aspect of the human organism interacting with its environment is sufficiently different that we label it "mental." We are not thereby positing a separate realm of substance—spirit—which we then oppose to another—matter; we are simply referring to the meaningful, symbolically mediated aspects of human existence, as opposed to those which are sufficiently understood in physiological terms. *There is no denial of the ontological unity of man.* There is no denial that neurobiological processes are necessary conditions for human mentation and behavior.

Second, having equated descriptive and heuristic propositions with ontological ones, Ryle then treats the statements about the *intention* of pulling the trigger and *pulling the trigger itself* as if they were propositions about two different orders of reality (the former mental, the latter physical). *In effect, it is Ryle himself who imposes the mind-body ontological split on his opponents so that he can then denounce them for it, so that he can then charge that two different orders of reality—a "ghost" and a "machine"—are being related.*

According to the theory, the workings of the body are motions of matter in space. The causes of these motions must then be either other motions of matter *or,* in the privileged case of human beings, thrusts of another kind. In some way which must forever remain a mystery, mental thrusts, which are not movements of matter in space, can cause muscles to contract. To describe a man as intentionally pulling the trigger is to state that such a mental thrust did cause the contraction of the muscles of his finger [Ryle's italics] (ibid, pp. 63–64).

What is in fact being related here? Is it spirit and matter? No. What is being related are the *symbolically mediated, meaningful aspects* of two human behaviors—"intending to pull the trigger" and "pulling it." This is *not* to deny that there are aspects of both these behaviors that are explicable in terms of neurological and neuromuscular physiology; it does not deny that the mechanical and physiological aspects of "intending to pull the trigger" and "pulling the trigger" could be causally related. It is simply that, at the psychological level, we are not concerned with the physiological explanation of these behaviors. Rather, we are preoccupied with relating the *meaningful act* of "wanting to pull the trigger of the gun pointed at Jones" to the *meaningful act* of "pulling the trigger of the gun pointed at Jones." If we also happen to be psychoanalysts, we shall be concerned with elucidating the history and determinants of the intention itself.

To recapitulate, if one inclines, as I do, toward a monist perspective on the mind-body problem (one that includes attention to interactions within the system and to properties emergent therefrom), then one views any split between 'mental' and 'somatic' as an explanatory and operational, but not an ontological, one. In such a paradigm, 'physiological' and 'psychological' are conceptualized as different explanatory and investigative approaches to a unitary set of phenomena—

each valid within the purview of the problems it addresses and the objectives it sets itself.

When we relate an intention to an observable behavior, as in the shooting of Jones, we are asserting a contiguous cause and effect relationship between the two activities in every respect—between those aspects of each behavior which are comprehended physiologically and between those aspects of each which are comprehended psychologically.

In sum, there is no need to relate a ghost to a machine because there is no ghost and there is no machine. There is only, or rather especially, a sentient and symbolizing material and energic entity—a human being—whose behaviors are unitary and causally related to one another and to a bewilderingly complex array of interacting determinants beyond our ken. (See also Searle's [1983, pp. 262–272] refutation of the "ghost in the machine" argument, in some respects similar to my own.)

Returning to Schafer, I concur with John Gach (personal communication) that Schafer's charge that metapsychological causal concepts are mechanistic and "thing-like" is based, in part, on the mistaken assumption that the referents of nominatives are always taken to be more statically material than those of verbs (whose referents are active). In fact, nouns can refer to activities, ongoing processes, conflict, and dynamic equilibria quite as much as can verbs. In other words, Schafer seems to assume that, because the analyst generally designates motives with nominatives and more often speaks of fantasies than fantasizing, the analyst must be conceiving of these motives as monolithic substances or entities.

I also believe that Schafer foreshortens the concept of psychic determinism in yet another way—by defining it as a theorem of causes acting upon the agent from without. In actuality, the causation whereof psychoanalysis speaks is, as I demonstrate later, intersectional, not transeunt (external). The dynamic concept takes account of the determinative role of the environment, but understands that the proximate cause of the behavior is always immanent to the actor himself. At no point in treatment, unless analysand or analyst are psychotic, does either conceptualize the patient's motives as overtaking him from outside. Both recognize that the analysand's immediate causes are his own mental activities. That which his motives are conceptualized as being apart from is his *center of consciousness*. It is the relationship between his unconscious mental processes and this center of consciousness that is the deterministic one. In other words, the cause-effect relationship is between one aspect (unconsciousness) of the agent's mental functioning and another (consciousness). Schafer splits off the motive from the agent and then accuses the metapsychologist of having done so.

That the psychoanalytic concept of causation is not mechanistic and transeunt undermines Schafer's criticism of the clinical implications of causal locutions. Freud, for example, could speak of dreams as determined and still acknowledge the dreamer's "responsibility" for them. He could do so precisely because he recognized that the *dreamer,* with his particular history and preoccupations, is the *cause* of his dream. Similarly, he could view the recurrent and troublesome situations confronting "fate neurotics" as both "determined by early infantile influences" and "arranged by themselves" (Freud, 1920a, p. 21). In short, the psychoanalytic concept of determinism is not opposed to a recognition of the autonomy of the agent and his active authorship of his behavior. It is opposed only to the naive notion that the actor is invariably *consciously* self determining.

Intersectional Causation

Nevertheless, although I disagree with Schafer's first two criticisms, I believe he is responding to at least one real difficulty in the concept of psychic causality—to wit, the often elliptical nature of causal propositions. Such explanations are sometimes couched in a way that does not do justice to the intricate interactions among the causes involved. Having demonstrated this earlier with examples from academic history, let me exemplify it with a clinical vignette.

Mr. D's father died on Monday. Two days later he attempted suicide. What do we mean when we say that the former event precipitated the latter? Do we mean that it caused it in approximately the way a gamma ray transforms a molecule? Of course not. This causal statement is a shorthand notation that omits reference to a complex array of *interacting* determinants. A more complete causal explanation would read as follows:

> Mr. D. had been ignored and intimidated by his well-known and highly successful father throughout childhood. He reacted to this by developing powerful fantasies of murdering and surpassing the father. At times he acted so obnoxiously that he actually aggravated the father's withdrawal and abusiveness. Eventually, because he feared his father's retaliation and the condemnation of his own conscience, he repressed these hostile fantasies. However, he continued to entertain them unconsciously and substitutively expressed them by entering into and rising in his father's profession. When the combination of his own success and his father's death fulfilled his unconscious wishes, Mr. D. reacted with an inordinate (unconscious) sense of guilt. In other words, *his* unconscious conflicts over patricidal aggression (themselves the effect of his early relationship with his father) *caused* him to misinterpret his father's death as a murder and himself as the murderer. He then punished himself as if he had actually committed this crime.

This was only one of many motives for his self destructiveness. My point is that the *cause* of the self-punitive fantasy that itself determined his suicidal behavior lay neither in the external event (the father's death) purely nor in the personality structure of the patient purely. Rather, the cause lay at the *intersection* of Mr. D's historically determined desires, fears, and interpretations with the external event itself. To belabor the obvious, the causal explanation of Mr. D's behavior asserts that "but for the death of the father and but for Mr. D's personality structure the behavior to be explained would not have occurred." I can conceive of no manner in which one could intelligibly explain the connection between the father's death and Mr. D's suicide attempt noncausally. Nor can I conceive of any way to relate the history of Mr. D's interaction with his father to Mr. D's father conflict noncausally. The suicide attempt was in every sense *caused* by the interaction between an event in external reality and the actor's neurotically determined misapprehension of it.[1] In other cases, such as with "fate neurotics," we have to deal, not merely with a neurotically determined misinterpretation of "precipitating" events, but with an active engineering of them.

In this context, Schafer is correct to remind us of the crucial role of the agent's interpretation of his situation, for this interpretation is the proximal cause of his behavior. Nevertheless, this interpretation does not arise de novo. It is itself determined by the current situation, the agent's unconscious fantasies, and the history of his prior interactions with significant others. In short, I argue that what is inadequate is not the concept of causation itself, but rather a unilinear view of causation. What is required is an interactional concept of

---

[1]This vignette also provides support for my prior speculation (Chapter 3, note 10) that aspects of symbolically mediated behaviors may forever defy reduction to physiological models. How could one ever adequately grasp the nature of the causal nexus between the father's death and Mr. D.'s self-destructiveness with purely physiological and physical concepts? All the latter could do is account for the physics and physiology of Mr. D.'s apprehension of one man's death and the resultant suicide attempt. But it is the symbolic dimension (i.e., the unconscious, historically determined interpretation) that made Mr. D.'s apprehension of *this particular death*— rather than his apprehension of countless others over the years— causally decisive. In other words, even if one had complete understanding of the physical and physiological aspects of Mr. D.'s interpretation of the death and of his self destructive response, one would still need to invoke the symbolic dimension to exhaustively explain the causal connection. Omitting psychological concepts here would be as flagrant an error as attempting to reduce the neurophysiology of the process entirely to physics.

multi-causation, with points of mutual feedback all along the way. I believe, furthermore, that this concept of causation is implicit in Freud's clinical formulations themselves (see, for example, Freud 1909a, pp. 198–199, and the Wolf Man case history, which illustrates brilliantly the mutually determinative interaction between the Wolf Man's fantasies and external reality; recall also Hartmann's thinking about the inner world and the developmental psychology of Erikson [1963], Spitz [1965], and Thomas and Chess [1977]). Consider, in this regard, Freud's (1938, pp. 184–185) aforementioned concept of infantile trauma, where the etiological factor is clearly placed at the interface between the external stimulus and the state of the psychic apparatus (i.e., its immaturity). Indeed, as early as 1896 Freud (p. 217) invoked an intersectional concept of causality to explain the apparently "abnormal, exaggerated, hysterical reaction to psychical stimuli": "It is not the latest slight—which, in itself, is minimal—that produces the fit of crying, the outburst of despair or the attempt at suicide, in disregard of the axiom that an effect must be proportionate to its cause; the small slight of the present moment has aroused and set working the memories of very many, more intense, earlier slights, behind all of which there lies in addition the memory of a serious slight in childhood which has never been overcome."

An intersectional model of causation holds, not merely for situations of psychopathological interaction with one's fellows, but for *perception and interpersonal relations and human communication in general*. This is true whether one is engaged in the most refined Socratic dialogue or reacting to the crassest insult from another. If, in the case of the former, we are led to adopt a novel position because of the superior logic of our partner, then he will be said to have given us good "reason" to do so; the cause lies at the intersection of his argument and our understanding. In regard to the latter, we can predict that the insult will cause (conscious or unconscious) anger in the recipient, but the final reaction—for example, fearful withdrawal, guilt feelings, anxiety, depression, aggressiveness, or self-destructiveness—will depend on the dynamics of the target. One man's erection, another's anxiety, and a third's guilt feelings in response to the lingering glance of a beautiful woman are all instances of intersectional causation, as are those subliminal, nonverbal communications that play so important a role in our conscious, preconscious, and unconscious reactions to others. A strain from a Mozart sonata may well elicit certain emotions common to the audience as a whole, but the specific constellation of affects and associations evoked will differ from person to person, according to the particular history and constitution of each.

The intersectional model also holds, of course, for the transactions between analyst and analysand. Mr. G's (Kohut, 1971, p. 93) precipitate haughty aloofness was caused by the interaction between Kohut's unwontedly unempathic and defensive tone when announcing his forthcoming absence and the patient's historically determined narcissistic psychopathology. But the effect of even the most empathic and clinically appropriate intervention (or nonintervention) is a function of its interaction with the personality structure of the patient; it is a truism that the same therapeutic comment or maneuver with two different patients may mean two quite different things to them—depending on the particular complexes and historically-constitutionally determined perceptual-interpretive set of each.

The same applies to the psychoanalytic concept of historical determinism. The causation here is an *interactive* and *mediate* one. It is the former in that: the infant is impinged upon by the behavior of his parents who, in every sense of the word, can be said to "shape" his nascent affective-conative-perceptual set; but they shape it in interaction with his idiosyncratic constitutional endowment; furthermore, the infant's innate activity level, emotional expressiveness, and so forth impinge upon the parents and to some extent shape their behavior toward, and expectations of, the infant.

After the first few months of life, the infant himself is developing, from the interaction between his neurobiological maturation and the parents' behavior, his own inner world and interpretive style. Henceforth, the parents impinge upon him through his psychological inner world; the infant's personality structure is then determined not by the parents' behavior per se, but by the impact of that behavior on his conative-interpretive set. This is what I mean by "mediate" determinism. The infant is thus not passively and mechanically buffeted about by his determinants, but "reaches out and grasps them" with his own mental set. Freud's (1930) assertion that the degree of superego aggressiveness is determined, not merely by the parent's aggressiveness, but by the child's as well, is a case in point, as is Kernberg's (1975) emphasis on the role of the child's affective state in determining how he perceives his parents. The concept of identification is an instance of mediate and interactive determinism. The child's identifications are not merely the passive effects of the parent's behavior. Identification is the *child's activity;* his mental set plays a role in determining not only whom he most identifies with but how he perceives them. (Indeed, the therapist's empathizing itself must be understood, like identification in general, as a manifestation of intersectional causation.) Furthermore, we are at times confronted with the development of symptomatic, defensive, or characterological modes for which it is not easy to discern a model in the child's environment—in which case we must acknowledge that the individual is capable of exercising creativity in the "choice" and construction of compromise formations. It is well known that the children of sexually permissive and provocative parents can develop, in direct contrast to their parental models, excessively puritanical superegos in order to ward off supercharged sexual and parenticidal fantasies. The child is part of a social structure in which he enacts a crucial role from the outset.

In short, by historical determinism we do not mean that one's history somehow sits outside one and determines him. We mean, rather, that he remains subject to a set of preoccupations, conflicts, and a self-world view formulated through his early interactions with others. His history thus lives on insofar as his personality structure is a precipitate of it; it persists in his *style* of interpretation and coping, as much as in specific conscious and unconscious memories and fantasies. Although aspects of one's personality structure continue to develop throughout adulthood and although one continues to make (determinate) choices that powerfully influence one's subsequent life course, the character structure (cognitive and affective style, pattern of compromise formations, and so forth) laid down at the close of childhood provides a direction for, and a range of limitations and possibilities to, subsequent behaviors, choices, and personality change.

Let me reemphasize that the intersectional approach to causation does not minimize the intrapsychic dimension or the capacity of the individual for self-initiated and self propagating behavior; rather it includes the latter within its purview, which is immanent, as much as transeunt. It is not a simple 'environmental stimulus-organismic response' model. Even when a person is responding to overwhelming environmental stimuli, one can choose to look at the resultant behavior from either side of the interaction. In other words, what we term the 'stimulus' is as much a function of the individual's perceptual-interpretive activity as of the matter and energy in his environment. From the outside we see an event impinging upon him, but from the inside we see his mental set impinging upon the event. Furthermore, the interactions whereof I speak are not limited to those between the individual and his environment—though such interactions are necessary for maintaining intact reality testing and self-concept—but refer also to those *within* the personality structure. In this regard, the mental activity of the contemplative seated atop his mountain is as much a manifestation of intersectional causation as that of his gregarious brother on the plain. Ego psychology has taught us that many of the functions which are interacting within the psyche are themselves the precipitate of prior interactions between psyche and world.

The intersectional aspect of causation in human behavior does not differentiate it from causality in the purely physical and biological realms. The effect, for example, of the addition of one chemical reagent to another depends on the properties of both compounds as they interact with one another. The "cause" of any infectious disease lies at the interface between the characteristics of the host and of the intruding organism.

Finally, the mediate and intersectional concept of historical determinism and psychic causality vitiates the false charge that psychoanalytic treatment is a hunt for victims and victimizers and an instrument for diminishing one's sense of personal responsibility for whence he comes and whither he is going.

Causation and Infinite Regress

Let us continue to address Schafer's criticisms of determinism before actually examining his alternative explanatory principles and comparing them to causal ones. His third criticism is that psychic causality commits one to an infinite regress of causal explanations. But it is difficult to see why causal formulations commit the psychoanalyst (or the historian, for that matter) to an infinite regress any more than they do the physical or biological scientist. The analyst simply acknowledges—unless, like Freud, he makes an instinctivist assumption—that he is uninformed on questions of ultimate causality. He stops with asserting that conscious and unconscious affect-laden fantasies somehow arise, from the inextricable interaction between body and world, and that these fantasies determine our behavior. I believe, in any event, that questions of ultimate causality are unanswerable and ill-conceived because of the circular interaction of events, feeding into one another at points all along the way.

The Identification and Nature of Causes

Schafer's fourth accusation, that psychoanalysts cannot identify causes in any "rigorous" sense and hence should forsake a concept of cause, is perhaps his most serious challenge. It is indeed true that the analyst (like the historian), because of the nature of his subject matter, cannot engage in the controlled, prospective experimentation that can enable one to make causal statements of such high statistical probability that, for all practical purposes, one can speak of discerning causes themselves. He cannot do this because many of the events to be explained have already transpired and are irreproducible, because the cause of a person's behavior is never in the external situation purely but in the intersection between the external conditions and his interpretations and fantasies, and because a certain amount of the analyst's evidence comes from the patient's impact upon the analyst's own subjective state. This ensures that no two situations are ever identical for any two patients—or even for any one patient!—and that there is no means of controlling for intrapsychic fantasies and the patient's interpretation of the situation (something behaviorists have never understood). Dynamic psychiatrists, like historians, encounter patterns, parallels, sequences, and correlations with varying degrees of regularity; from these they make retrospective *causal inferences*—as exemplified in the following vignettes, the first two from psychodynamic treatments, the third from intellectual history.

Ms. D. presented with the chief complaint of "accident proneness," the most recent episode of which began shortly after her boy friend's drowning. Anamnesis revealed that prior adult episodes followed broken relationships and that childhood accidents occurred during her parents' marital separations and after their eventual divorce. From the repetitive correlation between loss and accidents the therapist posited a causal connection between a complex of ideas and feelings associated with losses and the patient's accidents—an hypothesis which he then tested against the patient's subsequent verbalizations, behaviors, and recollections. After some months of therapy, the accident proneness, which had in the meantime subsided, resurrected itself in connection with the patient's fear that the therapist might leave her. It ceased when the patient realized her accidents had been a self destructive way of dealing with anger aroused by losses and rejections and a bid for the sort of attention she received as a child only when sick or injured.

In another patient, his most moderate, implied criticism of the parents would be consistently followed by a barrage of self castigation relating to other matters. From these repetitive connections the therapist posited a causal relation. The patient himself had been unconscious of this pattern. When it was pointed out to him he became conscious of hitherto repressed anger and guilt feelings vis-à-vis the parents. The self castigation had been motivated by his unconscious sense of guilt.

The intellectual historian encountered striking similarities in the form and content of some passages from Nietzsche's *Human, All Too Human* and Freud's *Interpretation of Dreams*. He hypothesized a causal connection and examined the evidence. He discovered that Freud made laudatory comments about Nietzsche, that Freud demonstrated embarrassment at Nietzsche's anticipations of psychoanalysis, and that at 17 he wrote a Rumanian friend that he had read all Nietzsche had written up to that point (the relevant text had been published by that time).

These hypotheses are not experimentally confirmed, but they are rendered plausible by the multiplication of several lines of evidence.

Freud himself, though generally unappreciative of the epistemological issues under consideration, occasionally acknowledged them. He confessed, for example, that the analyst can never know with certainty whether the patient's waking associations to a dream are really recollections of the antecedent causal fantasies or whether they arise de novo, after the fact of the dream itself (Freud, 1900, pp. 280, 311). This, it seems, is an admission of methodological weakness, one which is not fully obviated by Freud's (p. 311) contention that any novel associations are "only set up between thoughts which were already linked in some other way in the dream thoughts."[2]

---

[2]Wittgenstein (1967, pp. 50–51) opposed Freud's contention that the free association method leads to reliable information about the

Elsewhere Freud admitted that, in practice, the psycho-analyst can speak of "determinism" only retrospectively; the same holds true, of course, for the historian:

> So long as we trace the final development from its outcome *backwards,* the chain of events appears continuous, and we have gained an insight which is completely satisfactory or even exhaustive. But if we proceed the reverse way, if we start with the premises inferred from the analysis and try to follow these up to the final result, then we no longer get the impression of an inevitable sequence of events which could not have been otherwise determined. We notice at once that there might have been another result, and that we might have been just as well able to understand and *explain* the latter . . . in other words, from a knowledge of the premises one could not have foretold the nature of the result [my italics] (Freud, 1920b, p. 167).

---

determinants of the dream, although he nevertheless believed it could, perhaps, give one useful information about the dreamer himself: "The fact is that whenever you are preoccupied with something, with some trouble or with some problem which is a big thing in your life—as sex is, for instance—then no matter what you start from, the associations will lead finally and inevitably back to that same theme. Freud remarks on how, after the analysis of it, the dream appears so very logical. And of course it does. You could start with any of the objects on this table—which certainly are not put there through your dream activity—and you could find that they were all connected in a pattern like that; and the pattern would be logical in the same way. One may be able to discern certain thoughts about oneself by this sort of free association, but it does not explain why the dream occurred." See also Rieff's (1979, pp. 113–117) cogent comments on the matter. I would argue that, whether or not they lead one to the determinants of the dream, the associations are themselves determined by the conscious and unconscious complexes of the dreamer and hence give us valuable information about them. In short, the same personality structure that determined the dream determines the associations.

What this brings us to is the acknowledgment that psychic causality is in the nature of an axiom or scientific assumption. What I mean is that the hypothesis of the *omni*-causality, and hence (at least potential) omni-intelligibility, of human behavior must *first* be entertained before one would undertake the detailed and laborious clinico-historical investigations that in turn lend credence to the axiom. Dynamic psychiatrists, from their personal analyses and day-to-day work with patients, are so accustomed to the fruitfulness of this explanatory principle, and the abundance of thematic and contextual evidence for it, that they tend to forget that before Freud it was not taken for granted and that there are many today (psychiatrists among them) who do not subscribe to it.

One might counter that this is not the case, that the layperson's possession, in day-to-day interaction with his fellows, of a rough and ready notion of psychic causality proves that the concept is either purely empirical or a self-evident given. To do so, however, would be to overlook crucial differences between the everyday notion and the psychoanalytic one. The former admits of many gaps and exceptions and does not usually take account of unconscious motives; it leaves room for "chance," "meaninglessness," "accident," "arbitrariness," and the numerous devices with which people explain their parapraxes, amnesias, and so forth. The psychoanalytic concept, by contrast, is one of *exceptionless* causation in the behavioral sphere; if it were self-evident it would not have required a genius like Freud to alert us to it. Furthermore, we have seen that Freud's conceptualization itself was partly conditioned by a priori elements, that it was not purely the outcome of empiricism.

Nor can it be argued that one can be brought to the principle of exceptionless psychical causality merely through inspecting the evidence of his free associations, with no prior knowledge of the principle itself. This is manifestly *not* what occurs to the analysand in the course of his treatment; it is not that he enters analysis without a concept of ubiquitous psychic causality and, on the sheer strength of the evidence, leaves treatment with it. It is rather that he is brought to a working appreciation of the concept through the analyst's (and eventually his own) organization and interpretation of his life history in the light of this principle. Thus, I am not talking about "blind faith," but adherence to a principle which, once entertained, proves its utility and plausibility through its interaction with the data.[3]

---

[3]The implicit, everyday notion of psychic causality appears to be based upon relatively direct and immediate experiences of causation (à la Searle [1983]) and on Humean inferences from priority, regular conjunction, and contiguity. Examples of the former include: (a) I am thirsty and reach for a drink; (b) I smile in the face of a compliment; (c) I call my friend's name and he greets me; (d) my acquaintance mentions her recently deceased mother and then tears; and (e) I follow an intelligible line of communication from another. Although these appear to involve relatively direct and immediate experiences of causality I contend that the causal apprehensions in at least instances (c) through (e) also comprise Humean elements, as well as extrapolations from my own experience—both as one who causes and one who can be affected (i.e., empathy). Furthermore, although such direct "apprehensions" are often reliable they are not always so. My friend may have just caught sight of the person behind me and be greeting him or my acquaintance may be tearing secondary to a stab of pain from her dental abscess. Even in the case of (b) I certainly cannot claim direct awareness of all the psychobiological causes—perhaps even of the most effective ones—in me that intervene between the friend's compliment and my smile. Every analyst is aware of how misleading, when tested against subsequent patterns in the patient's behavior, "apprehensions" or "intuitions" of singular cause and effect relationships can sometimes be.

An example of Humean causal reasoning in everyday life would be the observation of regularities of conjunction between certain situations and behaviors in others or oneself and making causal inferences and low level predictions therefrom. (It is probable that a good deal of what Searle takes for direct experience of causation is actually the almost instantaneous drawing of such inferences.) From years of such cumulative experiences with oneself and others,

Since the psychoanalyst cannot go back in time and resurrect the actual conditions of origin—the situation, patient's state of mind, and so forth—of a symptom or dream, he must make the assumption, based on the psychoanalytic model of mind, that the patient's associations are in fact leading one to the antecedent causal fantasies. The closest approximation to experimental support for psychic causality is perhaps the phenomenon of post hypnotic suggestion—where one can observe the "implantation" of the unconscious fantasy and the subsequent behavior issuing therefrom.

Nevertheless, in its limitation to causal *inferences* psychoanalysis is not alone among the sciences. As previously mentioned, not all natural sciences utilize predominantly experimental methods. Some, such as paleontology, operate with a procedure that is historical and reconstructive, and others, such as ethology, with naturalistic observation. However, simply because they cannot formulate causal explanations with experimental degrees of probability, these sciences do not therefore abandon the idea of cause itself! Similarly, most physicists, unlike Heisenberg, do not conclude from our in-

---

one forms rough generalizations about what, in certain situations, he is likely to expect from himself and others and they from him. In short, I do not argue that the analyst does not utilize relatively direct causal experiences and apprehensions as much as (or more than) the layperson. Rather, I contend that the principle of *universal* psychical determinism is not empirical in the Searlian sense and that the unconscious, historical causes with which the analyst is mostly concerned are not directly apprehensible, but only inferable.

Again, as mentioned in Chapter 3, the psychoanalyst, like the historian, is engaged, not in identifying causes, but in constructing causal explanations. See Kohut's (1971, pp. 254–255 fn) distinction between the "genetic approach" of psychoanalysis and the "etiological approach" of experimental and developmental psychology. Nevertheless, this distinction can be overemphasized, for the experimentalist, like the analyst, *is still drawing causal inferences from patterns and correlations*—even if the correlations be more numerous and the variables better controlled.

ability to establish both the position and momentum of subatomic particles that their behavior is therefore not determined; rather, they draw conclusions about the adequacy of our instruments and the nature of the observational conditions, while retaining the principle of universal causation.

In its need to entertain a certain number of axioms, psychoanalysis is no different from mathematics and other scientific endeavors. The psychoanalyst, like every scientist, should not be embarrassed to acknowledge assumptions that cannot be experimentally proved. He should simply make as few as possible; they should accord with the rational canons of logic and the structure of science; they should square with, and coherently organize and explain the data; they should bear fruit in reality, and the psychoanalyst should honestly acknowledge where they occur.[4]

The point of contention is whether Schafer's explanatory schema escapes Occam's razor any more than does causal analysis. Schafer claims to have substituted "redescription" for causal explanation, thereby obviating the need to posit experimentally unprovable antecedent motives. "Redescriptions" are restatements of "particular actions and their corresponding situations so as to make the events in question more comprehensible to the questioner" (Schafer, 1976, p. 203). For Schafer, "reasons" are the content of these redescriptions (p.

---

[4]With some of his dreams and those of his patients (and occasionally with certain of his analysand's symptomatic behaviors) Freud's conviction in psychic determinism leads him to attempt causal explanations of virtually every item and aspect of the dream or behavior—down to the minutest detail regarding choice of word, symbol, and so forth. While Freud was correct, in principle, to do so, this drive to complete understanding at times involved him in formulations that seem a bit too intricate, clever, and contrived (that approximate the 'secondary elaboration' of the dream work itself). In most instances analysts must rest content with elucidating (some of) the probable causes of molar items of behavior—recurrent symptoms, lifelong patterns of action-reaction, typical modes of viewing the self and world, and so forth.

204). Consider Schafer's (ibid) redescription of a man's impotence:

> Unconsciously, he viewed intercourse as a filthy and destructive invasion of his mother's womb, and still unconsciously, he anticipated that he would react in a most painfully guilty and self-destructive way to his performing that action; not being in a predominantly genital sexual situation and intimate personal relationship, and not being engaged in sexual actions in a predominantly unthreatened, exciting, and pleasurable mode, he did not perform potently. That is why. These are his reasons.

Does that explanation in fact resort to fewer axiomatic assumptions than a causal one? I think not. One is still explaining actions *which have already transpired.* Even if one refers to the relationship between this man's Oedipus complex and his impotence "descriptively," rather than causally, how is one to prove, "rigorously and nontrivially," that this meaning was in fact present in each prior incident of sexual dysfunction, that the interpretation is not being retroactively imposed on the behavior? (If one counters that it makes no difference, that the analyst's and analysand's *present* construction or interpretation of his history is all that matters, he has abrogated the principle of historical objectivity and thereby gravely weakened the claim for psychoanalysis to be taken seriously epistemologically.) The patient's response to this interpretation and his subsequent associations may seem to bear it out; his characterological style, symptomatic acts, conversational themes, transferential behaviors, and reams of historical material may converge to support this formulation. But how is this different from the sort of evidence for causal propositions? Either way one is making a *retrospective inference about unconscious mental activity.* In short, I do not believe that Schafer's redescriptions are any more parsimonious than causal propositions. (See footnote 21.)

Furthermore, to recouch a causal explanation in descriptive terms does not prove the causal explanation invalid. Cannot any causal explanation in science be restated as a description? Indeed, insofar as causal propositions explain *how* something came about, are they not also descriptions?

Next, let us turn to Schafer's explanation of free associations, and then examine the causal explication of these most central of all analytic phenomena.

For Schafer, free associations are "creative actions which state or imply definition of self and other in relationship." Like all "actions," each is said to be *spontaneous and self-originated, and hence underived from mental events antecedent to it.* Rather, they are explained, not by their connections with one another, but as *rule following behaviors.* From the form and content of the associations, the analyst "makes surmises about the rules the analysand is following, the situations that are implied by these rules, and the conflictual historical antecedents and prototypes that may be the background of the conduct" (Schafer, 1978, p. 52). Examples of such rules would be (p. 55): "What is forbidden to think? What must one do to atone sufficiently? What is the way to get gratification in disguise, and why that disguise, and why any disguise? What is to be renounced and why and since when?" It is Schafer's (ibid) presupposition—that "however they [patients] act, they cannot do otherwise than perform ruled actions"—that seemingly allows him to ignore the causal question. In other words, the causal hinge is abandoned for 'behaving *in accord with* rules which imply a certain definition of situation.' Associations become simply "the things that a person would say or think in that situation, whatever it is" (p. 51).

Several queries are in order here. To begin with, it is obvious that Schafer is positing a relationship of direction and constraint between rules and actions. Does "in accord with" adequately express the nature of this direction and constraint or is it merely a euphemism for "determined by"? Similarly, how is one to relate both the actor's definition of his situation and the "conflictual historical antecedents and prototypes" (p. 52) to the rules other than deterministically. Schafer (ibid) does it with the words "situations that are implied by the rules" and "background." Again, are these phrases genuine alternatives to determinism or euphemisms for it? Even if "rule following," "in accord with," and "definition of the situation implied by" are genuinely different locutions from causal ones, they still require the analyst to make inferences quite as much as do deterministic propositions.

Furthermore, whence come the rules? Are they learned from interaction with one's parents? If so, could we not speak of them as simply another manifestation of historical determinism? Are they resultants of cognitive structures of the mind, themselves presumably based on underlying cerebral configurations? If so, then are they not biologically and genically determined?

If Schafer's explication of free association does not appear to be a viable alternative to causation, this does not mean that there are not difficulties in the latter. For example, no one has ever explained precisely how it is that one idea in a chain of associations elicits another. Is the paradigm that of one billiard ball banging against another or of our everyday experience of "making things happen" in our environment—or neither of these? Is the causal nexus not so much between the thoughts themselves as between an overriding set of purposive ideas and the associations?[5] Might there not be several species of causation involved, ranging from the more teleological—for example, when one is following one's train of thought to the end of recovering the memory of a misplaced object—to the more mechanistic—for example, clang associations or the sudden emergence of a long repressed idea or affect in response to an immediate sensory stimulus from the environment? Are not the causal relations between psychical events often more like, as Freud (1896b, pp. 196–197) himself opined, a tangled skein than a unilinear chain?: "The chain of associations always has more than two links; and the traumatic scenes do not form a simple row, like a string of pearls,

---

[5]More probably the cause and effect relationship between the items in a chain of associations must be understood as existing between the sequential 'total psychobiological activity states' of the individual, of which each idea is but one aspect.

but ramify and are interconnected like genealogical trees, so that in any new experience two or more earlier ones come into operation as memories."

Be that as it may, our inability to elucidate the precise nature of the causal linch pin gives us no warrant to abandon causality. What physicist or biologist can claim to have divined the nature of the causal linkages he studies? Like Hume, we are left with the recognition that causes are statements about regularity and succession; about the exact nature of this succession most scientists and philosophers remain agnostic. I believe the analyst must too.

Continuing our examination of psychic causality, let us move on to Schafer's explication of parapraxes, long considered among the strongest evidence for psychic determinism. For Schafer (1978, p. 56), to elucidate a parapraxis is "to define the analysand's situation in such a way that the action of saying the word makes more sense than can be established in any other way." It is assumed that the parapraxis, or "word surprise," is an action in accord with the analysand's sudden change in definition of the analytic situation. While Schafer is no doubt correct that understanding the analysand's interpretation of the situation is crucial to elucidating the parapraxis, is not the patient's interpretation itself *determined* by his desire, fear, and history? Is not this equally true of Schafer's patient's unconscious interpretation of intercourse as an invasion of his mother's womb? Examples from Freud (1901, p. 110) include the childless woman whose desire for children caused her to constantly misread "storks" for "stocks" and Freud himself whose antiquarian interests continually led him to misread "antiquities" on shop signs bearing the slightest resemblance to this word. Similarly, Mr. D's misapprehension, while driving to my office, of a dark station wagon as a hearse and his subsequent fantasy that I had taken ill and died were determined by (unconscious patricidal) wishes.

Furthermore, why can one not call the relationship between the interpretation and the subsequent behavior a causal one? "In accord with" versus "caused by" remains the

crux. Both explanatory models force us to make certain experimentally unprovable hypotheses about the patient's unconscious state of mind prior to, and during, the behavior to be
explained.

Schafer (1978, p. 56) contrasts his method of elucidating the
parapraxis—"set[ting] up the word-surprise as a curious text,
and ask[ing] how this text came to be written"—as an "historical," as opposed to a causal, approach. This argument rests on
the presupposition that causal explanations are not compatible with the historical enterprise—a position that, as we have
seen, most historians do not endorse. Furthermore, although
exegetes speak of the "meanings," rather than the "causes," of
their texts, they must often concern themselves with the historical and cultural determinants of their author's style and
thoughts—and there is a sense in which the author's ideas
and desires can be said to determine his text.

Historical Determinism

Turning now from psychic causality to the overlapping concept of historical determinism, we shall examine Schafer's
claim to have provided a superior alternative to the latter. Let
us permit Schafer to speak at length:

> Thinking historically, we do not say an agent is causally moti-
> vated to perform some action by all the relevant factors in the
> historical background of that action. We say that *this* agent did
> *that* and perhaps gave or could have given *these* reasons for
> doing so, while another observer might suggest other reasons
> for it. But, speaking of the historical factors that we consider
> relevant to the event, we do not designate them the *causes* of
> the agent's action; we use them to define the action, say, as a
> belated and displaced revenge on a younger sibling. . . . In per-
> forming a certain action, the analysand might or might not
> have been thinking of some life-historical conflict consciously
> or even unconsciously, and yet the analyst may legitimately
> claim that the conflict of long standing is an important fea-
> ture . . . in the sense that *the action will remain unintelligible*

or less intelligible if one does not suppose something of that sort [last italics mine] (Schafer, 1978, pp. 56–58).

The crucial question becomes: Is the locution "I interpret, and act in accord with, my history" a noncausal one? Again, can we express the relationship of *constraint* and *direction* between one's past experience and one's present self-world view and behavior, or the relationship between desire and interpretation, nondeterministically? For example, Schafer (1978, p. 23) speaks of the "archaic principles and categories that characterize the analysand's current construction of experience" as "historically founded." What is the difference between being *"historically founded"* and *"historically determined?"* Schafer (ibid, p. 12) himself lapses into causal language when talking about the regularities in childhood development: "Psychoanalysts . . . can say a lot about the conditions or *causes* of different types of development [my italics]"!

I believe that Schafer has wound up in a dilemma similar to that of existentialist writers such as Binswanger and Merleau-Ponty, who wish to avoid deterministic propositions while preserving the ordering and connecting principles that only determinism can supply:

It is one of the most impressive achievements of existential analysis to have shown that even in the realm of subjectivity nothing is left to chance, but that a certain organized structure can be recognized from which each word, each idea, drawing, acting, or gesture receives its particular imprint. . . . It is always this same world-design which confronts us in a patient's spontaneous verbal manifestations, in the systematic explanation of his Rorschach and word association responses, in his drawings, and also, frequently, in his dreams (Binswanger, 1958, p. 202).

The childhood memory which provides the key to a dream and the traumatic event which provides the key to an attitude (and which analysis succeeds in laying bare) are not therefore the *causes* of the dream or of the behavior. They are the means for the analyst of understanding a present structure or attitude (Merleau-Ponty, 1963, p. 178).

How are we to explain nondeterministically the regularly encountered relationships between certain habitual modes of interaction between parents and children, on the one hand, and certain adult character structures and psychopathological constellations, on the other? To continually relate everything to the individual's definition of, and action upon, his situation does no justice to the small child's vulnerability to his environment and biology and to his lack of conscious choice in such matters as how he comes to view himself, his world, and his desires. What are constructs such as the Oedipus complex if not causal propositions about what universally results from the interaction between enduring crosscultural aspects of social structure (i.e., the nuclear family) and the psychobiological endowment of the human infant. If psychoanalysis abandons the concept of determinism, must it not also relinquish its claims to be a nomothetic science demonstrating certain universalities in human development and certain regularities between antecedent conditions and subsequent behaviors?

Linguistic and Methodological Considerations

Now I shall turn to Schafer's fifth and sixth criticisms—that the metapsychological language of dynamics reflects neither the discourse of patient or analyst nor the analyst's methodology itself. It is on these grounds that he claims to have recovered the "native tongue" of psychoanalysis.

Schafer charges that people view themselves as whole and intentional agents who desire and act in accord with their view of the situation; they do not conceptualize themselves as caused or motivated. Having already refuted Schafer's charge that motives are "impersonal" and transeunt, his argument loses much of its force. I believe it is vulnerable on other grounds as well.

In fact, people do commonly experience and speak of themselves as unitary and volitional agents, as interpreters and world-makers. However—and psychoanalysts know this better than anyone—they also experience and speak of themselves as: "losing control" of their conscious volition and ability to refrain from certain behaviors; becoming overpowered by strong affect "for no reason"; repetitively, and against their conscious desires and better judgment, enacting maladaptive patterns of behavior; making, despite every conscious intention otherwise, embarrassing parapraxes; suffering from lapses of attention and forgetting important items; being "gripped" by painful or disabling symptoms; blocking on a train of thought; having thoughts "occur" to them; being "fragmented" rather than whole.

Schafer acknowledges such experiences and expressions, while redefining them as "disclaimed actions," that is, behaviors for which one disowns responsibility for originating. What, if anything, is actually being disclaimed here? It is not, unless the patient is psychotic, the authorship of the behavior itself. It is, rather, the motivating fantasy that is being unconsciously "disclaimed" or, as I prefer, "repressed."

In contrast to Schafer, I view patient's causal locutions as accurate renditions of their phenomenology and, consequently, as one of the strongest arguments *for* the necessity of motivational concepts. What they are experiencing and describing is, of course, conscious awareness of the derivatives of unconscious motives (each derivative being a mini-compromise formation) and of discontinuities in conscious mentation *caused* by the interaction between these motives. In this respect, the patient is not so much disclaiming any actions as expressing what it feels like when (unconscious) "disclaiming" fails—i.e., the return of the repressed or its derivatives. These unconscious motives are *both* the patient's mental activities and the causes of the conscious phenomenology he is describing. In theory-building such experiences and locutions deserve as much credence as those of secondary process mentation on which Schafer seems to rely.

Schafer charges that analysts are involved in thematic analyses, in placing behavior in progressively broader current and historical contexts, and in redescribing actions in more intelligible ways, rather than in discerning causes. Since this is what they are actually doing, their language should reflect it, he argues. I believe Schafer has stacked the deck; his argument is circular. He redefines what analysts are doing in such a way as to rule out causal explanations and then cites this redefinition as good reason that motivational concepts should be disallowed! With this instrument, and a few well placed verbs and adverbs, he can then transform any motivational explanation into a redescription. Indeed, the analyst, like the historian, *is* looking for patterns, themes, and contemporary and genetic contexts but, again like the historian, he is doing so to the end of constructing causal explanations. What is the premise of the genetic method but the proposition that later configurations of a phenomenon—whether it be a mountain or the structure of American government or Mr. Jones—are causally related to earlier ones? History and hermeneutics do not preclude causality; rather, they presuppose it.

At this point we leave our reevaluation of psychic causality via the writings of Schafer. Although he has neither refuted the concepts of psychic causality and historical determinism nor provided superior alternatives to them, I believe his contributions are manifold. They include: reawakening us to vital epistemological issues we would prefer to ignore, warning us that theory and reality are not one and the same, underlining the hermeneutic and historical character of psychoanalysis, emphasizing the unitary character of the human agent, and reminding us that the center of gravity is always the desiring, fearing, interpreting, and acting analysand. For this we are indebted to his bold and uncompromising thinking.[6]

---

[6]For critiques of other aspects of Schafer's "action language" see Meissner (1979) and Rawn (1979). In general, I disagree with Schafer's criticisms of structural theory. It is true that structural theory, like all scientific theory, is a complex model or metaphor aimed at corresponding to, organizing, and explaining, sense data; we understand the precise ontological status of its referents no more than we grasp the ontology of the referents of scientific theory in general. Psychical structures are certainly not to be understood, as

Historical Versus Situational Determinants

Let us return to an issue briefly addressed in Chapter One—the role of historical and intrapsychic determinants versus institutional and current contextual ones. Having discovered one great truth—the determinative role of early childhood experience—Freud and many other psychoanalysts

---

Freud (1895) warned, as neurobiological. Our immediate data—the most "real" aspect of the psychiatrist's subject matter—is that arising in the interpersonal relationship in the consulting room (which includes the patient's reports of prior experiences). All else are abstractions at varying degrees of removal from this data—attempts to organize, explain, and interrelate the data. Structural theory must be understood in this light. I believe that structural language is essential to addressing the continuity, amidst the flux, in human mental life and behavior. Nor are *id, ego,* and *superego* models without objective referents in human psychic functioning. Although one is always confronted by a biologically unitary human being, persons do behave as if they possess organized and more or less discrete mental functions corresponding to id, ego, and superego. Apparent psychical structures are of course most graphically demonstrated in dissociative states where alternate centers of consciousness take up, as it were, lives of their own. In his latest book Schafer (1983) himself utilizes structural language—the analyst's "second self"— in his discussion of empathy. For further consideration of idealist versus realist interpretations of structural theory see Wilson (1973) and Matte Blanco (1975, pp. 399–429); the latter considers that whatever the ontological status of 'mental structure,' whatever the ultimate nature of its referents, it is unlikely that we can think psychologically without spatial concepts.

It may well be that the very notion of 'analysis' (of the human being into component psychobiological structures and functions) requires the concept of causality—for causation appears to be the only way of connecting activities that are conceptualized as discrete from one another. From this perspective, Schafer's reluctance to talk structurally and his reluctance to talk causally would be logically consistent with one another.

lost sight of an equally important truth—the role of situational and social determinants. We have already examined
this as it manifested itself in Freud's sociocultural work
(Chapter 1, and Wallace, 1983c)—where, for example, complex, *institutionalized, adult* behaviors were collapsed entirely into their putative infantile meanings and motives.
Modern cultural institutions were collapsed into hypothetical
prehistoric events.

In the psychiatric sphere, Stanton and Schwartz (1954, p.
412) have criticized this indifference to the determinative role
of the current environmental context: "For instance, excellent
analyses are now available which deal with humor in terms of
the internal psychic economy; but whether or not laughter
follows a joke is preconditioned also by its setting—the laughter would not occur if the joke were told while sitting in a
stalled car on a grade crossing watching an approaching express." The same is true, they believe, of symptoms, which are
often determined, not only psychodynamically, but by a
"broader configuration whose interruption would be accompanied by a significant change in the symptom." An adolescent's obsessive-compulsive rituals might be a function, for
example, not merely of unconscious, historically determined
intrapsychic conflicts, but of their role in maintaining the
family equilibrium and the individual's adaptation to his environment (e.g., bringing otherwise estranged parents together around their concern for his symptoms, adapting to
conflicting parental demands for independence and depen-
dence, diverting attention from an even more disturbed family member, and so forth). Although Freud never confronted
such issues directly, he made an interesting statement in
1920 that suggests he was not unaware of them: "Every neurosis has a purpose: it is *directed toward certain persons* and
would disappear at once on a South Sea Island or in a similar
situation *for there would no longer be a reason for it*" (in
Gunther, 1974, p. 5, my italics).

A one-sided focus on the historical and intrapsychic determinants of the patient's behavior, when carried to the ward or
consulting room, entails dangers that Fromm-Reichmann and

Goffman grasped. The latter (1961) taught us that much that passes for psychotic behavior is determined by institutional pressures as well as by the individual's psychodynamics (e.g., mutism and social withdrawal as a means of adapting to hospital short-staffing and uninterested attendants and identity diffusion as a response to dehumanizing features of the environment). And the former (1950, p. 4) warns that, despite its usefulness, the "transference doctrine gave an opening to obviate the fact of the actual experiences between therapist and patient then and there. In practice, this at times carried with it the danger of inducing therapists to neglect the significance of the vicissitudes of the actual doctor-patient relationship as opposed to its transference aspects."[7]

Of course, in the final analysis, situational (including social) and psychodynamic factors are not totally separate from one another. There is, as previously stated, a fluid and mutually determinative line between "inner" and "outer" worlds. For example, the psychodynamics of the fate neurotic play a role in arranging the current environment to which he then reacts; his psychodynamics are themselves a function of still earlier interactions between personality and environment. Institutions and the associated normative pressures arise in part in response to individual needs, just as these individual needs arise in part in response to institutional pressures; similarly, the individual's psychodynamics influence his perception and interpretation of the current normative pressures. Furthermore, it must be appreciated that, insofar as one's personality structure is the proximate cause of all his behaviors, and insofar as that personality structure is a function of

---

[7]Freud's (1900, p. 562) earlier, topographic, conception of transference in some respects lessens the danger of the reductionistic collapse of all aspects of current mental life into their historical precursors: "an unconscious idea is as such quite incapable of entering the preconscious and . . . it can only exercise any effect there by establishing a connection with an idea which *already belongs to the preconscious,* by transferring its intensity on to and by getting itself 'covered' by it" (my italics).

one's history, it is correct to say that historical determinants participate in all one's behaviors. Nevertheless, operationally, in the psychoanalytic explanatory and therapeutic enterprise, it is necessary to draw some distinction between predominantly historical, intrapsychic determinants and predominantly situational and institutional ones (see also my comments on the therapeutic alliance-versus-transference controversy in the next section).[8]

Symmetry and Judgment

It is necessary to speak to a peculiar symmetry in the cause-effect relationship in psychoanalysis (and history): the past determines the present, the present determines the past. By this I intend to convey, of course, that the *meaning* of the present to the patient (the chronicler in the case of the historian), while in part a function of the past, also determines the patient's interpretation of the past. How an individual selects, organizes, interprets, and recounts the multitudinous data from his childhood at age 25 might sound quite different at age 50, depending on the vicissitudes of the intervening years. There are cases in which a single act of heroism or self-sacrifice has retroactively transformed the meaning of an otherwise prosaic or tragic life. The champion of historical deter-

---

[8]Attribution theorists have discovered that the observer tends to attribute the causes of his subject's behavior to factors within the subject, rather than to those within the subject's environment (whereas the subject tends to attribute causal primacy to the environment) (see Jones and Nisbett, 1971 and Strong, 1978). This suggests that the therapist (i.e., observer) will tend to overattribute the causes of his patient's behaviors during the session to factors within the patient (i.e., subject) and underattribute them to factors in the therapist's behavior (i.e., the patient's environment). This provides additional incentive for the therapist to monitor his behavior and its potential impact on the patient.

minism, Freud (1909, 1910) himself, reminded us that individuals, like nations, are forever rewriting their histories to accord with current concerns.[9]

Finally, and in line with this, the psychoanalyst, like the historian, cannot dispense with an element of judgment and interpretation in guaging the relative significance of the multiple causes under investigation—interpretation determined, not merely by the configuration of the data and the evidential and theoretical criteria of psychoanalysis, but by the clinician's particular perspective on his patient as well.[10]

---

[9]Freud's (1918, p. 20) discovery that the Wolf Man's memory of seducing his older sister was a defensively distorted recollection of the actual events—that *she* seduced him—is a case in point. This misremembrance was designed to protect the Wolf Man's shaky sense of masculinity. In this case report Freud (1918, p. 45fn) presented an example of the "deferred action" of experiences and events subsequent to the original trauma itself. The Wolf Man's primal scene at age 1½ was rendered its full pathogenic potency only when the patient became "able to understand it and to be moved by it when the impression [was] revived in him at the age of four . . ." See also Freud (1887–1902, p. 147) and Freud (1895, pp. 161–162) where the full pathogenic effect of childhood traumata manifested itself during pubescent reinterpretations of the earlier events.

[10]It is . . . a mistake to imagine that the historian is contradicting the journalist when he says that the Sarajevo assassination was not the true cause of the outbreak of the First World War. He is merely regarding the outbreak of war from a *different point of view,* talking about it upon a different level. The question "Why did the First World War occur?" is answerable in various ways: it is answerable upon the level of individual human purposes, desires, weaknesses, and abilities; it is answerable upon the level of national policies, traditions of diplomacy, plans; it is answerable upon the level of political alignments, treaties, the international structure of Europe in 1914; it is answerable upon the level of economic trends, social organization, political doctrine, ideology, and the rest" (Gardiner, 1961, p. 105) [my italics].

Inevitability Revisited

Let us return at this point to an issue, briefly addressed in Chapter 3, which serves as a bridge from our previous considerations to those on free will—do psychoanalytic causal propositions entail inevitability and invariancy clauses such as those in Strong's (1978, p. 115) definition of causation in psychology: "A cause is an event that precedes the event of interest and that can be shown to have an invariant relationship to the event (Heider, 1958, Popper, 1961). If the cause can be prevented from occurring, the event of interest will not occur. If the cause does occur, the event of interest is inevitable."?

To begin with, I have argued that, in practice, psychoanalysts, lacking access to controlled experimentation, cannot demonstrate invariant cause-effect relationships even if such exist. In principle, I do not believe there are such relationships to be found because the nexus of causes in even the simplest symbolically mediated behavior is too complex for precisely the same concatenation of events to occur twice. This is more obvious in some types of situations than in others—in the conjoined events of the death of Mr. D's father and Mr. D's suicide attempt, for example.

It is true that analysts look for factors common to otherwise idiosyncratic events—factors which give them clues to cause-effect relationships. It is also true that years of analytic experience have alerted us to regularities in the relationship between certain types of childhood events and certain types of adult behaviors. But in the former case, analysts are simply concerned to explain patterns and in the latter to express tendencies or probabilities rather than to assert that every time a certain cause is present the behavior to be explained will invariably and inevitably result. One can conceive of situations where a causal factor is present but its expectable effect is blocked by the action of a hitherto unappreciated opposing cause. For example, to hold that Mr. B's prior episodes of impotence with women physically resembling his mother were a function of his unconscious oedipal conflict is not to assert that he will invariably and inevitably be impotent with a certain type of woman. On his next attempt his anxieties might be allayed with drugs or alcohol, the understanding and reassurance of his partner, or through prior satisfaction of self punitive superego trends. To maintain, for instance, that parental rejection in childhood is a cause of adult depression is not to espouse an invariant relationship; the individual's constitutionally-historically determined coping mechanisms and the presence of nonparental nurturers could significantly affect what results. In short, the outcome of human affairs is determined by too many interacting variables for psychoanalysts to tie their causal explanations to invariancy and inevitability clauses.

Inevitabilists often attempt to salvage their position by invoking the *ceteris paribus* clause: "all other things being equal, if X and Y occur, then it is inevitable that Z will result." In theory, one could perhaps say that if precisely the same causal constellation were to occur twice (at the intersection between an individual's state of mind and environment), then precisely the same effect would occur. In reality, the problem is that one never confronts the identical causal nexus twice; in human affairs "all other things" are never equal. That certain personality factors may strongly predispose persons to behave in certain ways in certain situations is all that we want to be able to assert—and this, again, is a matter of *probability,* not *inevitability.*

The popular misconception that the proposition of psychic causality commits one to a Schopenhauerian concept of clockwork predeterminism is a prime cause of antipathy to psychological determinism. Schopenhauer's watch-spring determinism is a secularized and mechanistic version of Calvinistic predestinarianism. It involves the untenable assumption that the determinants of all the individual's subsequent behaviors are somehow present at the virtual inception of his personality—that, like a clock, he is wound up at the outset and that the course of his life is but a function of the recoil of the springs. In fact, the human personality is a complex and open system, constantly evolving and interacting with its environment; from this process novel determinants are continually arising.

Conscious, reality-oriented deliberation in the face of alternative options is a case in point. Unless our decision has been unconsciously determined from the outset (in which case what appeared to have been deliberation would in fact have been rationalization), conscious deliberation involves the weighing of considerations and perspectives and the active formulation of a novel position. The performance of thought experiments or the apprehension of hitherto overlooked factors may lead us to alter our initial proclivities on the matter at hand.

In this regard, when we speak of *inevitability* in behavior we are generally concerning ourselves with *novelty* versus *rigidity*. Repetitiveness and stereotypy are the hallmark of unconscious, neurotically determined behaviors. Here the possibility that the individual will arrive at innovative, creative, adaptive, and reality-oriented courses of action—at least in situations that impinge upon his complexes—is remote. It is to such behaviors that we usually append the adjective "inevitable."

Of course, "inevitability" applies to every behavior, not in the fatalistic Schopenhauerian respect, but in the sense that for the behavior under consideration *to have been different* some aspect of the determining antecedent conditions would had to have been different—a reality distorting unconscious wish or fear would had to have been absent, the conscious ratiocinative process would had to have been unimpeded by a particular unconscious intrapsychic conflict, the actor would had to have been privy to a piece of information of which he was unaware, some feature of the deliberation process would had to have gone differently, and so forth. In other words, what has happened *has happened* and the idea that it might have transpired otherwise involves a mystical alteration of the facts of the situation. One cannot even imagine that one might have done otherwise without fantasizing differences in one's precedent situation and state of mind.

This is perhaps also equivalent to saying that it is only at the end of the causal chain or the completion of the causal nexus, after the occurrence of all the necessary and sufficient conditions, that one can assert that the effect is inevitable. In other words, I am opposing inevitability in the sense of pre-determinism; I am not opposing the proposition that when all the necessary and sufficient conditions for an effect have occurred then the effect is inevitable. The predeterminists' error is that they would seem to require the effect to occur independently of whether the necessary and sufficient conditions are present.

Determinism does not assert inevitability in the *futuristic*, Schopenhauerian sense that offends the individual's sense of self determination—i.e., "posed as you are presently with options 'A' and 'B' you will inevitably choose 'B'": All one can say in the present is that one's future choice, whatever it will be, will be *determinate*—that is, that it will be *retrospectively* explicable with reference to the antecedent facts of one's personality structure, situation, and decisionmaking process. This is not to assert that one's decision was predetermined from the outset. The act of deliberation that determined the outcome occurred *after the fact* of one's confrontation by the options. To hold that for a different decision to have been made something would had to have been different in the antecedent conditions does not negate the fact that the deliberation occurred and that it affected the outcome. Even if one decides, on the basis of one's knowledge of one's past behavior, that one's response to a current delimma will inevitably be as it has to similar ones in the past is to make a decision—itself determined—that ensures that it will be. As Bunge (1979, p. 104) says, "past events have been necessary while future ones are contingent;" necessity resides in the backward glance at the event, contingency in the looking forward to it.

Determinism, Bunge (1979, pp. 103–105) asseverates again and again, is not fatalism, but, rather, the best antidote against it:

While fatalism holds an unconditional necessity and conceives it as transcendent, an essential mark of causality . . . is conditionality. Statements of causal laws and, in general scientific laws, do not assert *that* something will inevitably happen under *all* circumstances, regardless of past or present conditions; quite on the contrary, statements of causal laws assert that *if*, and only if, certain conditions are met, certain results will follow. A change in the conditions will therefore ensure a change in the results; the rule of fate is seen to be illusory, events not being predetermined once and for all, but improvised, so to say, along the way . . . causes may *interfere* with one another, so that the result may turn out to differ from what would follow from any of the separate causes. Since any given cause may be counteracted, or at least influenced, by another cause, *causality does not entail inevitability;* on the contrary, it leaves room for processes and deeds capable of changing the course of events, thereby affording a real—though certainly limited—ground for both chance and freedom . . . the conscious and planned handling of laws, of those asserting self-determination as well as of those expressing the way in which certain agencies may be counteracted by other agencies in a regular way, is the very condition for attaining a genuine *libero arbitrio* replacing the servitude to which ignorance of such laws condemns us (Bunge's italics).

The therapeutic optimism of psychoanalysis and psychoanalytic psychotherapy is founded upon just such a concept of determinism. For example, the therapist alerts a patient, currently facing a delimma of a recurrent sort, that past history suggests he will incline toward making such and such a maladaptive decision and that this seems yet another instance of such and such an historically determined conflict. If the patient is thereby enabled to avoid repeating his mistake, then this will be an instance of determinism triumphing over predeterminism (inevitability). It is only because the clinician viewed his patient's maladaptive choices as determined, but not predetermined or inevitable, that he would hazard an intervention (in effect, a new determinant) designed to affect the outcome; otherwise the therapist would do nothing because for the patient, as for the devout Muslim or Calvinist, all would have been written.

"FREE WILL" VERSUS DETERMINISM

No discussion of psychic causality and historical determinism would be complete without attention to the age old issue of determinism versus free will—a debate which cuts across the disciplines of psychology, psychiatry, philosophy, theology, jurisprudence, and ethics. Having surveyed a number of interdisciplinary authors, I can appreciate the sentiments of the eighteenth century Scottish philosopher, Sir William Hamilton (in Mill, 1874)

> The champions of the opposite doctrines [free will and determinism] are at once resistless in assault and impotent in defense. Each is hewn down, and appears to die under the home thrusts of his adversary; but each again recovers life from the very death of his antagonist, and, to borrow a simile, both are like the heroes in Valhalla, ready in a moment to amuse themselves in the same bloodless and interminable conflict (p. 275).

Those interested in definitive, logically watertight positions and conclusive arguments may find this the least satisfying portion of this monograph. I am not concerned to empirically confirm determinism or empirically refute free will because there does not appear to be, as the philosophical literature bears out, a decisive empirical test for either at this time. However, the evidential difficulties for free will are such that one seldom encounters "libertarians" who argue for the total indeterminacy of human behavior; typically they concede, in the face of multiple and increasingly suggestive lines of evidence from biology, psychology, and the social sciences, a sphere to determinism, the better to protect their hypothetical realm of indeterminate volition. By contrast, the epistemological advantages of the deterministic hypothesis of human behavior are manifold: it is more internally consistent than its opponent; it better squares with, organizes, and explains the data; it comprehends otherwise inexplicable discontinuities in conscious mentation and limitations in the capacity for what is experienced as "conscious volition;" its application has borne much fruit in reality; it does not commit us to positing two orders of explanation for human behavior—determinism and "freedom;" and it provides for continuity between the explanatory system of psychoanalysis and the rest of science. The acceptance of a deterministic universe leads one either to include all facets of human functioning within it or to posit an aspect of humanity which transcends that universe. And the latter position introduces an unbridgeable gap into the causal nexus and carries one, I would argue, inexorably to a mind-body, spirit-matter ontological dichotomy.

Operating from a determinist standpoint, I develop the thesis that the free will-determinism dichotomy, as it is usually conceived, is a mirage and that the tools for a good "working resolution" of the problem are at hand in Freud and ego psychology. I contend that determinism applies to all aspects of human mentation and behavior—from the most conscious, adaptive, secondary process, and conflict-free to the most unconscious, maladaptive, primary process, and conflictual—and that this in no way negates most of the capacities that are generally subsumed under "free will."

If by "free will" is meant that certain human activities escape the causal nexus into which the rest of existence is thrown, then I would deny the plausibility of the concept. Indeed, the more one thinks through the notion of free will—and its proponents are notoriously vague about its nature—the more difficult it becomes. How would such a will arise if not determinately; and, if its origin is determined, then how does it subsequently evade the causal matrix from which it arises? In what way can a will be free of the empirical individual who exercises it—be free of his conscious and unconscious desires, fears, and interpretations (and the latter be free of his history, constitution, and situation)? If a will is free in this sense, then who can be said to be exercising it? It seems that one would then be left with a latter day animism, the Kantian assertion of a noumenal self, what one libertarian (Chisholm, 1982) has frankly termed a "miracle," or the indeterminacy of quantum physics. And this last is a proposition of randomnesss, and surely the libertarian is no more eager to consider his will as chaotic then as determined!

Every human behavior is determined, in the sense that the necessary and sufficient condition for its occurrence was the interaction between (1) the antecedent state of the actor, with his particular constitutionally-historically determined, conscious and unconscious, desires, fears, preoccupations, and mode of interpreting the world and (2) the immediately precedent situation (i.e., the current environment). Because the individual's history lives on in the form of enduring unconscious fears, fantasies, prohibitions, affect-laden recollections, and styles of defense, compromise formation, and interpretation it is correct to say that *all* his behaviors partake of historical determinants. At the same time, because the determination of every behavior arises at the interface between the individual's historically-constitutionally determined psychic apparatus and his present environment, his behaviors are determined by current factors as well. Therefore, it is incorrect to oppose "historically determined" to "currently determined" behaviors, for historical and situational determinants invariably co-participate.

To avow historical determinism is not to disavow the self originating character of one's actions: as one side of those interactions which have determined him, it is correct to say that the individual is, in a real sense, part of that history which has shaped him. As the proximate cause of his behavior and barring situations of overwhelming external constraint or duress, it is true to say that the individual is invariably *self determining*.[11] Hence, determinism does not entail, as many

---

[11]It is useful to distinguish between the *fact* of human self determination and the individual's conscious *sense* of self determination. The former is a timeless truth about human behavior, the latter has slowly and painfully evolved over millenia. For example, there is considerable evidence, from anthropology and ancient and medieval history, that projection and "externalization" were once habitual and "normal" modes of thinking and of relating to one's impulses and feelings. For example, it is well known that the early Greeks,

seem to fear, the abrogation of individual autonomy and responsibility. Neither does it involve a denial of the unique and
idiosyncratic aspects of each human being; the constitution
and environment that converge to produce the personality
structure that determines behavior is never identical in any
two individuals. Nor, as outlined previously, is determinism

---

like young children and schizophrenics, experienced their thoughts
as originating from *outside* themselves. They were believed to be,
quite literally, *inspired* from the ambient air, produced by a spirit or
demon (*ate, menos*), or set in motion by a kind of independent voice
in the midriff (*thumos*). Only with time did the Greeks come to
perceive large aspects of their mental activity as self originated.
Similarly, Jung (1961) has stressed the relative unconsciousness of
the meaning and self-motivation of many of the behaviors of contemporary primitives he observed. Fate, Providence, and Satan
have long been assigned a causal role in events and behaviors unwittingly arranged by persons and societies. It can be argued that
one of the most salient features of the history of mankind is the
individual's and group's increasing ownership of the responsibility
for their thoughts, feelings, and behaviors; in this process psychoanalysis has played a preeminent role. The normal development of
the sense of conscious self determination in the individual recapitulates, to some degree, that in the history of the race—with each child
only gradually relinquishing mental mechanisms such as projection
and acquiring an increasing sense of the self-initiation of his
behavior.

In actual clinical practice, with certain types of patients, enhancing their *sense* of self determination can be as important as helping
them transform their mode of self determination itself. I am thinking of a severely schizoid young man who was so dominated by
internal representations of a sadistically controlling mother that he
felt, he said, "like an automaton with levers and strings leading to
my mother's hands." It was necessary to help him appreciate the
mother's causal role in his behavior and sense of self (and his feelings about this) while, at the same time, facilitating his awareness
that he was now himself assuming functions (vis-à-vis himself) formerly performed by his mother.

to be confused with predeterminism; it does not commit one to a fatalistic view of the human agent.

In short, it is always the individual who causes his behavior. The point to be differentiated is not whether a particular behavior is determined or "free," for all human activities are equally determined, but the degree to which it accords with the reality principle and secondary process or with the pleasure principle and primary process, the extent to which it is adaptive or atavistic, and whether it is relatively conflict-free or conflict-laden.

The ego psychological concept of conflict-free and autonomous ego functioning corresponds roughly to what I mean by "reality-oriented self determination." Such self determination often—though not always—involves a heightened consciousness of one's motives and mental processes (hence the ego psychologist's "conscious volition"). In this context, recall Freud's (1901) distinction between conscious and unconscious motivation:

> According to our analysis, it is not necessary to dispute the right to the feeling of conviction of having a free will. If the distinction between conscious and unconscious motivation is taken into account, our feeling of conviction informs us that conscious motivation does not extend to all our motor decisions. *De minimis curat lex.* But what is thus left free by the one side receives its motivation from the other side, from the unconscious; and in this way determination in the psychical sphere is still carried on without any gap (p. 254).

Now this is not to assert that conscious motivation is itself undetermined. "Once before I ventured to tell you that you nourish a deeply rooted faith in undetermined psychical events and in free will, but that this is quite unscientific and must yield to the demands of a determinism whose rule extends over mental life" (Freud, 1915–1917, p. 106). Conscious motivation is as much a function of the individual's historically-constitutionally determined personality structure as is unconscious motivation. At issue is not how one's motives originate, but whether one is conscious of them. In any event, the conscious motive that leads to a subsequent behavior is no less a cause of that behavior simply because the conscious motive is itself determined. Where Freud opposed "free will" he (1915–1917, p. 49) made it plain that he was against, not the concept of conscious and reality-oriented self determination, but the idea that a mental act could be arbitrary, that it could bear no meaningful and causal relationship to the physiology, history, prior mental set, and situation of the actor.

The processes of consciousness are as determined as those of unconsciousness. Consciousness somehow emerges and develops from the interaction between various aspects of constitution and between constitution-nascent personality structure and environment. Its mode of functioning is thenceforth determined in that it proceeds along definite lines, in that it continues to derive from the interaction between components of constitution-personality structure and environment, and in that its range of operation can be delimited by constitutional, historical, unconscious, and situational factors. Thus both the *origin* and *manner of functioning* of consciousness are determined. To argue otherwise is to accord to certain activities (those of consciousness) the capacity to arise *de novo,* out of nothing, as it were, to escape the chain of cause and effect as a *primum mobile*—and, since any mental event takes its meaning from its relationship to antecedent and subsequent mental events, to escape the nexus of meaning as well.

Nevertheless, although the degree to which the individual is conscious of his determinative mental set and antecedents is important, it is not the primary consideration. More significant is the dichotomy between reality-oriented, secondary process, adaptive, relatively conflict-free self determination on the one hand, and primary process, atavistic, conflict-laden self determination on the other. The preparation of some of our most adaptive behaviors proceeds largely preconsciously or unconsciously. Much of the fruit of such sophisticated activities as creative synthesis and logical analysis is the product of mental processes of which the individual is unconscious. Just as it is incorrect to oppose "historically" to "currently"

determined behaviors, it is erroneous to oppose "unconsciously" to "consciously" determined behaviors, for psychobiological factors outside consciousness participate in the determination of every mental activity.

In focusing on the historically determined, unconscious
conflicts that limit our capacity for reality-oriented self determination, psychoanalysis does not thereby dispute the existence of the latter. If analysts write briefs for the impact of the
former, it is because there is no lack of advocacy for the role of
the latter. Analysts, in day to day clinical discourse, have
concepts of both atavistic and reality-oriented self determination. The latter is expressed in the notion of the therapeutic or
working alliance, the distinction between "real" (current reality-oriented) and transferentially distorted aspects of the doctor-patient relationship, and the very aim of psychoanalysis
("where id was, there shall ego be").

Consider Freud's (1933) characterizations of the healthy
ego as a case in point:

> But what distinguishes the ego from the id quite especially is a
> tendency to synthesis in its contents, to a combination and
> unification in its mental processes which are totally lacking in
> the id. . . . The ego develops from perceiving the instincts to
> controlling them; but this last is only achieved by the
> [psychical] representative of the instinct being allotted its
> proper place . . . the ego stands for reason and good sense
> while the id stands for the untamed passions. . . . The ego's
> relation to the id might be compared with that of a rider to his
> horse. The horse supplies the locomotive energy, while the
> rider has the privilege of deciding on the goal and of guiding
> the powerful animal's movement (pp. 76–76).

> [The ego's] constructive function consists in interpolating, be-
> tween the demand made by an instinct and the action that
> satisfies it, the activity of thought which, after taking its bear-
> ings in the present and assessing earlier experiences, endeav-
> ors by means of experimental actions to calculate the conse-
> quences of the course of action proposed. In this way the ego

comes to a decision on whether the attempt to obtain satisfaction is to be carried out or postponed or whether it may not be necessary for the demand by the instinct to be suppressed altogether as being dangerous (Freud, 1938, p. 199).

The analyst enters the picture when the "horse" begins to guide the "rider." By forging a "pact" with the patient's weakened ego, the analyst aims to enhance the patient's self knowledge and to "give his ego back its mastery over lost provinces of his mental life" (Freud, 1938, p. 173). "The ideal situation for analysis is when someone who is otherwise his own master is suffering from an inner conflict which he is unable to resolve alone, so that he brings his trouble to the analyst and begs for his help. The physician then works hand in hand with one portion of the pathologically divided personality, against the other party in the conflict" (Freud, 1920, p. 150).

From this it seems clear where Freud would place himself in the "therapeutic alliance versus transference" controversy: "not every good relation between an analyst and his subject during and after analysis was to be regarded as transference; there were also friendly relations which were based on reality and which proved to be viable" (1937a, p. 222). To acknowledge that each of us perceives others through an unconscious, historically determined lens of wishes, fears, and expectations is not to deny that—in all but the severest cases of psychosis— we are capable of apprehending, to greater or lesser degree, current and concrete aspects of others as individuals in their own right.

If one wants to speak of "reasons," as a *sub*species of causation, then the sphere of secondary process, reality-oriented self determination is their domain of operation. "Reasons" are those motives or mental activities which we can deliberate upon—anticipating the consequences of our potential choices, weighing and considering with an eye to the possibilities and limitations of our environment and our own capabilities. Frequently, the same behavior is motivated both by reality-oriented reasons and unconscious affect laden fantasies. For example, Mr. D's choice of career was dictated in part with an eye to his aptitudes and the realistic opportunities for advancement and comfort it afforded him, but in part by deeply unconscious, historically determined conflictual desires.

Logical and scientific discourse, and that aspect of the psychoanalytic dialogue that transpires between the analysand's observing ego and the analyst, operate in the sphere of reasons. If, for example, a person should accept or reject the thesis of universal determinism because he examines its arguments and finds them compatible or incompatible with experience and the canons of logic and science, then his decision could be said to be motivated by reasons. If, on the other hand (or in addition to), he endorses or repudiates it out of neurotic compulsion or overwhelming unconscious desire, then we are dealing with another variety—atavistic, conflict-laden self-determination—of causation altogether.[12]

This concept of reality-oriented self determination is akin to what Locke (1690) and Reid meant by "liberty." Liberty, for the former, consisted not in the power to consciously determine one's desires, but in the power to consider whether, and how, to gratify them:

> There being in us a great many uneasinesses, always soliciting and ready to determine the will, it is natural, as I have said, that the greatest and most pressing should determine the will to the next action; and so it does for the most part, but not always. For, the mind having in most cases, as is evident in experience, a power to suspend the execution and satisfaction

[12]My treatment of "reasons" as a *subspecies* of causation, rather than considering them (as do many theorists) an acausal explanatory principle, seems to tally with the popular wisdom of etymology. The *Oxford English Dictionary* demonstrates that throughout history, and at present, there is considerable overlap between the usage of "cause," "reason," and "motive." Freud as well used "reason" and "cause" interchangeably (see, for example, 1901, p. 9).

of any of its desires . . . is at liberty to consider the objects of
them, examine them on all sides, and weigh them with others.
In this lies the liberty a man has (1690, p. 48).

Similarly, liberty, for Reid (1813–1815, p. 66), was the capacity to interpose judgment between the impulse and the final
action itself. He recognized that this sphere of deliberation
could be delimited by strong passion, constitution, and
madness.

I believe that Freud's therapeutic maxim, "where id was
there shall ego be," speaks precisely to the enlargement of
this domain of what Locke and Reid termed "liberty." Psychoanalytic treatment attempts to make the analysand affectively and cognitively aware of maladaptive patterns of behavior, and the historically based conflictual motives and
distortions in view of self and world from which these patterns
result, to the end of broadening his reality-oriented and secondary process operations upon reality. To bring a patient to
conscious awareness of previously repressed motives is to
make it possible for him to deliberate upon them, to transform
them from "causes" into "reasons."[13] Through insight formation and deliberation we can enter into the determination of
our behaviors in a manner in which the rest of the animal
kingdom cannot.

Another important aspect of adaptive and reality-oriented
self determination is the capacity to form what Frankfurt
(1982, pp. 82–83) terms "second-order desires and volitions."
"Besides wanting and choosing and being moved to do this or
that [first-order desires] men may also want to have (or not to
have) certain desires and motives [second-order desires]. They
are capable of wanting to be different, in their preferences and
purposes, from what they are." When a person, in addition to
having "second-order desires" wants, not merely to have these

---

[13]Freud (1920, p. 151) analyzed the dynamics of homosexuality in
order that the patient might be enabled "to *choose* whether he
wished to abandon the path that is abandoned by society [my
italics]."

desires, but for them to move him to action (i.e., to become his "effective will"), then he can be said to have "second-order volitions" (p. 86)—a state of affairs which, Frankfurt asserts, is not true of all persons. Although Frankfurt remains neutral on the free will versus determinism issue, he thinks it "conceivable" that a person could be "causally determined" to be able to "want what he wants to want" (p. 92).

An individual's desire to alter his character, affective state, and behavior patterns is an example of a second-order desire. Should this motive become powerful enough to bring him to treatment, then it would have become a second-order volition. In the course of a detailed anamnesis clinicians invariably encounter factors which can be plausibly denominated the "causes" of the desire to be different, the desire for this to be one's effective will, and the decision to implement it. Precipitating events (created by the conscious and unconscious conspiracy between the patient and his environment) cause the second order desire to be different to become the second order volition to enter treatment.

Nevertheless, it is crucial to recognize that the conscious, reality-oriented, secondary process self determination of which Locke and Freud speak is *itself determined.* By this I mean that one's mode and range of operation of reality-oriented self determination are a function of the prior interaction between the biological substrate of the psychic apparatus and its psychologically emergent properties on the one hand and the environment on the other. The capacity for Locke's liberty, the situations in which one exercises it, and whether one aspires to it at all are equally determined. The individual who accepts or rejects universal determinism because he weighs and sifts the arguments according to his experience and the canons of rationality is engaging in behavior that is no less determined than that of his neurotic counterpart—determined by constitution, prior experience, education, the cognitive structures of the human mind, the rules of logic and science, and so forth. And the position of the determinist, like that of the indeterminist he opposes, will be partly a function of mental tendencies beyond his ken.

Again, acknowledging the exceptionless determination of human behavior does not carry, as some charge, fatalistic implications. The determinist, no less than the indeterminist, exercises reality-oriented self determination to the extent (and in the manner) which his historically-constitutionally determined desire, capacity, and conflict and his current situation allow; the former simply does not contend his behavior is indeterminate. Nor does determinism negate the importance of *conscious* effort, attitudes, deliberations, and volition. Such activities are as real and efficacious as the unconscious psychobiological processes from which they derive. What is crucial to human actors in their day to day lives is, not whether their will is indeterminate, but whether they have the will that they want and whether they can negotiate the world in an adaptive and reality-oriented manner. The indeterminist need not fear determinism, for in a deterministic universe people continue to do whatever it is that they can do—and they do it irrespective of their position on the truth value of determinism!

The following excerpt from the treatment of Ms. C., encountered in Chapter One, illustrates the expansion of conscious and reality-oriented self determination that can result from awareness of hitherto unconscious dynamics.

Early in her second year of treatment Ms. C's mother was killed in a car crash—tragically ill timed, considering the matricidal fantasies with which the patient was then contending in therapy. For some weeks following this, Ms. C. did not experience much affect, though she became plagued with insomnia, psychosomatic ailments, and phobias (including fear of ghosts). During this time she was confronting the question whether to sell her mother's house or move into it. (It is significant that the patient's dependent ten-year-younger sister was still living in this house; shortly after her birth, this sister had been "handed over" to Ms. C. to raise—an event about which Ms. C. had always harbored considerable resentment.) Ms. C's strong initial impulse was to move into her mother's house and live with the dependent (now adult) sister. She was not able to more rationally and realistically weigh this decision and ponder a recent job offer that would advance her career (but necessitate a move) until she appreciated that her precipitous inclination to occupy her mother's home and role with the infantile sister was a function of a number of unconscious trends: (1) identifying with the mother as a way of denying her death; (2) taking care of the sister as a reaction formation to, and atonement for, death wishes toward both mother and sister; (3) vicarious identification with the sister, whom Ms. C. would then "mother" as Ms. C. herself wanted to be "mothered"; (4) Ms. C's identification of the sister with her mother—the two latter having many character traits in common; (5) deferred obedience to the mother—"doing what Mama would want"; and (6) attempting to regain the unrecapturable home (and father) of her childhood, in which she played, one recalls, a special role. When she had identified these factors and begun her grief work, she was eventually able to arrive at a decision that took into account her psychological, financial, and occupational interests—as well as those of her sister.

It is important to point out that psychodynamic therapy had not moved Ms. C. from a state of determinism to one of "free will." Her behavior thereafter was no less determined than before. Rather, it was her *mode* of self determination that had changed. And it changed deterministically—by which I mean the changes resulted from the interaction between her historically-constitutionally determined psychic apparatus and my interventions. Furthermore, the attitude toward her psychopathology that led her to seek treatment and the psychological mindedness that enabled her to profit from it were themselves the effect of prior interactions between constitution-personality and environment.

On a different, but related note, let us delve more deeply into the relationship between capacity and determinism. Determinism recognizes that persons possess capacities for adaptive behavior that they do not always—much to their disadvantage—utilize. Determinism, as we have seen, explains the capability for reality-oriented self determination without negating it. If an individual fails to utilize capacities for adaptive self-determination which he has hitherto possessed, the question becomes not "Why is he recalcitrantly and freely choosing to suspend his capacities?", but "What, in the nexus between his current situation and his historically-constitutionally determined motivational and interpretive set, is leading him to act as if he wants for capacities he has heretofore demonstrated?"

It is clinically, and not merely theoretically, important to distinguish between the patient who is behaving maladaptively because he has never developed the requisite ego strength to cope with particular impulses, feelings, and situations or because he is gripped by a psychotic process, and the patient who is behaving maladaptively because unconscious motives, anxieties, and misinterpretations are interfering with his ability to utilize ego strengths to which he has previously attained and to which he typically has access. Of course in the strict sense, it is a matter of capacity for the latter patient as well—an incapacity to behave adaptively in this particular situation at this particular time.

Consider, for example, a generally well functioning hysteric, frantically phoning for an extra appointment or immediate hospitalization, protesting his inability to weather a situation similar to those which he has successfully negotiated in the past. The therapist's questions then become: "What are the factors impeding his exercise of ego strengths which he has developmentally obtained and which he has utilized in prior situations similar to this one? What are his unconscious motives for feeling incapable and what is causing him to interpret the situation as beyond his control? What is the source of the anxiety that is undercutting his capacity?"

It may be, for example, that unconsciously the patient wants to feel incapable so that he can act out dependent or oedipal fantasies by calling the therapist, or so that he can regress to a preconflictual psychosexual position, or so that he can act out a morally or sexually masochistic fantasy, and so forth. If the clinician's intervention succeeds in calming the patient, restoring his sense of competence, and augmenting his adaptive self control, then this will not be an instance of the patient's being persuaded to "buck up" and use his "free will." Rather, it will be a case of an interpretation or suggestion assisting the patient to regain access to ego strengths he was hitherto denying. Again, as with Ms. C., any change in behavior would be a function of the causal intersection between the clinician's intervention and the patient's personality structure.

It remains to consider three items that are often invoked in support of free will and against determinism: (1) that people experience themselves as acting "freely," arbitrarily, or whimsically and that they believe they might have acted otherwise than they actually did; (2) that people make choices; and (3) that people sometimes behave unpredictably or "out of character" and are capable of arriving at novel and creative solutions and positions.

(1) Indeterminists have long considered the phenomenology of free will and the sense that "I could have chosen and done otherwise" as the best evidence for their position. (Recall, in this regard, Johnson's response to Boswell's flirtation with determinism: "Sir, we *know* that our will is free, and *there's* an end on't"! Such phenomenological arguments are similar to the ontological proof of the existence of God—i.e., since we have the idea of God there must be an objective reality that corresponds to it.) Determinists have traditionally countered "if you could have desired to will otherwise you would have," or "if you could have willed otherwise you would have," or "if you could have implemented your will to do otherwise you would have." For example, determinists argue that enacting an impulse one has hitherto demonstrated the capacity to check does not prove that one has exercised a transcendently free choice to suspend self-restraint; rather, it means that some causal factors in the individual's (conscious and unconscious) state of mind and situation were different such that he no longer desired to restrain himself or desired to, but could not. Because one cannot resurrect the original state of affairs

it is impossible to decisively confirm or refute either the determinist or indeterminist interpretation. Each side makes its assumptions.

Psychoanalysis does not deny the phenomenology of free will; it simply denies that is accurately reflects the actual state of affairs. Psychoanalysis has demonstrated that conscious experience is only one aspect of mental functioning, that it is not a reliable indicator of the individual's total state of mind, and that the continuities and discontinuities in conscious experience and limitations in conscious volition cannot be adequately explained without reference to factors outside consciousness. Psychoanalytic treatises such as *The Psychopathology of Everyday Life* and day-to-day clinical work provide, not experimental proof, but impressive evidence for the historical and unconscious determination of even the most apparently arbitrary and trivial mental acts.

In these matters we are continually confronted by the discrepancy between what the individual feels to be the case and what scientific observation and explanation lead us to believe. For example, the normal mother, nursing her infant, feels quite free in her behavior, and yet we appreciate that it is partly determined by hormonal factors and aspects of prior socialization beyond her awareness. Mr. G, abruptly leaving off the topic of his mother for the nth time, felt he was freely doing so and yet the therapist understood his behavior as motivated by unconscious defensive trends. The citizen in the polling booth believes he is exercising free choice and yet the social scientist comprehends his preference as largely shaped by his socioeconomic and religio-ethnic background. As Hume (1777a, p. 108) said, "however we imagine we feel a liberty within ourselves, a spectator can commonly infer our actions from our motives and character . . ."

When the individual is functioning smoothly, in relative freedom from conflict, with adpative compromise formations, with predominantly secondary process modes of mentation, and in reality-oriented interactions with the environment he has no inkling that his behavior is nonetheless constrained and directed by aspects of psychobiology beyond conscious awareness. In mental equilibrium he wants, and is able, to do the adaptive thing; his conscious fantasies and behaviors are ego syntonic. At such moments the individual may experience—and is eager to consider—his will as "free." It is only when confronted with ego dystonic fantasies, obsessive-compulsive symptoms, depression, phobias, sexual disabilities, work inhibitions, troublesome discontinuities in conscious mental functioning, and so forth that he can be brought to some understanding of determinism.[14] But it is more difficult

---

[14]The reluctant and narcissistically injuring confession that one's conscious volition is "resolute but powerless" to alter a troublesome state of affairs—compulsive rituals, anxiety attacks, ego dystonic desires, sexual impotence is the most common reason people go to a therapist. A successful treatment may involve any or all of the following: (1) increasing one's sense of personal agency, and of how one has often been exercising one's will in a manner inimical to self and others; (2) helping one see where one has been unrealistically assuming responsibility for what it was humanly impossible for one to affect; (3) enhancing one's awareness of situations where conscious wilfullness not only avails nothing but can get in the way— such as artistic activity, athletics, relaxation, sexual behavior, and participation in psychotherapy—where a certain amount of "letting go" is required; and (4) helping one appreciate that one does not *consciously* decide how to feel—i.e., from the point of view of one's center of consciousness, feelings, although they are one's own (self-originated) activities, *occur*. Where conscious volition has proved ineffective it would be absurd for the therapist to tell his client, as have his friends and family members, to "snap out of it." It is in this sense that Sullivan (1953, pp. 300–302) correctly warned the psychiatrist against the "illusion" of an excessively "voluntaristic" concept of will. In the treatment of neurotics, where the therapeutic alliance and the ego are strong, there is seldom any indication for educating the patient to refined distinctions between conscious and unconscious self determination. With the borderline patient, however-er, as Kernberg and others have suggested, it is occasionally necessary to address the extent to which a behavior is consciously, versus unconsciously, motivated. In short, one must at times address the

for him to appreciate—partly because its phenomenology is so different, partly because of human narcissism—that the domain of adaptive and ego syntonic mental functioning is no less determined than its psychopathological counterpart.[15]

(2) People are confronted with options and do make choices, as the existentialists are fond of reminding us. Psychoanalytic determinism does not deny that we stand before possibility, that we choose, and that our choices influence the subsequent

---

degree of his conscious commitment (itself determined) to the therapeutic process and to controlling destructive and self destructive acting out. If the therapist has correctly guaged the strength of the positive transference and therapeutic alliance and the state of the patient's ego functioning, then the latter may be enabled to alter his behavior; and such alteration would be a manifestation of intersectional causation.

[15]But let us step back a moment and consider that on the matter of phenomenology we may have given the libertarian more than his due. I am not convinced that phenomenology involves the experience of "free will" to the extent that the indeterminist would have us believe. It is primarily when consciously confronting a decision and weighing alternatives that we experience our will as free. For the most part, however, we are simply aware of thinking, interacting, doing, and feeling and not of consciously deliberating over and choosing every item in our chain of associations or behaviors; indeed, affects and moods usually feel anything but freely chosen. When we are painting or dancing, composing a poem, playing an instrument by ear, engaging in casual conversation, or playing tennis we do not generally experience that we are in total conscious control of the choice and preparation of our every activity. In such cases we may even consider ourselves most "free" when we are least aware of preparing and willing our behaviors—when our ideas and moves "just come to us," so to speak. As for the sense that "we could have done otherwise" I argue that this is a retrospective interpretation rather than a primordial experience. In fine, I contend that when we experience ourselves as "free" what we generally feel is not so much that our will is transcendently free and arbitrary, but that we are self determining and free from external constraint or duress.

direction of our lives, that, in this sense, we make ourselves. What it does deny is that our range of potential desires and choices is limitless and that it is uninfluenced by history, constitution, and situation. It is not only psychoanalysts who appreciate this; the advertising industry is predicated on the assumption that persons' backgrounds influence their desires and choices and that these preferences can be shaped through appropriate (liminal and subliminal) current stimuli.

(3) That an individual may act other than he typically does, behave unpredictably, and be creative and innovative I have treated in the inevitability discussion. Much of what is termed "free will" resides in these unpredictable aspects of human behavior. They are to be comprehended, not as free or undetermined, but as the result of novel interactions between previously existing components of constitution-personality structure and between constitution-personality structure and environment—in other words, as the result of novel causes or interactions among causes. It is the intersectional nature of causation that permits the novelty, unpredictability, and capacity for change that indeterminists are anxious to retain.

To recapitulate, history and constitution determine the range and intensity of our desires and the particular unconscious and conscious fantasies through which they express themselves, the nature of our anxieties and aversions, the pattern of our defenses and compromise formations, the degree to which we can consciously restrain or divert our impulses (and the extent to which we want to), our style of conscious and unconscious cognition and interpretation, our capacity for reality-oriented operations upon our environment (as well as the situations in which we are capable of exercising these functions), the degree to which we are cognizant of and satisfied or dissatisfied with our character structures, and the extent to which we are motivated to and capable of engaging in a psychoanalytic dialogue.[16] Psychoanalysis exerts its

---

[16]If it is charged that "personality structure" is an abstraction and that, as such, it cannot logically be invoked as a determinant of concrete human behaviors, I would counter that: (1) the investiga-

transformative impact by becoming part of the deterministic universe of the patient.

From our consideration of "free will" and determinism it follows that the analysand is always self determining, hence "free" in Spinoza's (1677, p. 44) sense of the word: "That thing is called free which exists from the necessity of its nature alone, and is determined to action by itself alone." The analyst's task is facilitating the analysand's awareness that he is and has been self determining, albeit in ways and to ends often inimical to the well being of himself and others. From this enhanced self awareness and from collaboratively induced changes in the structure of the patient's personality, his mode of self determination will change.

I believe the "free will"—determinism dichotomy is a false one. Our behavior, insofar as it is not externally constrained, is free; as a function of our history and personality structure it is determined. The valid dichotomy is not "determined" versus "free," for psychoanalysis comprehends all behaviors as equally determined, but pleasure principle versus reality principle, primary process versus secondary process, relatively conflict-laden versus relatively conflict-free, atavistic versus adaptive, and unconscious versus conscious.[17,18]

---

tor's description and conceptualization of the *behavior* is itself an abstraction from another abstraction (e.g., the subject's conceptualization and description of his experience); (2) the subject's immediate experience of his behavior is itself, in part, a signifier for aspects (unconscious and preconscious) of his behavior of which he is unaware; and (3) the *referents* of the abstraction "personality structure"—the individual's more or less enduring conscious and unconscious mode of interpreting self-in-world, cognitive and affective style, preferred mental mechanisms, and pattern of conflicts and compromise formations—are as real as the behaviors the concept is invoked to explain. Once more, it is important to keep in mind that in psychology, *as in every other discipline,* we work, not with noumenal reality directly, but with abstractions—signs and symbols—through which we apprehend and explain the universe.

[17]One motive for antipathy to determinism may be the groundless fear that causal explanations abrogate or attempt to

SUMMARY

In concluding my reevaluation of psychic causality and historical determinism, let me say that the concept of causation—its

---

explain away the phenomenological dimension of human life. Although determinism comprehends all aspects of human behavior and experience as equally determined it does not depreciate the richness of individual experience or devalue the phenomenological approach. For example, Coleridge's *Kubla Khan* is determined through and through, every element and nuance of it, just as is any reader's response to it. But to say that one "understands" the poem, in the literary and aesthetic sense, is not to say that one has elucidated its determinants. To do the latter is to explain the genesis of the poem, to do the former is to grasp it experientially. In most aspects of everyday life we are simply concerned to experience and understand in the phenomenological mode; we bracket the causal question unless it appears relevant to the task at hand.

[18]It must be acknowledged that there is layer upon layer of complexity behind and beneath that into which this brief analysis has gone. At this point any position on the matter rests primarily upon assertions, assumptions, inferences and, at best, generalizations and extrapolations from relatively indirect evidence. Among the assumptions central to my argument are, of course, an acceptance of the universal ontological validity of determinism and of the axiom that mental events invariably begin unconsciously. Furthermore, when one considers the narcissistic, "superego," "id," and "ego" motives which this topic allows full play, it is difficult to conceive how anyone could approach the matter totally dispassionately.

Nor is the issue clearcut within analysis itself. At times Freud (1923, p. 50 fn) himself espoused versions of libertarianism: "analysis does not set out to make pathological reactions impossible, but to give the patient's ego *freedom* to decide one way or the other" (Freud's italics). A similar ambivalence and ambiguity pervades much of the subsequent psychoanalytic literature. The philosopher and psychoanalyst Hanly (1979, pp. 224–227), while mounting a closely reasoned argument against libertarianism, notes that Glover, Rycroft, Winnicott, and Kohut are among the many analysts who have implicitly or explicitly espoused some version of free explanatory, methodological, and ontological status—is far from elucidated; we may well have need for more than one concept of causation in psychoanalysis (and in history). Deterministic explanations of psychopathology and aspects of character style seem much more clearly developed than those of

---

will, alongside that of determinism. He (p. 225, fn) correctly adds that "ego psychology and the structural theory have been used to formulate an ambiguous concept of psychic determinism that allows the ego some kind of freedom of choice." Hartmann writes at times as if mentation and motivation can somehow arise de novo in the ego's structure of consciousness. There may be some validity to the charge of Schafer and others that structural theory has spawned a multitude of intrapsychic homunculi which have become endowed with the free will that is no longer permitted to the whole person. Consider Freud's numerous anthropomorphisms in elaborating upon the intersystemic relations of the psyche. Recall, in this regard, Rieff's (1979) trenchant observation that Freud's concept of mind is, in many respects, a microcosm of that of the polity—comprising a number of freely acting citizens and interests clashing or collaborating with one another.

The positions of Knight (1946, pp. 251–262) and Brierly point further to this ambiguity. The former asserts that the phenomenology of freely choosing "has nothing whatever to do with free will as a principle governing human behavior but is a subjective experience which is itself causally determined." Nevertheless, this illusion of free choice is declared to be, among other factors, causally necessary for change! "As psychotherapy progresses," note Gatch and Temerlin (in May, 1969, pp. 195–196) in a review of Knight's article, "the experience of freedom increases, so that successfully analyzed people report experiencing more freedom in the conduct of their lives than they did prior to psychotherapy. If this freedom is illusory, the purpose of therapy, or at least the result of successful therapy, is to restore an *illusion* even though most therapists believe that successful therapy increases the accuracy with which the patient perceives himself and the world" (my italics).

And for Brierly (1951), as well, "The real situation appears somewhat paradoxical. The validity of psychoanalytic determinism is seldom questioned by psychoanalysts, because clinical evidence re-the relatively conflict-free and adaptive features of conscious and preconscious mentation. Logical analysis and creative synthesis (insofar as they are conflict free) are only two of the activities not in the purview of psychoanalysis as a clinical discipline; whether they will ever be exhaustively explained

---

proves from hour to hour that we are what we have become as a result of our past history and that what we are now becoming is shaping our future. But, equally, there can be no question that living is creative and that, within limits variously circumscribed for different people, the ego appears to have some possibilities of choice. Every decision is a fresh decision, which may represent a new beginning, a readaptation not necessarily always predictable in advance, though explicable after the event. It would seem that the ego is fulfilling its proper functions when it tries to make the most reasonable decision on the evidence before it, as if it were a responsible free agent. But the sounder the internal and external reality-sense of the ego, the better will it recognize the limiting conditions of its own choices and the more likely will it arrive at integrative, predictable decisions."

Likewise, my experience bears out the paradox that most dynamic psychiatrists espouse universal determinism while living their lives as if they possess some degree of what is generally considered "freedom of will." In short, this age-old issue is far from resolved. It may even need reframing in categories that transcend those of determinism versus free will.

The bugbear may have been the equation of "free" with "indeterminate" will. I believe that what most of us want to retain is not the notion that our "willing" (and it would require volume upon volume to unpack the very word and examine its ontological status) is undetermined by aspects of *ourselves* outside of consciousness (including aspects of the environment which are nonetheless filtered through *our* perceptual-interpretive apparatus) and that that willing is unaffected by constitution and history. It would be difficult to imagine what such willing would be like.

Rather, I think that what we want to retain is: (1) the idea of self mastery, self control, and autonomy—that is, that we, in our psychobiological totality and to whatever degree of consciousness or unconsciousness, are the locus of the initiation, direction, and con-by psychodynamic causal propositions is a moot point at this time. As Freud (1914, p. 50) said, "Psycho-analysis never claimed to provide a complete theory of human mentality in general, but only expected what it offered should be applied to

---

trol of our volition, wishing, thinking, feeling, and acting; (2) the idea that we stand before possibility—in the sense that, through unconscious and preconscious interactions among aspects of psycho-biology and between these functions and our environment, new modes of behavior, interpretation, compromise formation and, ultimately, of consciousness may emerge; and (3) the idea that we stand before yet another form of possibility, that at times (however rare) all but the most handicapped or psychopathological confront *consciously,* and however momentarily, two or more options—either or any of which is, *at least at that instant of conscious awareness,* actually open to us; and that this be the case, in whatever manner such capacity arises and to whatever degree it is itself derivative of unconsciousness.

Of these three posited capacities determinism clearly, in my opinion, logically permits the first two. Whether it allows the third (which I shall term "genuine possibility") remains an open question. What follows is very speculative, lays claim to less logical and evidential assurance than the rest of the monograph, and may even contradict earlier aspects of my argument. It points toward the unknown and aims to open up and facilitate further consideration of the matter.

That there are times (however infrequent) when most of us feel, quite consciously, poised before 'genuine possibility,' before Kierkegaard's "seventy thousand fathoms" (that is, before situations in which we view the consequences of our choices as important and in which we believe ourselves really capable of choosing one way or the other—perhaps even of opting for the "line of most resistance") is an important *empirical* datum of human experience— one which we might well ponder before martyring it to the fires of any supposed logical consistency. (That such a sense of genuine possibility can often be plausibly explained, after the fact, as a wishful or defensive distortion does not prove that such is always the case.) If the earlier argument that determinism does not entail predeterminism or inevitability is correct, then this second form of

supplement and correct the knowledge acquired by other means." In short, a discipline need not pretend to explain everything in order to claim to be able to understand anything at all.

---

possibility may indeed be logically consistent with a deterministic universe; alternatively, if determinism is taken to imply that, at the instant of conscious awareness of options, prior events have *already determined* the ensuing deliberation and choice, then *present* (i.e., conscious awareness of options) and *future* (i.e., deliberation process and eventual choice) are collapsed into the *past* and determinism becomes, in effect, predeterminism. Conversely, as I argued in 'Inevitability Revisited,' it is where one's psychopathology bears overwhelmingly on his situation that we speak of probabilities and inflexibilities that approximate to predeterminism or inevitability. This may be what Freud had in mind when he spoke of analysis "giv[ing] the patient's ego *freedom* to decide one way or the other."

To argue that we may at times stand before genuine possibility is not to suggest that we do so indeterminately; historically-constitutionally determined personality structure and situation will determine when, and the degree to which, we possess such possibility. And the ensuing deliberation process and eventual choice will be retrospectively explicable determinatively (and with reference to many factors in the subject that were operating outside of consciousness). Furthermore, *after the chain of events has occurred*— conscious recognition of the options and their consequences, the belief that one has the capacity to choose one way or the other, deliberation upon the alternatives, and the resultant choice—one can even assert that the choice could not have been otherwise (unless something in the antecedent mental events had been different).

If this sensation of genuine possibility (i.e., of being actually open, however momentarily, to two or more options) is an illusion, then it may indeed be an illusion that is causally necessary for the adaptive, socialized, and moral behavior of many or most individuals. (It may even be an "illusion" that is causally determined by an accurate perception of the actual state of affairs or, if it is an illusion, it appears to be one in which most, if not all, people are causally determined to believe—in which case it would be yet another instance of "nature"'s wry trickery of mankind.) If belief in

Nevertheless, despite all the unresolved problems, the thesis of determinism appears essential to expressing the relationship of constraint and direction between unconscious and conscious mentation, between history and current behavior,

---

genuine possibility in fact bears an important influence on many persons' behavior and since we possess no decisive—prospective, experimental, quantitative, or even logical—means of confirming or disconfirming it (nor have we solved the "mind-body" problem, the resolution of which must be anterior to any closure on the genuine possibility issue), then we are facing what William James (1896, pp. 3–4), the master servant of theory, logic, empiricism, and ambiguity, terms a *"genuine* option"—that is, one which is *"living"* (in which both alternatives make some appeal to one's interest or concern), which is *"forced"* (in which "there is no standing place outside of the alternative . . . [a] dilemma based on a complete logical disjunction with no possibility of not choosing"), and which is *"momentous"* (which is important and which excludes one from the alternative possibility altogether) (all italics James'). In face of James' *"genuine* option" one *will* choose, one way or the other, and, if I am correct, that choice will have a determinant influence on the course of one's subsequent choice and behavior. And one's historically-constitutionally determined personality structure will determine whether, and the degree to which, belief in genuine possibility is for him a genuine possibility!

Before this issue—of whether we ever possess genuine possibility—the mind boggles. Precise and clear-headed positivistic and analytical philosophers may deplore the often murky, ambiguous, *non* (not necessarily *ir*)rational, and internally inconsistent language of many Romantic psychologists, theologians, phenomenologists, and existentialists (e.g., "the will in bondage" versus the "will in freedom," "facticity" versus "possibility," the mixing of deterministic and "libertarian" terminology, and so forth), but it may be that in such obscurity shines a clear confession of the awesome deep before which we stand and of the inability of our current logical and scientific categories to plumb the phenomenon confronting us. It may be that logic, when penetrating to depths it cannot yet elucidate, snuffs itself out and darkens that which it seeks to illumine. The story continues; but for the present I wager that deter-

and between desire and interpretation. Adherence to determinism also preserves the continuity between the explanatory principles of psychoanalysis and the other sciences concerned with investigating man and his environment—
physics, chemistry, biology, and sociology—and hence en-
hances the likelihood that the contributions of psychoanalysis
can be integrated with those of these other disciplines. But
the determinism I advocate is a complex and interactive one,
taking account of the fact that the human being is always,
consciously and unconsciously, part of that which determines
him. He grasps his environment with his interpretations and
desires—interpretations and desires all too often determined
atavistically, but *his* interpretations and desires nonetheless.
In this respect, it is the patient who constructs his psychopathology and his world.[19]

Such a concept of causality fosters the view of psychoanalysis as a collaborative enterprise, rather than one of the
analyst modelling his analysand like a lump of clay or applying levers to a system of forces. The therapist plays a role in

---

minism holds universally and I am open to the possibility that it in
some manner permits, though far less often than pre-Freudians
imagined, some degree of genuine possibility.

[19]Appreciation of the intersectional nature of causation, and the
consequently intimate intertwining of psychical and actual reality
would have quelled much of the current furor (see Masson, 1984) over
Freud's seduction theory. While Masson is correct that Freud under-
estimated the extent to which seduction occurs, and that this has led
some analysts to erroneously minimize the role of actual events, he
errs in adopting a unilinear concept of causality and a sharp either-or
view of psychical and actual reality. In any trauma it is always a
matter of participation from the side of both psychical and actual
reality; what is clinically important is dissecting out the strands of
each and assessing their relative contribution. An actual seduction is
indeed much more likely to produce pathological sequelae than a
fantasied one; but the traumatization of the former will not be adequately worked through if the fears, fantasies, and interpretations
both preceding and following the seduction are not worked through
as well.

effecting personality restructuring by entering into a causal nexus in which the patient himself remains the primary determinant. The analyst intervenes, but it is the analysand who determines what this intervention means and what to do with it.

> In every encounter with reality the structures of self and world are interdependently present. The most fundamental expression of this fact is the language which gives man the power to abstract from the concretely given and, after having abstracted it, to return to it, to interpret and transform it. The most vital being is the being which has the word and is by the word liberated from bondage to the given. In every encounter with reality man is already beyond this encounter. He knows about it, he compares it, he is tempted by other possibilities, he anticipates the future and he remembers the past. This is his freedom (Tillich, 1952, p. 82).[20,21]

---

[20]The ethical implications of determinism is a topic I hope to explore at some point. For consideration of some related issues, see my "Freud as Ethicist" [*Freud Studies,* Volume 1, P. Stepansky (ed.), Hillsdale, New Jersey, The Analytic Press, in press]. With respect to the pivotal concept of 'responsibility,' determinism clearly ascribes 'causal' responsibility to the agent. It is only because the individual's behaviors are determined by his personality structure — rather than being purely arbitrary — and because he is self determining in certain relatively enduring ways that reward, punishment, and education can affect his behavior. At the interpersonal level, moreover, the notion that persons can, through their actions, participate in the causation of distress in others is fundamental to moral discourse. The relationship between 'causal' and 'moral' responsibility and the impact of determinism on moral evaluation has been long debated and remains an open question. See Freud's (1925) essay on the moral responsibility of the dreamer.

[21]Postscript to "The Identification and Nature of Causes": The fact that the subject of a post-hypnotic suggestion can, when requested to free associate to the behavior, often recollect its unconscious, antecedent mental cause — i.e., the hypnotist's suggestion — seems a powerful warrant, in principle, for the causal epistemological claims of the associative method.

Conclusion

In this essay I have been concerned to demonstrate the affinities between history and psychoanalysis and to examine methodological and epistemological issues that they share, including a number of dichotomies: historicism versus positivism, subjectivism versus objectivism, presentism versus antiquarianism, and art versus science. I have consistently argued for a middle ground that recognizes the intimate and inextricable interaction between the elements in each of these polarities. I continue to believe that psychoanalysis is a fundamentally historical enterprise, that Freud's greatest contribution was his genetic method for the study of human behavior, and that further contemplation of the similarities and differences between psychoanalysis and history will bear fruit for both disciplines.

On the matter of causation I sought to clarify some historical issues that contribute to our understanding of the concept. Key here was an unpacking of Freud's thinking on the matter. Through analyzing the concepts of psychic causality and historical determinism and through evaluating the arguments of their critics, I have attempted to defend the principle of causation in psychoanalysis and to explicate the purposive, intersectional concept of multi-causation that has been, I believe, native to psychoanalysis all along. I hope my critique will awaken further interest in the nature of determinism in psychoanalysis and human behavior.

More questions remain unanswered—or even unasked—than have been satisfactorily resolved. What exactly is theory in science, in history, in psychoanalysis? How are they alike and how different? What is the relationship between interpretation and theory, and between interpretation in history, in psychoanalysis, and in textual studies? Precisely how is it that theorization and observation "interact" with one another? What is the relationship between hermeneutics & causation?

The philosophy of psychoanalysis is still in its infancy—in a position comparable to that of the philosophy of history in the 1930's. Nevertheless, when one considers what has been accomplished in little more than a decade, there are grounds for optimism. Increasingly detailed reproductions of the analytic process (such as the audiotapes of Hartvig Dahl, 1972, and the verbatim transcripts of Merton Gill, 1982), while not a panacea, will permit more refined observation and thought about the relationship between theory and data and make it harder for "suggestion" to be invoked as a facile criticism of the analyst's work. Longitudinal studies such as those of the Yale Child Study Center will continue to refine our understanding of constitutional and historical determinism. It is to be hoped that professional philosophers will continue to interest themselves in psychoanalytic epistomology and that they will seek first-hand familiarity with psychoanalytic theory and practice.[1]

---

[1]It is difficult for philosophers whose exposure to psychoanalysis is limited to the writing of Freud and a few other key figures to appreciate the clinical methodology of psychoanalysis. It is primarily by familiarizing themselves with psychoanalytic practice that philosophers will come to appreciate such points as the following: (1) that psychoanalytic formulations are not built upon one piece or type of evidence, but from the multiplication and convergence of a variety of data; (2) that clinical hypotheses are tested against the configuration of the data as a whole rather than, as in experimental science, against any single datum whose presence or

Let me conclude by way of expressing an "Hegelian" conviction about the nature of the process of knowledge that also constitutes a caveat to the reader of this essay. I believe that knowledge progresses dialectically—in the sense that a point is put forward which is found, upon further scrutiny, to be extreme, simplistic, or inadequate in various respects; what was taken for analytical rock bottom is found to be false flooring, inconsistencies have been overlooked, and violence has otherwise been done to logic and reality. A corrective counterpoint emerges, following which the whole process begins anew.

It is in this spirit that I put forward this monograph which is tentative and incomplete. After centuries of logical and empirical analysis there remains an overplus of mystery and ambiguity to concepts such as determinism, freedom, autonomy, mind, body, rationality, irrationality, interpretation, evidence, and so forth.[2] We have further to contend with the fact that logical and instrumental analysis, or what Heidegger terms "calculative thinking" is only one mode of relating to the self and universe; there are also the "existential" and "essential" approaches, which may well make their own contribution to our understanding of the world.

This essay is cast into this dialectical stream in the hope that it will contribute to further clarification of the issues at

---

absence would decisively confirm or refute them; (3) that the ambiguity and complexity of the human psyche necessitate hypotheses that often lack the neat and clean "either-or" logic of which philosophers are fond; and (4) that there is a distinct method and coherent logical structure to psychoanalytic thinking and practice. See Hospers (1959) for an excellent example of psychoanalytically versed philosophizing. See Nagel (1959) and Hook (1959) for good instances of failure to appreciate the aforementioned points.

[2]See Toulmin (1976) for a discussion of the dialectic, ambiguity, and paradox in these and other issues in the philosophy of science and for exemplification of an "inclusive" approach to philosophy that amalgamates the formal logical, contextual-commonsensical, and critical orientations.

hand. It does not intend to resolve any reader's mind or close him off to further examination of these issues—for they are fraught with paradoxes and antitheses that are far from settled. Future consideration of these topics may well lead to concepts which transcend our current explanatory dichotomies.

Only one thing appears certain, as my friend John Gach suggests: reality is always more complicated than any mind or theory which addresses it—particularly, I might add, when that reality is mind itself. Psychoanalysts and historians must walk a painful, but exciting tightrope between dogmatic certainty and skeptical nihilism. Tolerating the ambiguity inherent in their subject matter, while continuing to refine their interpretive approach is the most difficult dialectic for both.

References

Alexander, F. (1963). *Fundamentals of psychoanalysis* (Revised edition). New York: Norton.

Alexander, F., & Selesnick, S. (1966). *The history of psychiatry.* New York: Mentor Books.

Arlow, J., & Brenner, C. (1964). *Psychoanalytic concepts and the structural theory.* New York: International Universities Press.

Aron, R. (1969). Evidence and inference in history. In R. Nash (Ed.), *Ideas in history: Vol. 2.* New York: E. P. Dutton.

Atkinson, R. (1978). *Knowledge and explanation in history.* Ithaca, New York: Cornell University Press.

Barash, D. (1977). *Sociobiology and behavior.* New York: Elsevier.

Barrett, W. (1961). Determinism and novelty. In S. Hook (Ed.), *Determinism and freedom in the age of modern science.* New York: Collier.

Bartlett, F. (1939). The limitations of Freud. *Science and Society* 3:64–105.

Barzun, J., & Graff, H. (1970). *The modern researcher* (Revised edition). New York: Harcourt, Brace, Jovanovich.

Beard, C. (1934). Written history as an act of faith. In H. Meyerhoff (Ed.), *The philosophy of history in our time.* New York: Anchor Books, 1959.

Beard, C. (1935). The noble dream. In R. Nash (Ed.), *Ideas in history: Vol 1.* New York: E. P. Dutton, 1969.

Beard, C. (1936). *The discussion of human affairs.* New York: Macmillan.

Becker, C. (1958). *Detachment and the writing of history*. Ithaca: Cornell University Press.

Berlin, I. (1954). *Historical inevitability*. Oxford: Oxford University Press.

Bhaskar, R. (1975). *A realist theory of science*. Leeds, Eng: Leeds Books.

Binswanger, L. (1958). The existential analysis school of thought. In R. May, E. Angel, & H. Ellenberger (Eds.), *Existence*. New York: Basic Books.

Blake, C. (1959). Can history be objective? In P. Gardiner (Ed.), *Theories of history*. New York: Free Press.

Bloch, M. (1953). *The historian's craft* (P. Putnam, Trans.). New York: Vintage Books.

Boisen, A. (1936). *The exploration of the inner world*. New York: Harper.

Boss, M. (1963). *Psychoanalysis and daseinsanalysis* (L. Lefebre, trans.). New York: Basic Books.

Braithwaite, R. (1966). Causal and teleological explanations. In J. Canfield (Ed.), *Purpose in nature*. Englewood Cliffs, N.J.: Prentice-Hall.

Brenner, C. (1973). *An elementary textbook of psychoanalysis* (Revised edition). New York: International Universities Press.

Brenner, C. (1982). *The mind in conflict*. New York: International Universities Press.

Breuer, J., & Freud, S. (1895). *Studies on hysteria*. Standard Edition Vol. 3. London: Hogarth Press, 1962.

Bridgman, P. (1961). Determinism in modern science. In S. Hook (Ed.), *Determinism and freedom in the age of modern science*. New York: Collier.

Brierly, M. (1951). *Trends in psychoanalysis*. London: Hogarth Press.

Buckle, H. T. (1862). *History of civilization in England: Vol. 1* New York: Appleton.

Buckley, W. (1967). *Sociology and modern systems theory*. Englewood Cliffs, N.J.: Prentice-Hall.

Bunge, M. (1979). *Causality and modern science* (3rd revised edition). New York: Dover.

Buss, A. H., & Plomin, R. (1975). *A temperament theory of personality*. New York: Wiley.

Campbell, D., & Misanin, J. (1969). Basic drives. In P. Mussen, & R. Rosenzweig (Eds.), *Annual review of psychology: Vol. 20*. Palo Alto, Calif.: Annual Reviews.

Carr, E. (1961). *What is history?* New York: Vintage.

Cash, W. J. (1941). *The mind of the South*. New York: Vintage.

Chisholm, R. (1982). Human freedom and the self. In *Free Will* (Ed. G. Watson), pp. 24–35. Oxford: Oxford University Press.

Chomsky, N. (1968). *Language and mind*. New York: Harcourt, Brace, and World.

Cohen, M. (1931). *Reason and nature*. New York, 1931.

Collingwood, R. (1940). *An essay on metaphysics*. Oxford: Oxford University Press.

Collingwood, R. (1946). *The idea of history*. Oxford: Oxford University Press.

Collingwood, R. (1965). *Essays in the history of philosophy*. Austin: University of Texas Press.

Copleston, F. (1962). *A history of philosophy: Vol. 1, Part 1*. Garden City, N.Y.: Image Books.

Croce, B. (1921). *History: Its theory and practice*. (S. Ainslee, trans.). New York: Harcourt, Brace.

Dahl, H. (1972). A quantitative study of a psychoanalysis. *Psychoanalysis and Contemporary Society*. 1, 237–257.

Demos, R. (1969). The language of history. In R. Nash (Ed.), *Ideas in history: Volume 2*. New York: E. P. Dutton.

Dilthey, W. (1944). *Wilhelm Dilthey: An introduction* (Ed. H. Hodges). London: Routledge and Kegan Paul.

Dorer, M. (1932). *Historische grundlagen der psychoanalyse*. Leipzig: Meiner.

Dray, W. (1969). The historical explanation of actions reconsidered. In R. Nash (Ed.), *Ideas in history: Vol. 2*. New York: E. P. Dutton.

Dray, W. (1980). *Perspectives on history*. London: Routledge and Kegan Paul.

Edelson, M. (1975). *Language and interpretation in psychoanalysis*. New Haven: Yale University Press.

Edwards, P. (1961). Hard and soft determinism. In S. Hook (Ed.), *Determinism and freedom in the age of modern science*. New York: Collier.

Elton, G. (1970). *The practice of history*. New York: Thomas Crowell.

Erikson, E. (1958). *Young man Luther*. New York: Norton.

Erikson, E. (1963). *Childhood and society*. New York: Norton.

Erikson, E. (1975). *Life history and the historical moment*. New York: Norton.

Farrell, B. (1981). *The standing of psycho-analysis*. Oxford: Oxford University Press.

Fenichel, O. (1945). *The psychoanalytic theory of neuroses*. New York: Norton.

Fischer, D. (1970). *Historians' fallacies: Toward a logic of historical thought*. New York: Harper.

Flew, A. (1954). Psychoanalytic explanation. In M. McDonald (Ed.), *Philosophy and analysis*. New York: Philosophical Library.

Floderus-Myrhed, B., Pedersen, N., & Rasmusson, I. (1980). Assessment of heritability for personality, based on short-form of the Eysenck personality inventory: A study of 12,898 twin pairs. *Behavior Genetics, 10,* 153–162.

Florovsky, G. (1969). The study of the past. In R. Nash (Ed.), *Ideas in history: Vol. 2*. New York: E. P. Dutton.

Frankel, C. (1962). Explanation and interpretation in history. In P. Gardiner (Ed.), *Theories of history*. New York: Free Press.

Frankfort, H., Frankfort, H. A., Wilson, J., & Jacobsen, J. (1967). *Before philosophy*. Baltimore: Penguin Books.

Frankfurt, H. (1969). Alternate possibilities and moral responsibility. *Journal of Philosophy 65,* 829–839.

Frankfurt H. (1982). Freedom of the will and the concept of a person. In *Free Will (Ed. G. Watson), pp. 81–95. Oxford: Oxford University Press*.

Freud, E., Freud, L. & Grubrich-Simitis, I. (1978). Sigmund Freud: His life in pictures. New York: Harcourt, Brace, Jovanovich.

Freud, S. (1873–1939). *The letters of Sigmund Freud* (Ed. E. Freud). New York: Basic Books, 1975.

Freud, S. (1887–1902). *The origins of psychoanalysis: Sigmund Freud's letters, drafts, and notes to Wilhelm Fliess* (Eds. M. Bonaparte, A. Freud, & E. Kris). New York: Basic Books, 1954.

Freud, S. (1892–1893). A case of successful treatment by hypnotism. *Standard edition of the Complete Psychological Works of Sigmund Freud* (hereafter referred to as 'Standard Edition'), *Vol. 1*. London: Hogarth Press, 1966.

Freud, S. (1895a). *Project for a scientific psychology. Standard Edition, Vol. 1.* London: Hogarth Press, 1966.

Freud, S. (1895b). *A reply to criticisms of my paper on anxiety neurosis. Standard Edition, Vol. 3.* London: Hogarth Press, 1962.

Freud, S. (1896a). *Heredity and the aetiology of the neuroses. Standard Edition, Vol. 3.* London: Hogarth Press, 1962.

Freud, S. (1896b). *The aetiology of hysteria. Standard Edition, Vol. 3.* London: Hogarth Press, 1962.

Freud, S. (1898). *The psychical mechanism of forgetfulness. Standard Edition, Vol. 3.* London: Hogarth Press, 1962.

Freud, S. (1899). *Screen memories. Standard Edition, Vol. 3.* London: Hogarth Press, 1962.

Freud, S. (1900). *The interpretation of dreams. Standard Edition, Vols. 4 and 5.* London: Hogarth Press, 1953.

Freud, S. (1901a). *Fragment of an analysis of a case of hysteria. Standard Edition, Vol. 7.* London: Hogarth Press, 1953.

Freud, S. (1901b). *The Psychopathology of everyday life. Standard Edition, Vol. 6.* London: Hogarth Press, 1960.

Freud, S. (1905a). *Three essays on the theory of sexuality. Standard Edition, Vol. 7.* London: Hogarth Press, 1953.

Freud, S. (1905b). *Jokes and their relation to the unconscious. Standard Edition, Vol. 8.* London: Hogarth Press, 1960.

Freud, S. (1906). My views on the part played by sexuality in the aetiology of the neuroses, *Standard Edition, Volume 7.* London: Hogarth Press, 1953.

Freud, S. (1907). *Obsessive actions and religious practices. Standard Edition, Vol. 9.* London: Hogarth Press, 1959.

Freud, S. (1909a). *Notes upon a case of obsessional neurosis. Standard Edition, Vol. 10.* London: Hogarth Press, 1955.

Freud, S. (1909b). *Analysis of a phobia in a five-year-old boy. Standard Edition, Vol. 10.* London: Hogarth Press, 1955.

Freud, S. (1909c). *Five lectures on psycho-analysis. Standard Edition, Vol. 11.* London: Hogarth Press, 1957.

Freud, S. (1910a). *Future prospects of psycho-analytic therapy. Standard Edition, Vol. 11.* London: Hogarth Press, 1957.

Freud, S. (1910b). *Leonardo Da Vinci and a memory of his childhood. Standard Edition, Vol. 11.* London: Hogarth Press, 1957.

Freud, S. (1911a). *Formulations on the two principles of mental functioning. Standard Edition, Vol. 12.* London: Hogarth Press, 1958.

Freud, S. (1911b). *Psycho-analytic notes on an autobiographical account of a case of paranoia. Standard Edition, Vol. 12.* London: Hogarth Press, 1958.

Freud, S. (1912). *Recommendations to physicians practicing psychoanalysis. Standard Edition, Vol. 12.* London: Hogarth Press, 1958.

Freud, S. (1913). *Totem and Taboo. Standard Edition, Vol. 13.* London: Hogarth Press, 1958.

Freud, S. (1914). *On the history of the psycho-analytic movement. Standard Edition, Vol. 14.* London: Hogarth Press, 1957.

Freud, S. (1914). *On narcissism: An introduction. Standard Edition, Vol. 14.* London: Hogarth Press, 1957.

Freud, S. (1915a). *The uncanny. Standard Edition, Vol. 17.* London: Hogarth Press, 1955.

Freud, S. (1915b). *Repression. Standard Edition, Vol. 14.* London: Hogarth Press, 1957.

Freud, S. (1915c). *The unconscious. Standard Edition, Vol. 14.* London: Hogarth Press, 1957.

Freud, S. (1915d). *Instincts and their vicissitudes. Standard Edition, Vol. 14.* London: Hogarth Press, 1957.

Freud, S. (1915–1917). *Introductory lectures on psycho-analysis. Standard Edition, Vols. 15 & 16.* London: Hogarth Press, 1963.

Freud, S. (1917). *Mourning and melancholia. Standard Edition, Vol. 14.* London: Hogarth Press, 1955.

Freud, S. (1918). *From the history of an infantile neurosis. Standard Edition, Vol. 17.* London: Hogarth Press, 1955.

Freud, S. (1920a). *Beyond the pleasure principle. Standard Edition, Vol. 18.* London: Hogarth Press, 1955.

Freud, S. (1920b). *The psychogenesis of a case of homosexuality in a woman. Standard Edition, Vol. 18.* London: Hogarth Press, 1955.

Freud, S. (1923a). *The ego and id. Standard Edition, Vol. 19.* London: Hogarth Press, 1961.

Freud, S. (1923b). *Remarks on the theory and practice of dream-interpretation. Standard Edition, Vol. 19.* London: Hogarth Press, 1961.

Freud, S. (1925). *An autobiographical study. Standard Edition, Vol. 20.* London: Hogarth Press, 1959.

Freud, S. (1926). *Inhibitions, Symptoms, and Anxiety. Standard Edition, Vol. 20.* London: Hogarth Press, 1959.

Freud, S. (1927a). *The future of an illusion. Standard Edition, Vol. 21.* London: Hogarth Press, 1961.

Freud, S. (1927b). *Fetishism. Standard Edition, Vol. 21.* London: Hogarth Press, 1961.

Freud, S. (1930). *Civilization and its discontents. Standard Edition, Vol. 21.* London: Hogarth Press, 1961.

Freud, S. (1932a). *Why war? Standard Edition, Vol. 22.* London: Hogarth Press, 1964.

Freud, S. (1932b). *My contact with Josef Popper-Lynkeus. Standard Edition, Vol. 22.* London: Hogarth Press, 1964.

Freud, S. (1933). *New introductory lectures on psycho-analysis. Standard Edition, Vol. 22.* London. Hogarth Press, 1964.

Freud, S. (1937a). *Analysis terminable and interminable. Standard Edition, Vol. 23.* London: Hogarth Press, 1964.

Freud, S. (1937b). Constructions in analysis. Standard Edition, Vol. 23. London: Hogarth Press, 1964.

Freud, S. (1938). *An outline of psycho-analysis. Standard Edition, Vol. 23.* London: Hogarth Press, 1964.

Freud, S. (1939). *Moses and monotheism. Standard Edition, Vol. 23.* London: Hogarth Press, 1939.

Fromm-Reichmann, F. (1950). *Principles of intensive psychotherapy.* Chicago: University of Chicago Press.

Gallie, W. (1964). *Philosophy and historical understanding.* New York: Schocken.

Gardiner, P. (1961). *The nature of historical explanation.* Oxford: Oxford University Press.

Gershoy, L. (1963). Some problems of the working historian. In S. Hook (Ed.), *Philosophy and history.* New York: New York University Press.

Gill, M., & Hoffman, I. (1982). *The analysis of transference, Vol. 2: Studies of nine audio-recorded psychoanalytic sessions.* New York: International Universities Press.

Glover, E. (1955). *The technique of psycho-analysis.* (Revised edition). New York: International Universities Press.

Goffman, E. (1961). *Asylums.* Chicago: Aldine.

Gottschalk, L. (1950). *Understanding history.* New York: Alfred A. Knopf.

Gould, S. J. (1982). *The panda's thumb: More reflections on natural history*. New York: Norton.

Green, H. (1964). *I never promised you a rose garden*. New York: Holt, Rinehart, & Winston.

Greenson, R. (1967). *The technique and practice of psycho-analysis*. New York: International Universities Press.

Grünbaum, A. (1979). Epistemological liabilities of the clinical appraisal of psychoanalytic theory. *Psychoanalysis and Contemporary Thought, 2,* 451–526.

Grünbaum, A. (1982). Can psychoanalytic theory be cogently tested on the couch? *Psychoanalysis and Contemporary Thought, 5,* 155–255, 311–436.

Gunther, M. (1974). Freud as expert witness: Wagner-Jauregg and the problem of war neuroses. *The Annual of Psychoanalysis, 2,* 3–23.

Hamlyn, D. (1967). History of epistemology. In *Encyclopedia of philosophy, Vol. 3*. New York: Macmillan.

Hanly, C. (1979). *Existentialism and psychoanalysts*. New York: International Universities press.

Hart, H. L. A., & Honoré, A. (1959). *Causation and the law*. Oxford: Oxford University Press.

Hart, H. L. A. (1961). Legal responsibility and excuses. In S. Hook (Ed.), *Determinism and freedom in the age of modern science*. New York: Collier.

Hartmann, H. (1927). Understanding and explanation. In H. Hartmann's *Essays on ego psychology*. New York: International Universities Press, 1964.

Hartmann, H. (1960). *Psychoanalysis and moral values*. New York: International Universities Press.

Hartmann, H., & Kris, E. (1945). The genetic approach in psychoanalysis. *The Psychoanalytic Study of the Child, 1,* 11–30.

Heider, F. (1958). *The Psychology of Interpersonal Relations*. New York: Wiley.

Hempel, C. (1965). *Aspects of scientific explanation and other essays in the philosophy of science*. New York: Free Press.

Hempel, C. (1969). Explanation in science and history. In R. Nash (Ed.), *Ideas in history, Vol. 2*. New York: E. P. Dutton.

Herbart, J. (1824). *Psychologie als wissenschaft*. Leipzig.

Hobbes, T. (1651). *Leviathan*. New York: Collier, 1962.

Holt, R. (1976). Drive or wish?: A reconsideration of the psycho-analytic theory of motivation. In R. Holt, (Ed.), *Psychology versus metapsychology: Psychoanalytic essays in memory of George S. Klein*. New York: International Universities Press.

Hook, S. (1950). *The hero in history*. New York: Humanities Press.

Hook, S. (1959). (Ed.) *Psychoanalysis, scientific method, and philosophy*. New York: New York University Press.

Hook, S. (1961). Necessity, indeterminism, and sentimentalism. In S. Hook (Ed.), *Freedom and determinism in the age of modern science*. New York: Collier.

Hospers, J. (1959). Philosophy and psychoanalysis. In S. Hook (Ed.), *Psychoanalysis, scientific method, and philosophy*. New York: New York University Press.

Hughes, S. (1964). *History as art and as science*. New York: Harper and Row, 1964.

Hume, D. (1777a). *An inquiry concerning human understanding*. In R. Cohen (Ed.), *Essential works of David Hume*. New York: Bantam, 1965.

Hume, D. (1777b). *A treatise on human nature*. In A. Flew (Ed.), *David Hume: On human nature and the understanding*. New York: Collier, 1962.

James, W. (1896). *The will to believe and other essays in popular philosophy*. New York: Dover, 1956.

Johnson, A. (1926). *The historian and historical evidence*. New York: Charles Scribner's Sons.

Jones, E. (1953, 1955, 1957). *The life and work of Sigmund Freud, 3 vols*. New York: Basic Books.

Jones, E. E., & Nisbett, R. E. (1971). The actor and the observer: Divergent perceptions of the causes of behavior. In E. E. Jones, D. E. Canouse, H. Kelley, R. E. Nisbett, S. Valine, & B. Weiner (Eds.), *Attribution: Perceiving the causes of behavior*. Morristown, N.J.: General Learning Press.

Jung, C. C. (1961). *Memories, dreams, reflections*. Princeton: Princeton University Press.

Kant, I. (1933). *Critique of pure reason*. (N. K. Smith, trans.). London.

Kant, I. (1909). *Critique of practical reason* (T. Albret, trans.). London.

Kardiner, A. (1939). *The individual and his society.* New York: Columbia University Press.

Kernberg, O. (1975). *Borderline conditions and pathological narcissism.* New York: Jason Aronson.

Klein, G. (1976). *Psychoanalytic theory.* New York: International Universities Press.

Kline, P. (1972). *Fact and fantasy in Freudian theory.* London: Methuen.

Knight, R. (1946). Determinism, freedom, and psychotherapy. *Psychiatry, 9,* 251–262.

Koestler, A. (1967). *The ghost in the machine.* New York: Random House.

Kohlberg, L. (1974). Moral development. In Gamson, W., & Modigliani, A. (Eds.), *Conceptions of social life.* Boston: Little, Brown.

Kohut, H. (1971). *The analysis of the self.* New York: International Universities Press.

Kohut, H. (1979). The two analyses of Mr. Z. *International journal of Psycho-Analysis, 60,* 3–27.

Kubie, L. (1939). A critical analysis of the concept of a repetition compulsion. *International Journal of Psycho-Analysis, 20,* 390–402.

Kubie, L. (1950). *Practical and theoretical aspects of psychoanalysis.* New York: International Universities Press.

Kuhn, T. (1970). *The structure of scientific revolutions.* Chicago: University of Chicago Press.

Lacan, J. (1968). *Speech, language, and psychoanalysis.* (A. Wilden, trans.). Baltimore: Johns Hopkins University Press.

Langer, W. (1958). The next assignment. *The American Historical Review, 63,* 283–304.

Langlois, S., & Seignebos, C. (1898). *Introduction to the study of history* (G. Berry, trans.). London: Duckworth.

Leavy, S. (1980). *The psychoanalytic dialogue.* New Haven: Yale University Press.

Levinson, D. (1978). *The seasons of a man's life.* New York: Alfred A. Knopf.

Lévi-Strauss, C. (1963). *Structural anthropology.* (Tr. C. Jacobsen and B. Grundfest). New York: Basic Books.

Lifton, R. (1979). *The broken connection*. New York: Simon and Schuster.

Locke, J. (1690). *An essay concerning human understanding*. In R. Taylor (Ed.), *The empiricists*. Garden City, N.J.: Dolphin Books, 1961.

Loehlin, J., & Nichols, R. (1976). *Heredity, environment, and personality*. Austin: University of Texas Press.

Leowald, H. (1977). *Psychoanalysis and the history of the individual*. New Haven: Yale University Press.

Lovejoy, A. D. (1959). Present standpoints and past history. In H. Meyerhoff (Ed.), *The philosophy of history in our time*. New York: Anchor Books.

Lowes, R. (1927). *The road to Xanadu*. New York: Houghton Mifflin.

Mackie, J. (1980). *The cement of the universe: A study of causation*.

Mandelbaum, M. (1938). *The problem of historical knowledge*. New York: Liveright.

Mandelbaum, M. (1963). Objectivism in history. In S. Hook (Ed.), *Philosophy and history*. New York: New York University Press.

Mandelbaum, M. (1969). Historical explanation: The problem of covering laws. In R. Nash (Ed.), *Ideas in history, Vol. 2*. New York: E. P. Dutton.

McMurtrie, D., et al. (1946). *Theory and practice in historical study: A report of the committee on historiography*. Social Science Research Council Bulletin 54.

Marrou, H. (1966). *Meaning in history*. Baltimore: Helicon Press.

Masson, J. (1984). Freud and the seduction theory. *The Atlantic, 253*, 33–61.

Matte Blanco, I. (1975). *The unconscious as infinite sets: An essay in bi-logic*. London: Hogarth Press.

May, R. (1969). *Love and will*. New York: W. W. Norton.

Meissner, W. (1979). Methodological Critique of the action language in psychoanalysis. *Journal of the American Psychoanalytic Association, 27*, 79–105.

Meissner, W. (1981). Subjectivity in psychoanalysis. In J. Smith (Ed.), *Kierkegaard's truth: The disclosure of self*. New Haven: Yale University Press.

Melden, A. I. (1961). *Free action*. Oxford: Oxford University Press.

Melden, A. I. (1969). Historical objectivity. In R. Nash (Ed.), *Ideas in history, Vol. 2.* New York: E. P. Dutton.

Menninger, K. (1958). *Theory of psychoanalytic technique.* New York: Basic Books.

Merleau-Ponty, M. (1963). *The structure of behavior* (A. Fisher, trans.). Boston: Beacon Press.

Meyer, A. (1906). Principles in grouping facts in psychiatry. In A. Lief (Ed.), *The commonsense psychiatry of Dr. Adolf Meyer.* New York: McGraw-Hill, 1948.

Meyerhoff, H. (1959). Introduction. In H. Meyerhoff (Ed.), *The philosophy of history in our time.* New York: Anchor Books.

Meyerhoff, H. (1962). On psychoanalysis as history. *Psychoanalytic Review, 49,* 3–20.

Mill, J. S. (1874). *An examination of Sir William Hamilton's philosophy.* New York: Holt.

Mill, J. S. (1969). Ethology—the science of the formation of character. In R. Nash (Ed.), *Ideas in history, Vol. 2.* New York: E. P. Dutton.

Morgan, L. (1907). *Ancient society.* New York: Holt.

Murphey, M. (1973). *Our knowledge of the historical past.* New York: Bobbs-Merrill.

Nagel, E. (1959). The logic of historical analysis. In H. Meyerhoff (Ed.), *The philosophy of history in our time.* New York: Doubleday.

Nagel, E. (1963). Relativism and some problems of working historians. In S. Hook (Ed.), *Philosophy and history.* New York: New York University Press.

Nagel, E. (1969). Determinism in history. In R. Nash (Ed.), *Ideas in history, Vol. 2.* New York: E. P. Dutton.

Niederland, W. (1974). *The Schreber case.* New York: Quadrangle.

Novey, S. (1968). *The second look: The reconstruction of personal history in psychiatry and psychoanalysis.* Baltimore: Johns Hopkins University Press.

Noy, P. (1969). A revision of the psychoanalytic theory of primary process. *International Journal of Psycho-Analysis 50,* 155–178.

Oakeshott, M. (1933). *Experience and its modes.* Cambridge: Cambridge University Press.

Pap, A. (1962). *An introduction to the philosophy of science.* New York: Free Press.

Penfield, W., & Rasmussen, T. (1950). *The cerebral cortex in man.* New York: Macmillan.

Peters, R. (1966). *Authority, responsibility, and education.* New York: Atherton Press.

Piaget, J. (1929). *The child's conception of the world.* London: Routledge and Kegan Paul.

Piaget, J. (1951). *The child's conception of physical causality.* New York: Humanities Press.

Popper, K. (1952). *The open society and its enemies, Vol. 2.* London: Routledge and Sons.

Popper, K. (1965). *The logic of scientific discovery.* New York: Harper.

Popper, K., Eccles, (1981). *The self and its brain.* London: Springer International.

Prior, A. (1967). Correspondence theory of truth. In *Encyclopedia of Philosophy, Vol. 2.* New York: Macmillan.

Rado, S. (1932). The paths of natural science in the light of psychoanalysis. *Psychoanalytic Quarterly, 1,* 683–700.

Ranke, L. von (1973). *The theory and practice of history* (G. Iggers, K. von Moltke, Eds. and trans.). New York: Bobbs-Merrill.

Rawn, M. (1979). Schafer's action language: A questionable alternative to metapsychology. *International journal of psycho-analysis, 60,* 455–465.

Reid, T. (1813–1815). *Essays on the active powers of the human mind.* Cambridge, Mass.: M.I.T. Press, 1969.

Reik, T. (1949). *Listening with the third ear.* New York: Farrar, Straus, & Cudahy.

Reiner, M. (1932). Causality and psychoanalysis. *Psychoanalytic Quarterly, 1,* 701–714.

Renier, G. (1950). *History: Its purpose and method.* Boston: Beacon Press.

Ricoeur, P. (1970). *Freud and philosophy.* New Haven: Yale University Press.

Ricoeur, P. (1974). *The conflict of interpretations.* Evanston, Ill.: Northwestern University Press.

Rieff, P. (1953). History, psychoanalysis, and the social sciences. *Ethics, 63,* 107–120.

Rieff, P. (1959). *Freud: The mind of the moralist.* New York: Viking Press.

Rieff, P. (1979). *Freud: The mind of the moralist,* 3rd Edition. Chicago: University of Chicago Press.

Rosen, V. (1955). The reconstruction of a traumatic childhood event in the case of derealization. *Journal of the American Psychoanalytic Association, 3,* 211–221.

Russell, B. C. (1929). *Mysticism and logic.* New York: Norton.

Ryle, G. (1949). *The concept of mind.* New York: Barnes and Noble.

Sachs, D. (1967). Distinctions between fantasy and reality elements in memory and reconstruction. *International Journal of Psycho-Analysis, 48,* 416–423.

Schafer, R. (1976). *A new language for psychoanalysis.* New Haven: Yale University Press.

Schafer, R. (1978). *Language and insight.* New Haven: Yale University Press.

Schafer, R. (1980). Narration in the psychoanalytic dialogue. *Critical Inquiry, 7,* 29–53.

Schafer, R. (1983). *The analytic attitude.* New York: Basic Books.

Schmidl, F. (1962). Psychoanalysis and history. *Psychoanalytic Quarterly, 31,* 532–548.

Schopenhauer, A. (1960). Free will and fatalism. In T. B. Saunders (Ed. and Trans.), *On human nature.* London: Allen and Unwin.

Schur, M. (1969). *The id and the regulatory principles of mental functioning.* New York: International Universities Press.

Schwarz, J. (1979). Childhood origins of psychopathology. *American Psychologist, 34,* 879–885.

Scriven, M. (1966). Causes, connections, and conditions in history. In W. Dray (Ed.), *Philosophical analysis and history.* New York: Harper and Row.

Searle, J. (1983). *Intentionality: An essay in the philosophy of mind.* Cambridge: Cambridge University Press.

Searles, H. (1965). *Collected essays on schizophrenia and related subjects.* New York: International Universities Press.

Serota, H. (1964). Home movies of early childhood: Correlative developmental data in the psychoanalysis of adults. *Science, 143,* 1195.

Sherwood, M. (1969). *The logic of explanation in psychoanalysis.* New York: Academic Press.

Siegal, R. (1973). *Galen on psychology, psychopathology, and function and diseases of the nervous system.* Basel: S. Karger.

Sigerist, H. (1935). Introduction. In G. Zilboorg, *The medical man and the witch in the Renaissance*. Baltimore: Johns Hopkins University Press.

Skinner, B. F. (1971). *Beyond freedom and dignity*. New York: Alfred A. Knopf.

Smith, P. (1966). *The historian and history*. New York: Alfred A. Knopf.

Spence, D. (1982). *Narrative truth and historical truth: Meaning and interpretation in psychoanalysis*. New York: Norton.

Spencer, H. (1898). *Principles of sociology, 3 Volumes*, New York: Appleton.

Spinoza, B. (1677). Ethics. In R. Elwes (Ed. and Trans.), *Works of Spinoza, Vol. 1*. New York: Dover, 1951.

Spitz, R. (1965). *The first year of life*. New York: International Universities Press.

Sprio, M. (1965). Religious systems as culturally constituted defense mechanisms. In M. Spiro (Ed.), *Context and meaning in cultural anthropology*. New York: Free Press.

Stannard, D. (1980). *Shrinking history: On Freud and the failure of psychohistory*. Oxford: Oxford University Press.

Stanton, A., & Schwartz, M. (1954). *The mental hospital*. London: Tavistock.

Stover, R. (1967). *The nature of historical thinking*. Chapel Hill, N.C.: University of North Carolina Press.

Strawson, P. (1982). Freedom and resentment. In *Free Will* (Ed. G. Watson), pp. 59–80. Oxford: Oxford University Press.

Strong, S. (1978). Social psychological approaches to psychotherapy research. In S. Garfield, & A. Bergin (Eds.), *Handbook of psychotherapy and behavior change*, 2nd ed. New York: Wiley.

Sullivan, H. S. (1947). *Conceptions of modern psychiatry*. Washington: William Alanson White Psychiatric Foundation.

Sullivan, H. S. (1953). *The interpersonal theory of psychiatry*. New York: Norton.

Sulloway, F. (1979). *Freud: Biologist of the mind*. New York: Basic Books.

Taylor, A. E. (1955). *Aristotle*. New York: Dover.

Taylor, R. (1967). Causation. In *The Encyclopedia of philosophy, Vol. 2*. New York: Macmillan.

Thomas, A., Chess, S. (1977). *Temperament and development.* New York: Brunner/Mazel.

Tillich, P. (1952). *The courage to be.* New Haven: Yale University Press.

Toulmin, S. (1954). The logical status of psychoanalysis. In M. Macdonald (Ed.), *Philosophy and analysis.* New York: Philosophical Library.

Toulmin, S. (1976). *Knowing and acting: An invitation to philosophy.* New York: Macmillan.

Trosman, H., Simmons, R. (1973). The Freud library. *Journal of the American Psychoanalytic Association, 21,* 646–687.

Turner, F. J. (1938). The significance of history. In *The early writings of Frederick Jackson Turner.* Madison: University of Wisconsin Press.

Tylor, E. (1874). *Primitive culture, 2 volumes.* New York: Holt.

Von Wright, G. H. (1972). *Causality and determinism.* New York: New York University Press.

Waelder, R. (1963). Psychic determinism and the possibility of predictions. *Journal of the American Psychoanalytic Association, 32,* 15–42.

Wallace, E. (1978). Freud's mysticism and its psychodynamic determinants, *Bulletin of the Menninger Clinic, 42,* 203–222.

Wallace, E. (1979). Freud and Leonardo, *Psychiatric Forum 8,* 1–10.

Wallace, E. (1980a). Freud and cultural evolutionism. In E. Wallace & L. Pressley (Eds.), *Essays in the history of psychiatry.* Columbia, S.C.: S.C. Dept. of Mental Health Publications.

Wallace, E. (1980b). The primal parricide. *Bulletin of the History of Medicine, 54,* 153–165.

Wallace, E. (1983a). Historiography in history and psychoanalysis. *Bulletin of the History of Medicine, 57,* 247–266.

Wallace, E. (1983b). *Dynamic psychiatry in theory and practice.* Philadelphia: Lea and Febiger.

Wallace, E. (1983c). *Freud and anthropology: A history and reappraisal.* New York: International Universities Press.

Wallace, E. (1983d). The repetition compulsion. *Psychoanalytic Review, 69,* 455–469.

Wallace, E. (1983e). Essay review of D. Stannard's *Shrinking History. Clio Medica 17,* 247–252.

Wallace, E. (1984). Determinism, possibility, and ethics. *International Forum for Psychoanalysis,* in press.

Walsh, W. (1958). *Philosophy of history: An introduction.* New York: Harper and Brothers.

Walsh, W. (1969). Positivist and idealist approaches to history. In R. Nash (Ed.), *Ideas in history, Vol. 2.* New York: E. P. Dutton.

Weinstein, F., Platt, G. (1973). *Psychoanalytic sociology: An essay on the interpretation of historical data.* Baltimore: Johns Hopkins University Press.

White, A. (1967). Coherence theory of truth. In *Encyclopedia of philosophy, Vol. 2.* New York: Macmillan.

White, M. (1959). Can history be objective: In H. Meyerhoff (Ed.), *The philosophy of history in our time.* New York: Doubleday.

White, M. (1963). The logic of historical narration. In S. Hook (Ed.), *Philosophy and history.* New York: New York University Press.

Wilson, E. (1973). The structural hypothesis and psychoanalytic metatheory: An essay on psychoanalysis and contemporary philosophy of science. *Psychoanalysis and Contemporary Science, 2.*

Wilson, E. O. (1975). *Sociobiology: The new synthesis.* Cambridge, Mass.: Belknap Press of Harvard University.

Wilson, E. O. (1977). Foreword In Barash, D. *Sociobiology and behavior.* New York: Elsevier.

Wilson, E. O. (1978). *On human nature.* Cambridge, Mass.: Belknap Press of Harvard University.

Wittgenstein, L. (1967). *Lectures and conversations on aesthetics, psychology, and religious belief.* Berkeley: University of California Press.

Wollheim, R. (Ed.) (1977). *Philosophers on Freud.* New York: Jason Aronson.

Wolman, B. (1971). Sense and nonsense in history. In B. Wolman (Ed.), *The psychoanalytic interpretation of history.* New York: Basic Books.

Zilboorg, G. (1935). *The medical man and the witch in the Renaissance.* Baltimore: Johns Hopkins University Press.

Zilboorg, G. & Henry, G. (1941). *A history of medical psychology.* New York: Norton.

Zinn, H. (1964). *The Southern mystique.* New York.

Index

About the Author

Edwin R. Wallace, IV, M.D. completed his psychiatric training at the Yale University School of Medicine and his historical training at the Johns Hopkins University, from which he holds the M.A. in the history of medicine. Formerly on the faculty in psychiatry at Yale and Chief of Individual Psychotherapy at the Connecticut Mental Health Center, Dr. Wallace is currently Director of Psychotherapy Education and Associate Professor of Psychiatry at the Medical College of Georgia. The author of *Dynamic Psychiatry in Theory and Practice* (which has also appeared in Japanese and Spanish language editions) and *Freud and Anthropology: A History and Reappraisal,* he has co-edited *Essays in the History of Psychiatry* and written numerous articles and chapters on the history and philosophy of psychoanalysis. Dr. Wallace is a member of the Editorial Boards of the *Bulletin of the History of Medicine* and *The Review of Psychoanalytic Books*. He lives in Augusta, Georgia, with his wife, Laura, and children, Laura and Win.